PREHISTORY AND HUMAN ECOLOGY
OF THE VALLEY OF OAXACA

Volume 5

Part 1

THE VEGETATIONAL HISTORY OF
THE OAXACA VALLEY

Part 2

ZAPOTEC PLANT KNOWLEDGE:
CLASSIFICATION, USES, AND COMMUNICATION
ABOUT PLANTS IN MITLA, OAXACA, MEXICO

PREHISTORY AND HUMAN ECOLOGY OF THE VALLEY OF OAXACA

Kent V. Flannery and Richard E. Blanton
General Editors

Volume 1 *The Use of Land and Water Resources in the Past and Present Valley of Oaxaca, Mexico,* by Anne V. T. Kirkby. Memoirs of the Museum of Anthropology, University of Michigan, No. 5. 1973.

Volume 2 *Sociopolitical Aspects of Canal Irrigation in the Valley of Oaxaca,* by Susan H. Lees. Memoirs of the Museum of Anthropology, University of Michigan, No. 6. 1973.

Volume 3 *Formative Mesoamerican Exchange Networks with Special Reference to the Valley of Oaxaca,* by Jane W. Pires-Ferreira. Memoirs of the Museum of Anthropology, University of Michigan, No. 7. 1975.

Volume 4 *Fábrica San José and Middle Formative Society in the Valley of Oaxaca,* by Robert D. Drennan. Memoirs of the Museum of Anthropology, University of Michigan, No. 8. 1975.

Volume 5 Part 1. *The Vegetational History of the Oaxaca Valley,* by C. Earle Smith, Jr.

Part 2. *Zapotec Plant Knowledge: Classification, Uses and Communication about Plants in Mitla, Oaxaca, Mexico,* by Ellen Messer.

Memoirs of the Museum of Anthropology, University of Michigan, No. 10. 1978.

MEMOIRS OF THE MUSEUM OF ANTHROPOLOGY
UNIVERSITY OF MICHIGAN
NUMBER 10

PREHISTORY AND HUMAN ECOLOGY
OF THE VALLEY OF OAXACA

Kent V. Flannery and Richard E. Blanton, General Editors

Volume 5

Part 1:

THE VEGETATIONAL HISTORY OF THE OAXACA VALLEY

BY C. EARLE SMITH, JR.

Part 2:

ZAPOTEC PLANT KNOWLEDGE: CLASSIFICATION, USES, AND COMMUNICATION ABOUT PLANTS IN MITLA, OAXACA, MEXICO

BY ELLEN MESSER

ANN ARBOR
1978

© 1978 Regents of The University of
Michigan The Museum of Anthropology
All rights reserved

Printed in the
United States of America

ISBN 978-0-932206-72-5 (print)

ISBN 978-1-951538-17-0 (ebook)

AN INTRODUCTION TO VOLUME 5 OF THE SERIES

by Kent V. Flannery

This *Memoir* is the fifth in our series of final volumes on the University of Michigan Museum of Anthropology project, "The Prehistoric Human Ecology of the Valley of Oaxaca," supported by National Science Foundation grants GS-1616, GS-2121, and GS-42568. As indicated on the cover, beginning with this volume, I will be joined as series editor by Richard E. Blanton, director of the Valley of Oaxaca Settlement Pattern Project. Since there is close collaboration between his project and mine, it seemed advisable to bring out the results of both projects within a single publication series. A few monographs in the series which would be extraordinarily difficult and expensive for the Museum of Anthropology to produce will be commercially published, with royalties accruing to the publication fund for the Valley of Oaxaca *Memoirs*.[1]

Volume 5 deals with the plant world of the Valley Zapotec, past and present. As an archeologist interested in human ecology, one of my concerns has been to know how the Precolumbian Zapotec utilized the wild and domestic plants of the Valley of Oaxaca. To begin with, this required a botanical study of the present-day vegetation and an analysis of the archeological plant remains. In addition, since the Zapotecs' perception and classification of plants affected their usage, I needed an ethnobotanical study of the present-day Valley Zapotec. This would give me a look at the valley's vegetation both through the eyes of a 20th century botanist and through the eyes of a 20th century Zapotec-speaking *campesino*. Finally, I needed a study that would bridge the gap between the Precolumbian world and the present-day, highly-acculturated Zapotec—an ethnohistoric study, based on the way the Zapotec perceived and classified their environment at the time of the Spanish Conquest. Such an analysis could never have the detail of a botanical or ethnobotanical study done today, but would provide a crucial check on acculturation.

For the botanical study, I turned to the "dean of Mesoamerican archaeological plant remains," C. Earle Smith, Jr., already a veteran of Richard S. MacNeish's Tehuacán Archaeological-Botanical Project (Smith 1965a, 1965b, 1967). Smith's reconstruction of the Precolumbian vegetation of the Valley of Oaxaca appears in this volume, and his analyses of archeological plant remains will appear in future volumes. For the ethnobotanical study I turned to Ellen Messer, then a graduate student at Michigan and now an Assistant Professor at Yale University, whose analysis of Mitla Zapotec plant knowledge also appears in this volume. The ethnohistoric work is being undertaken by Joyce Marcus as part of a larger study of 16th century Mesoamerican Indians which will appear in the future (see Marcus 1978; Marcus and Flannery 1978).

Smith spent more than five field seasons in the Valley of Oaxaca, climbing mountains, wading rivers, and searching isolated canyons for surviving patches of undisturbed vegetation. It is not an easy task to reconstruct the original wild vegetation of a valley whose flat floor has been disturbed by agriculture for more than 7000 years, whose piedmont has been grazed by goats for at least 400 years, and whose mountains are filled with woodcutters and charcoal burners. However, Smith found remnants of the original vegetation, and drawing on his long experience in the southern Mexican highlands, combined these remnants with (1) principles of plant growth as they apply to the physiographic features of the

---

[1] The first of these is Blanton's *Monte Albán: Settlement patterns at the ancient Zapotec capital.* New York: Academic Press (1978).

valley; (2) knowledge of vegetation in similar environments in neighboring valleys; and (3) plant remains recovered by the screening of dry caves and the flotation of ashy debris from open-air sites.

In this report, Smith has reconstructed the Valley of Oaxaca as an area originally covered by forest, brush, or low *monte*—not the open, grassy valley we see today, which is a product of agricultural land clearance. Along the Atoyac River and its major tributaries he sees a riverine forest of alder, willow, *ahuehuete,* fig, and *anona.* On the alluvium, where the subsurface water lies between 3 and 6 meters below the surface, there would have been a lower forest of mesquite, acacia, and members of the Burseraceae, Malvaceae, and Euphorbiaceae. The piedmont (from the 6-meter water table zone up onto the lower slopes of the mountains) would have had a thorn-scrub-cactus forest, of which patches survive near Guilá Naquitz Cave; prickly pear, organ cactus, leguminous trees, yucca and maguey characterize this community. In the higher mountains grew a forest of oak, pine, manzanita and madroño, now greatly thinned.

Messer also made a collection of plants from the Mitla area in connection with her work. Because Smith identified his specimens at the U.S. National Herbarium in Washington, D.C., and Messer's were identified in collaboration with Rogers McVaugh at the University of Michigan Herbarium, there are occasionally slight differences in nomenclature. These are for the most part minor differences which result from still-unresolved decisions about the lumping or splitting of various species of Mexican plants, and are of no consequence for the purposes of this volume.

Messer lived for four field seasons at Mitla, the "town of the souls" already immortalized by Elsie Clews Parsons and Charles Leslie; additional work was done at Abasolo, a village some 25 kilometers west. The data she recovered show a system of classification that should probably be called "folk" rather than "Indian," with fascinating accomodations made to the bewildering number of plants and concepts introduced by the Spanish in the 1500s. Among the largely bilingual population of Mitla, there are words which Spanish has borrowed from Zapotec (Sp. *togoles,* from Zap. *gi togol*) and words which Zapotec has borrowed from Spanish (Zap. *lečug,* from Sp. *lechuga*). There are also Spanish introductions for which the Zapotec have "invented" a term; because its seeds resemble corn kernels, the pomegranate is called *žob štil* (*žob* = Zapotec for corn kernel, *štil* = from the Spanish, *Castilla*).

Messer's study has already answered a number of significant archeological questions. For example, some archeological pollen samples from our Formative village sites (1350-100 B.C.) show high frequencies of chenopod and amaranth pollen that do not match modern surface pollen samples from any known environment in the valley. They do, however, match pollen samples from the floors of houses in present-day villages. For some years, therefore, we suspected that these high "Cheno-Am" pollen frequencies reflected cultural activities rather than climatic fluctuation. Messer's study reveals that Zapotec farmers encourage several major genera of "weeds" in their milpas because they can be used as edible greens at various stages in the growth cycle. Not only does this raise the pollen frequency of these "weeds" in the cornfield, it also increases its frequency in floor debris because the plants themselves are brought back to the house and their pollen carried home on the maize crop. These "edible weeds" include not only *Chenopodium* and *Amaranthus,* but other genera like *Anoda, Crotalaria, Galinsoga,* and *Portulaca.* Thus one archeological mystery was solved.

I expect Messer's data to contribute to our understanding of prehistoric human ecology in many other ways, so long as we do not lose sight of the fact that it is a study of acculturated Indians. Our ethnohistoric data indicate that even some things which appear superficially "Zapotec"—for example, the division of plants into *yahg* ("trees"), *kʷan* ("herbs"), and *giš* ("grass"), reported by Messer—have changed substantially since the 16th century. In 1578, the Valley Zapotec did not distinguish "herbs" from "grass"; these were categories emphasized by the Spanish. Thus, over the 400 years since the Conquest, the 16th century Zapotec term *nocuana,* "fruit," has gradually taken on the meaning of Spanish *yerba* while it evolved to *kʷan;* and the 16th century Zapotec term *quijxi,* "weed," has gradually taken on the meaning of Spanish *pasto* while it evolved to *giš* (Marcus and Flannery 1978).

Still other plants have retained names that in Precolumbian times had religious or supernatural significance, some of which survives even in the milieu of Oaxacan Catholicism. An example would be *Datura meteloides*, for which Messer collected the term *binij̆ bido*. This is all that remains of *nocuana pinijchi pitào* ("fruit of [the plant called] ghost of the great spirit"), one of several 16th century terms for hallucinogenic plants. Of *Datura*, the early Spanish chroniclers wrote, *"fruta como erizo de castaña, con que los indios ven visiones comiéndola."*

With the publication of this volume, we now see the dim outlines of the Precolumbian Zapotec plant world. We see the vegetation itself through Smith's reconstruction, which uses the principles of botany to reason back from the tiny remnants that have survived to be studied. We see the Precolumbian classificatory system by reasoning back from Messer's rich, though acculturated, ethnobotanical data, using ethnohistory as our bridge to the past.

Ann Arbor, Michigan
May 1, 1978

REFERENCES CITED

Marcus, Joyce
   1978 Archaeology and Religion: A Comparison of the Zapotec and Maya. World Archaeology, Vol. 10(2).

Marcus, Joyce, and Kent V. Flannery
   1978 Ethnoscience of the 16th Century Valley Zapotec. *In:* The Nature and Status of Ethnobotany, edited by Richard I. Ford. Museum of Anthropology, University of Michigan, Anthropological Papers, No. 67. Ann Arbor.

Smith, C. Earle, Jr.
   1965*a* Agriculture, Tehuacán Valley. Fieldiana: Botany 31:49-100.
   1965*b* Flora, Tehuacán Valley. Fieldiana: Botany 31:101-143.
   1967 Plant remains. *In:* The prehistory of the Tehuacán Valley, Vol 1: Environment and Subsistence, edited by Douglas S. Byers. University of Texas Press. Austin.

Part 1

THE VEGETATIONAL HISTORY OF THE OAXACA VALLEY

Frontispiece. Tlacolula arm of the Oaxaca Valley in the vicinity of Mitla. The thorn-scrub vegetation in the foreground once occupied all of the valley floor except the dark area at the center. The dark area at the valley center represents the original extent of riverine forest along the Río Mitla (Río Salado). The ecotone between the thorn-scrub and the oak-pine forest can be clearly seen on slopes on the other side of the valley.

MEMOIRS OF THE MUSEUM OF ANTHROPOLOGY
UNIVERSITY OF MICHIGAN
NUMBER 10

PREHISTORY AND HUMAN ECOLOGY
OF THE VALLEY OF OAXACA

Kent V. Flannery and Richard E. Blanton, General Editors

Volume 5

Part 1:

THE VEGETATIONAL HISTORY OF THE OAXACA VALLEY

BY C. EARLE SMITH, JR.

ANN ARBOR
1978

CONTENTS

Illustrations 6
Preface 7
I. Geographical Overview 9
II. Present-Day Vegetation in the Oaxaca Valley 13
III. Original Vegetation of the Valley 17
IV. Summary 23
    Resumen en Español 27
    References 29

ILLUSTRATIONS

MAPS

1. The Valley of Oaxaca, showing all localities mentioned in the text 8
2. Reconstructed vegetational map of the Oaxaca Valley in prehistoric times 19

PLATES

Frontispiece. Tlacolula arm of the Oaxaca Valley ii
1a. Cultivation of the Oaxaca Valley 31
1b. Cultivation of the Río Atoyac Valley 31
2a. Mitla arm of the Oaxaca Valley 32
2b. View of the Oaxaca Valley 32
2c. The Mitla River 32
2d. Vegetation of the Mitla River bank 32
3a. Mitla mesquite forest 33
3b. Vegetation at the edge of Gheo-Shih 33
4a. Thorn-scrub around Caballito Blanco 34
4b. Cleared land near Mitla 34
4c. Thorn-scrub near the ignimbrite cliffs 34
4d. Corral del Cerro 34
5a. *Quercus impressa* near Guilá Naquitz Cave 35
5b. Vegetation near Guilá Naquitz Cave 35
6a. Thorn-scrub and oak-pine zones above 1700 meters 36
6b. Shrubby members of the thorn-scrub 36
7a. Hedgerows along the old Oaxaca-Tlacolula road 37
7b. Mounds throughout the valley offer refuge for perennial plants 37
7c. Hedgerow plants 37
7d. Willow trees along the Rio Atoyac 37
8a. The only valley floor forest remnant left in 1965 38
8b. Sites of old hedgerows in the fields near Zaachila 38
8c. Alders and willows 38
8d. Various stages of usage of the hills at the north end of the Oaxaca Valley 38
9a. Valley sides behind Tierras Largas illustrate centuries of land use 39
9b. Clearing for fields and pastures continues on the ridges 39
9c. Ridges above San Gabriel Etla show the results of repeated clearings 39
9d. Slopes along the road from the Oaxaca Valley to Guelatao support the best second-growth oak-pine forest left near the valley 39

TABLES

1. Mesophyllic vegetation at similar elevations at localities north and south of the Oaxaca Valley 21

PREFACE

In cooperation with the University of Michigan project "Prehistory and Human Ecology of the Valley of Oaxaca," under the direction of Kent V. Flannery, I surveyed the current vegetation of the Oaxaca Valley in order to establish a comparative collection by which archeological plant remains could be identified (Flannery et al. 1967). When these data were combined with Michael and Anne Kirkby's data concerning the water resources of the valley (Kirkby 1973), it became obvious that rather far-reaching changes have occurred in the Oaxaca Valley vegetation due to human manipulation. In this report, I shall attempt to present a picture of the current vegetation and reconstruct the valley's post-Pleistocene vegetation as it was at the time that it was first utilized by man.

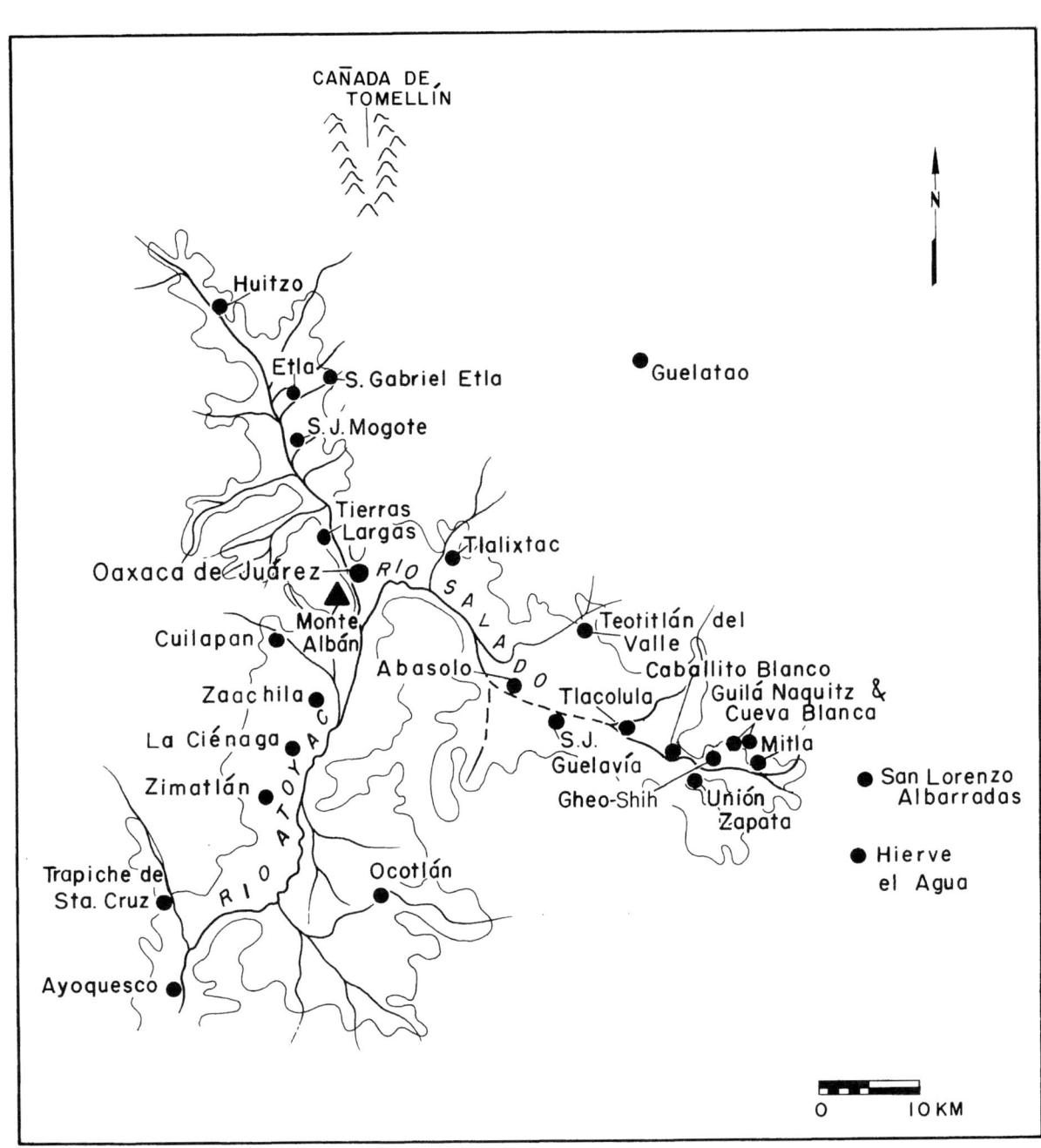

Map 1. The Valley of Oaxaca, showing all localities mentioned in the text.

I

GEOGRAPHICAL OVERVIEW

The Oaxaca Valley is an anomalous formation in the jumbled highlands of southern Mexico. Where narrow, rivercut valleys thread the mountains in all directions, the Oaxaca Valley spreads a broad plain between 16°40' and 17°20' N and between 96°15' and 96°55' W. (Pl. 1a, b). The Atoyac River, originating to the north in the mountains, has deposited a broad alluvial bed from near Etla almost to Ayoquesco. The Río Salado, joining the Atoyac from the southeast, has undoubtedly added its share, although this stream now has a much smaller flow than the main river. The remarkably level valley floor is about 1550 m above sea level. The major elevation in the valley is the mountain mass between Tlacolula and Ocotlán, which divides the southern end of the valley into two major arms.

The arm extending to the southeast from the center of the valley contains the site of Mitla, a major pre-Conquest center. This is undoubtedly the driest section, since the Mitla River (Río Salado) flows with vigor only during the rainy season (Pl. 2c, d), and this arm receives less rainfall than the remainder of the valley. It is obvious from the vegetation that Mitla receives less precipitation than the nearest meteorological station, Tlacolula. Here the annual precipitation has ranged from 382 to 886 mm over the period of recorded data since 1921 (in contrast to Oaxaca where the range has been from 420 to 896 mm).

A comparison of the meteorological records for the Oaxaca Valley stations of Oaxaca and Tlacolula shows some interesting variations (Boletín Hidrológico and Boletín Hidrométrico, 1955-60). It should be noted that Tlacolula is at an elevation of 1650 m, approximately 100 m higher than Oaxaca which is 1563 m. Over about ten years, precipitation peaks for both stations have generally occurred in June and September. The earlier peak has consistently had less rainfall than the later peak for Oaxaca, while the reverse sometimes occurs at Tlacolula. This is emphasized by the recorded precipitation for the 1955-1960 period, when the highest recorded precipitation for June at Oaxaca for all years was 220 mm, but 211 mm is the highest recorded for Tlacolula. During the September precipitation peak, a maximum high for the period recorded at Oaxaca was 236 mm (16 mm more than the highest June peak) while a maximum high for the same period at Tlacolula was only 160 mm. Another variation is shown by the dry season records, which show that Oaxaca generally has no recorded precipitation during December, January and February, while Tlacolula frequently records no rainfall for the entire November through March period. As mentioned above, rainfall at Oaxaca averages about 500 to 800 mm per year, whereas Tlacolula records about 500 to 650 mm per year.

In any evaluation of meteorological conditions in relation to vegetation, factors other than the overall precipitation are generally considered although the relationship of the meteorological data to the plant life is still imperfectly understood. One of the factors which must be considered is the loss of moisture through evaporation. The only figures available to me are from the Oaxaca station, where a high of 2611 mm was recorded in 1949. Generally, evaporation for this station is about 1950 mm, which obviously exceeds the precipitation by a margin of at least a thousand millimeters. With the considerably longer dry season at Tlacolula, the water deficit due to evaporation must be even greater than that recorded at Oaxaca.

Part of the effectiveness of available precipitation is associated with the temperatures in which it is operative. The records for mean annual temperatures for Oaxaca and Tlacolula from 1921 to 1960 indicate that the two stations are about 1°C apart (Tlacolula generally recording the cooler temperature because of elevation). The pattern is disturbed from 1940 onward when the differences recorded at the two stations diverge more widely (1.6° C in 1940 to a maximum of 6.2° C in 1955). While it is not the place of this discussion to explain the greater divergence, it may be a result of expanding urban settlement in the city of Oaxaca.

The minima and maxima are frequently more important than are the means of temperature in delimiting plant growth. Maximum temperatures are less liable to be limiting than are minimum temperatures, but they must be noted because they function in the mean annual temperature computations and illuminate the divergence in mean annual temperature between Oaxaca and Tlacolula noted above. Over the period from 1921 to 1960, maximum recorded temperatures at both stations never exceeded 39° C. This temperature was recorded in Tlacolula in 1941 and 1945 but in Oaxaca only in 1954. In general, the spread of the highest temperatures between Oaxaca and Tlacolula has seldom exceeded two degrees; on the average one degree has been normal, with the highest temperatures recorded in Tlacolula prior to 1942. In that year, the highest temperature was recorded in Oaxaca, as it was in all subsequent years for which comparisons are available except 1945. During this period, the spread between maximum temperatures at the two stations frequently exceeded two degrees and in 1954 reached 7.5° C.

Minimum annual temperatures exhibit another anomaly over the 1921-1960 observation period which must complement the shift noted above. As is to be expected, the Tlacolula station, which is about 100 m higher in elevation than that at Oaxaca, consistently reports lower temperatures. For many years, the difference is similar to that noted for maximum termperatures of 2.0° C to 4.0°C. Frost (0.0°C) was reported for Tlacolula on several occasions, but after 1950 this station consistently reports several degrees of frost (-3.5°C to -8.5°C) every year for which a summary report is available. During these years, the differential between Oaxaca and Tlacolula varies from as little as 6.0°C to as much as 9.0°C. The warming trend noted in maximum and mean annual temperature reports for Oaxaca is thus reinforced by a lowering of minimum annual temperatures at Tlacolula.

While the interplay of precipitation and temperature and the less precise value of evaporation rate can be plotted with finality, the effect on vegetation must be calculated in terms of other factors. Less clearly understood are edaphic factors, particularly those involved with the moisture regimen which is so critical to the success or failure of individual plants or to certain species of plants.

The relationship between the soil and soil solution and the vegetational cover is very difficult to study because any disturbance of the soil disrupts the normal pattern of moisture dispersal. Likewise, any disturbance of plant tissue to insert devices to monitor fluid flow similarly disrupts the normal sap flow, and the plant immediately begins to modify all adjacent living tissue to seal off the area. Thus, all observations have been made from disrupted systems or by the erection of models against which comparisons of natural phenomena have been made. Once man has begun to clear or otherwise modify vegetational cover, it is nearly impossible to reestablish the original conditions.

However, some observations have been made which appear to have validity over wide areas of the arid and semiarid parts of the world. Amount of precipitation reaching the soil is directly conditioned by the amount and kind of vegetational cover. Milthorpe (1960) reports interception of as much as 55% of the precipitation during light showers, but during showers of total fall greater than 40 mm, only 10% were lost to interception. Other work has shown that channelization by leaves and stem flow has resulted in redistribution of 20% of the precipitation in the California chaparral.

Obviously, the precipitation which finally reaches the soil surface will be absorbed according to the degree of slope, the smoothness of the surface, the size of the soil particles, the porosity of the soil and many other factors. Both the compacting action of raindrops on bare soil and the swelling of clay particles with wetting tend to decrease the rate of absorption, and in some arid area soils, surface colloids swell with wetting to the extent that they slow intake of water to zero within two hours. Once the precipitation has been absorbed into the soil, it may percolate downward until an equilibrium has been established between the amount of water entering the soil and the amount clinging to the constituent soil particles by adhesion, or until it reaches the water table. However, a portion of the soil moisture from a wet soil is lost by evaporation. Some workers have found that as much as 20 mm of water can be lost from the upper soil quite rapidly, and an additional 7 to 8 mm may be lost slowly over a prolonged period. Of course, the amount and kinds of vegetational cover modify the rate of evaporation also, but vegetation introduces losses through transpiration.

Unfortunately, transpiration data are derived principally from cultivated crops, because of the difficulties in measuring transpiration in the mixed vegetation of a natural area and because crop plants are economically more important on a day-to-day basis. One of the few measurements which have been made by comparing the transpiration of a stand of trees with the same area completely cleared indicates that forest in the eastern United States transpires about one-third of the annual precipitation (Hoover 1944). No measurements have been made in areas of restricted rainfall such as the Oaxaca Valley. However, the evidence suggests that vegetation both increases soil uptake of precipitation in various ways and retards evaporation from the soil solution. Although measurements are not available, it appears that the balance is higher on the side of soil covered with vegetation; i.e., the uptake of rainfall is better and water is retained more readily than on bare soil.

Salt apparently has a marked effect on the availability of soil water to plants, as well as on the actual dynamics of mechanical water retention in the soil. Downes (1961) suggests that all of the salts added to soils are of oceanic origin, although salt is transported inland more than 100 miles in only very small amounts. Whatever the origin of the salts, they are frequently a concern in arid and semiarid areas because lack of water for flushing means that they may accumulate in low areas. Milthorpe (1960) suggests that salt in surface layers results in lower vapor pressure and, therefore, lower evaporation rates for soil water. It has long been known that the presence of salts above certain concentrations greatly affects the vegetational cover of an area through the elimination of those plants which are intolerant of salt. Even in concentrations low enough to allow the persistence of salt-intolerant plants, salts can lower the osmotic pressure of the soil solution so that normal uptake of soil solution into a root system is hampered.

Altogether, the many factors impinging on the proportions of species of plants occurring in a specific place (precluding the disturbing effects of man), are imperfectly known and often nearly impossible to measure. However, the patterning of vegetation on the earth's surface is regular enough so that observations of major meteorological and edaphic factors can allow a reasonably, if not absolutely accurate, prediction of the nature of a plant cover. Further, by comparison with other areas of like elevation, soil and climate at the same latitude, some confirmation of the prediction can be achieved.

II

PRESENT-DAY VEGETATION IN THE OAXACA VALLEY

The present-day vegetation of the Oaxaca Valley is much changed from the original plant cover of the area. Today, the greater part of the valley floor and the gentler slopes of the valley sides are in cultivation. Steeper slopes have been cultivated and are currently pastured. Even the steepest slopes and ridge tops have been markedly changed by the activities of the charcoal burners, timber harvesters and herders even if they have not been under cultivation.

The valley floor is a mosaic of cultivated fields, divided by boundary lines which are the only areas in which plants grow undisturbed over a long period of time (Pl. 2a). Occasional trees are left standing along the Río Atoyac and the Río Salado (Mitla River) (Pl. 2). These are principally willow (*Salix bonplandiana* HBK.). The southeastern arm of the valley rises gradually and receives less rainfall than the Atoyac Valley proper. Thus, some areas of thin soil are still seen in fallow vegetation which is undoubtedly all secondary. However, it may approach the original cover for this area more closely than does vegetation in other parts of the valley.

In the Mitla arm of the valley, the valley of the Río Mitla-Río Salado has some trees, principally willow, along it. However, the flood plain is well used and the vegetation is disturbed and weedy (Pl. 2d). Where land is unused for one reason or another at a greater distance from the river, the principal tree is mesquite (*Prosopis juliflora* [Sw.] DC.) intermixed with much *nopal* or prickly pear (*Opuntia* spp.) (Pl. 3a). Further removed from the river on the higher valley slopes, the less disturbed vegetation gives way to a mixed thorn-scrub which varies according to drainage and soil. For example, in some of the arroyos near Mitla, the soil is very thin and the area is heavily grazed. Here heavy use has resulted in a formation of weedy shrubs and herbs more equivalent to meadow in more northerly regions. Rocky prominences have probably never been severely disturbed except for the removal of firewood and harvesting of wild foods. However, these have never supported a very rich sample of the flora. Those of larger extent, like the volcanic tuff mesa at Caballito Blanco (Paddock 1966: Fig. 89), are continuously exploited by grazing, for poles, for fuel and for other uses (Pl. 4a). These activities have undoubtedly changed the species composition of the area to the extent that it bears little resemblance to the original vegetation. The thorn-scrub extends outward from the Mitla area into the hills where the cave sites of Guilá Naquitz, Cueva Blanca, etc. are located (Flannery et al. 1967). Little of this area is currently under cultivation, but everywhere evidences of former cultivation can be seen. Today, this is principally pasturage for herds from Unión Zapata ("Loma Larga," an *agencia* of Mitla), which exert their influence by selective grazing, removal of seedlings and cropping of annuals before they have set seed.

Currently, vegetation in the Mitla arm of the Oaxaca Valley is marked by a few prominent species of plants (Pl. 2d). Along the river itself, the *sauce*, or willow, *Salix bonplandiana* HBK., is the principal tree around which grow weedy shrubs, largely of the Compositae or sunflower family. In much of the area, *Selloa glutinosa* of the Compositae is abundant, particularly in areas of land abuse (Pl. 2c). In the river valley, *Prosopis juliflora* (Sw.) DC. predominates wherever the vegetation has been uncleared for a long enough period of time. It is frequently accompanied by small trees or large shrubs of *huizache*, *Acacia farnesiana* (L.) Willd. In this area, *Solanum* aff. *laurifolium* Mill., *Opuntia pumila* Rose with its yellow to salmon flowers, and *Lantana involucrata* are common.

Perhaps the thorn-scrub of the Oaxaca Valley can be best characterized as a zone of loosely scattered shrubs and small trees liberally punctuated with arborescent cacti (Pl. 4a). The most common large cacti are the *tunillo, Lemaireocereus treleasei* (Vaupel) B. & R., whose dark red fruit is seasonally available for harvesting; *Myrtillocactus schenkii* (Purpus) B. & R., with small edible fruit; and several large species of *nopal, Opuntia* spp. (Pl. 4b). The shrubs are many and varied. Perhaps the most ubiquitous is *Croton ciliato-glandulosus* Ort., which has inconspicuous cream-white flowers. Others like *Lantana involucrata,* and the *mala mujer, Jatropha urens* L., are more conspicuous, as is *Bouvardia xylosteoides* H. & A. The yellow flowers of *Bunchosia montana* Juss. often vie with the yellow flowers of *Acacia farnesiana* (L.) Willd.

The trees of the thorn-scrub are all small in stature with spreading crowns and, often, tortuous branches. Except in better watered areas, the trees are scattered. Perhaps the most conspicuous of these is *Cassia polyantha* Moc. & Sesse, although *huizache* often becomes a tree conspicuous because of its long white spines. Less frequently, trees like *Randia watsonii* form a local colony which is well known to the shepherd boys, who gather the fruit for its bitter dark brown pulp. However, over much of the thorn-scrub area, trees are conspicuous for their absence (Pl. 5a-b). In fact, the shallow depth of soil and the persistent misuse of the area has resulted in virtual elimination of woody plants from the site known as Gheo-Shih. (Flannery and Marcus 1976: 206-207).

The Gheo-Shih area has a scattered ground cover of herbaceous plants like *Cyperus densicaespitosus* Mattf. & Kuek., *Tridax coronopifolia* (HBK.) Hemsl., and *Pectis saturejoides* (Mill.) Sch.-Bip. Perhaps the most common shrub is *Bunchosia montana* Juss., which is conspicuous with yellow flowers and orange or red fruit.

The northeastern side of the Mitla arm of the Oaxaca Valley is today largely uncultivated, although it is intensively grazed. Evidences for former use are numerous, and the secondary vegetation in the area has been much modified from the original vegetation. The thorn-scrub and cactus continue up the barrancas in all directions to an elevation of about 1700 m. At this elevation, oak trees become mixed with the more abundant thorn-scrub species (Pl. 6a). It is probable that the tops of the hills in this area (above the site of Guilá Naquitz) were once covered with an oak-pine forest. In the ecotone, other species of the oak-pine forest association have also persisted including *Arctostaphylos polifolia* HBK. (*manzanilla*) and *Amelanchier denticulata* (HBK.) Koch (*madroño*), both of which bear fruits which were probably once exploited. The oaks persisting at the present time are *Quercus impressa* Trel., although other species must have been present in the original forest in the area (Pl. 6a). Unfortunately, the tops of the hills will probably remain somewhat impoverished because of the heavy use of this area for grazing.

The broad bottom of the valley near Mitla has little native vegetation remaining because of the very long history of agriculture here (Pl. 4b). However, the presence of the Mitla River furnishes moisture year around in an otherwise dry area, and upward from Mitla, the valley must have supported ever more dense vegetation. Currently, such colorful flowers as the orange and yellow of *Castilleja tenuiflora* Benth., the purple flowers of *Solanum peduncularis* (Schlect.) Bitter and the scarlet flowers of *Lamourouxia rhinanthifolia* HBK. suggest that this must have been a beautiful area (Pl. 4c). In this area the *Oxalis* sp. locally called *chiciule* is not uncommon. The roots of the plant are known to be edible.

Not far above Mitla toward San Lorenzo Albarradas are found the first pine trees. *Pinus michoacana* Martínez appears to be common. Other woody plants include the *palo cuchi, Cassia villosa* Mill., *Ceanothus coeruleus* Lag., *Arbutus xalapensis* HBK. (*madroño*), and *Xolisma squamulosa* (Mart. & Gal.) small. During the rainy season, herbaceous plants like *Commelina elegans* HBK. with blue flowers and *Setcreasea australis* Rose with rose colored flowers grow close to the rocks or beneath spiny shrubs. The fern, *Pellaea allosuroides* (Mett.) Hieron., and the fern ally, *Selaginella lepidophylla* (Hooke & Grev.) Spring (the "resurrection fern" of U.S. novelty shops), lend an apperance of somewhat more moist conditions although both are well adapted to dry areas.

The hedgerows of the valley floor provide the only habitat of little disturbance for native vegetation (Pl. 7a). They are also the refuges for introduced foreign species such as *pirul, Schinus molle,* which has become a prominent tree in the Mexican landscape. Perhaps the most common species are a shrubby composite, *Verbesina* sp., and the rangy *rompecapa* or hackberry, *Celtis pallida* Torr. The fruit of the latter is edible; for this reason, the plant is probably encouraged. Often, larger trees like mesquite, *Prosopis juliflora,* or, in the Zaachila area, *guamuchil, Pithecolobium dulce,* are occasionally allowed to persist. In the Mitla arm of the valley, the *lechuguilla (Agave karwinskii)* forms an impenetrable barrier (Pl. 7c). To the north around Etla, hedgerows include a number of trees of the spiny *Pereskiopsis rotundifolia* (DC.) B. & R. and the conspicuous, large-leaved *Jatropha ciliata* Sesse in Cerv. In the same area, hedgerows at San José Mogote are often largely *tunillo, Lemaireocereus* cf. *treleasei,* and *isote, Yucca* sp. Thus, it is obvious that local preferences control the species to be favored in the hedgerows, and they cannot be taken as any indication of the original composition of the valley floor vegetation.

Over many parts of the valley floor, the only refugia for species of the native vegetation are the archaeological mounds. Near San José Mogote in the Etla region (Flannery and Marcus 1976:208-219) the mounds harbor a miscellany of spiny shrubs, trees and cacti such as mesquite, *Prosopis juliflora,* and *Opuntia* which are favored because of their edible parts (Pl. 7b). In the same area, a few old willows (*Salix*) are allowed to persist on or near the river bank (Pl. 7d). The only remnant of original vegetation on the entire valley floor is a small portion of forest along the Panamerican Highway near Etla (Pl. 8a, c). This has been thoroughly high-graded for firewood (perhaps without the knowledge of the absentee owner) so that the only tree species left are willow and alder. However, it is the refuge for a number of interesting shrubby and herbaceous species like *Passiflora subpeltata* Ort., climbing over the shrubs and into the trees, *Solanum nudum* L. and *Solanum hispidum* Pers., both of which are shrubby or tree-like. The most conspicuous herbaceaous plant sprawling on the ground is *Teucrium* cf. *vesicarium* Mill. In the vicinity of La Ciénaga and Zaachila, the *guamuchil, Pithecolobium dulce,* is frequently left standing because of the sweet material around the seeds (Pl. 8b).

As the valley is limited in all directions by uplands, the 1700 m contour is soon approached, where a change to oak-pine forest takes place. On many of the slopes, this has been removed for fields and pastures or has been heavily utilized for firewood or charcoal. To the north, the hills nearer the valley obviously have been repeatedly cleared, so that one can now see vegetation in all stages—from newly plowed fields, to grassed-in shrubby pastures, to poor quality second-growth woods with many scrub oaks (Pl. 8d). Elevations to the west and to the south are less. There the rainfall or accumulated runoff is less, but the gentler slopes have been heavily exploited (Pl. 9a). All show extensive clearing and second growth, and many slopes show marked gully erosion. As on the slopes behind the Tierras Largas site (Winter 1972), regrowth of trees is now largely restricted to the gullies or *barrancas* (Pl. 9b). In the southeast, where rainfall is more limited, trees have not regrown, but the secondary vegetation is largely shrubby.

The oak-pine forest zone above the Mitla arm of the valley has probably never supported as luxuriant a tree cover as have the slopes to the north, because of the paucity of rainfall in the Mitla region. The pressure of population has meant the constant scavenging of fuel from the upper slopes so that the better species for this purpose were removed first, and inroads have continued to be made on the rest of the species (Pl. 9c). Thus, no forest within reach of the Oaxaca Valley is today untouched. The best, easily accessible examples of secondary forest are those along the Guelatao road leading up slope to the east of the valley center (Pl. 9d). Here mixed oak-pine forest is composed of several species each of oaks and pines. Pines dominate on well-drained soils toward ridgetops. Oaks predominate overall. In this area are some of the unusual plants of the Oaxaca area such as *Salvia tricuspidata* Mart. & Gal. with blue flowers and the vine *Metastelma macropodum* Greenm. Straggling shrubs of *Fuchsia minutiflora* Hemsl. with numerous small flowers with red sepals and white petals are much less common than *Bouvardia viminalis* Schlecht. with conspicuous, vividly scarlet flowers and the ubiquitous *Bidens pilosa* L. with its white and yellow heads and achenes which cling to any rough surface. Herbaceous plants are more numerous in this habitat than in the drier lower areas of the valley.

A similar oak-pine area to the southwest along the *quebrada* of the Río Serrano south of Trapiche de Sta. Cruz has a large population of *Dahlia coccinea* Cav. often mixed with *Russelia sarmentosa* Jacq. both of which bear conspicuous red flowers. Near the greater humidity of the river, *Mirabilis sanguinea* Heimerl. bears rose colored flowers among the silvery bracts of *Eryngium scaposum* Turcz. Along this stream, the *ahuehuete*, *Taxodium mucronatum* Ten. supported plants of *Tillandsia fasciculata* Sw. (called *biliuh* in Zapotec) with brilliant red and yellow inflorescences. It is impossible to determine if the ahuehuete is native or planted here, because of the obvious disturbance of the area by man.

III

ORIGINAL VEGETATION OF THE VALLEY

At the present time, the major part of the Oaxaca Valley is under urban areas, villages, cultivation or grazing. Even the slopes of the valley walls are cultivated or grazed and the upper slopes of the oak-pine zone (roughly elevations above 1700 m) often are grazed. In any event, preparation of charcoal and the removal of firewood has been disturbing this forest for at least 3000 years as evidenced by charcoal braziers with pine charcoal recovered at San José Mogote (K. Flannery, personal communication). The vegetation of the Oaxaca Valley is obviously now highly modified from that which grew here when the first attempts at plant cultivation were undertaken.

In spite of the fact that the present vegetation is either highly disturbed, or consists of weeds imported from elsewhere, a number of lines of evidence can be utilized to reconstruct the original vegetational pattern. It is obviously impossible to completely reconstruct the original species associations without ample evidence in the form of pollen, fossils or subfossils. Even each of these kinds of evidence is limited. Pollen most frequently found and identified is that which is wind borne, and the majority of species in any flora are insect pollinated or, less frequently, bird or bat pollinated. Also, local conditions may cause a severe loss of pollen so that only the most abundant grains persist or the analyst finds no pollen at all. Fossils are even more rarely formed than is pollen preserved. While the process of fossilization is not thoroughly understood, most paleobotanists feel that plant material must be in a constantly wet environment to prevent rotting, with the deposit of fine sediments of the proper chemical composition to ensure the development of impressions with details. Since these conditions are rarely attained, fossils are rare. Furthermore, the need for submersion of plant material in water means that plants which grow at a distance from a body of water are seldom fossilized. Fossils of the vegetation of the recent past are unknown from the Valley of Oaxaca, but dessicated plants from dry caves number in the thousands, and the pollen record is reported to reflect no major climatic changes since the end of the Pleistocene (Schoenwetter 1974).

Utilizing the observable factors affecting vegetation can provide clear indications of the kinds of vegetation which might grow in areas of human disturbance. Obviously, the climatic, edaphic, and hydraulic factors cited earlier in this paper provide facts which may be considered. Another set of facts is provided by the survey of soils and the valley water table (Kirkby 1973). In spite of our lack of concrete knowledge concerning interactions, certain observable phenomena certainly occur. For instance, meteorological techniques measure precipitation with standard gauges and evaporation from open containers of water. Absorptions of water by various soil types can be physically measured in the laboratory as can the evaporations from these soils. However, none of these can properly express the modifications introduced by vegetation. It is observable, though, that under the cover of vegetation during the day, temperatures may be considerably lower and a domino effect leads to lower evaporation of water from the soil surface under vegetation, because the cooler air physically holds less water and is less absorbent. Further, observations have shown that erosion is less liable to occur under a vegetational cover because less runoff occurs. This apparently is due to a number of factors, including greater tilth due to higher organic content in the soil, as well as greater activities of burrowing animals, and more debris on the soil surface. Included is the breaking of raindrops by the interference of stems and leaves so that compaction of soil is less, and the channeling of precipitation to areas near the base of the plant where more duff provides a greater surface for absorption.

Along with such observations, one must be aware of the potential species which might inhabit an area under a certain climatic regimen at a specific latitude, longitude, and elevation. Along with these must be considered the vegetation of nearby areas which might be able to furnish propagules for such colonization, and this consideration must recognize the fact that not years, but hundreds of centuries were available for such movements of plant species to take place. Sometimes, the local animals and birds follow specific routes of movements and they may have been influential in transporting propagules intentionally or unintentionally. For instance, many birds follow habitual routes between feeding areas and roosting areas. If fruit is ingested with intact seeds, these seeds are often voided during the return flight from the feeding area to the roosting area, thus providing transport and planting with a fertilizer, which, of course, will only be successful if the seed falls on a suitable habitat.

A glance at the topographic map of southern Mexico shows that several land routes are available for the movement of plants into the Oaxaca Valley. To the north, a way through the mountains via the Tomellín Canyon and the Tehuacán Valley exists, which connects along the Papaloapan River with the lowlands of Veracruz. To the south and east, via the Miahuatlán Valley, and the course of the Ríos Grande and Tehuantepec, plants have access from the Isthmus of Tehuantepec. Finally, to the south and west via the course of the Ríos Atoyac and Verde, plants could immigrate from the Pacific coastal lowlands.

Finally, the highland ridges overlooking the Oaxaca Valley on either side are well watered and have served as a corridor for north-south movement of many species of plants. Many of these species are present on the highlands from Guatemala to northern Mexico along the Sierra Madre Oriental and the Sierra Madre Occidental. Wherever a tributary stream has formed a barranca on the mountainside, conditions have been favorable for the movement of some of these species down into the Río Atoyac Valley.

Thus, at the time of first human colonization in the Oaxaca Valley, the vegetation must have presented a far different appearance than it does at the present time. Based upon a study of the water table and soils of the valley, some concept of the original vegetation can be given. Map 2 represents a reconstruction of this vegetation. Along the course of the Río Atoyac and its principal tributaries which are permanent streams, the water table is high. Except for some areas of sand, soil is frequently a loam or clay loam. Utilizing the present water table, the forest is depicted as occupying all of the tributary bank and river bank area where the water table lies 3 m or less beneath the surface. It is designated as willow-alder or willow forest because these are the dominant species along streams at the present time.

The map depicts a very conservative estimate of the former extent of the riverine forest in the Oaxaca Valley. Considering the many meteorological and edaphic factors which change under conditions of fully developed forest, and the probable changes in the hydrostatic state of the valley, it is obvious that the 1 m water table once extended much further from the water courses, particularly in areas of heavier soil. The overall effect of a considerably more dense forest cover would have been the absorption into the water table of a large part of the summer precipitation and holding of this water reserve longer into the dry season, in spite of the increased loss due to transpiration. In fact, the microclimatic conditions under forest cover usually result in a slightly lowered mean annual temperature and a corresponding decrease in the need for water by organisms in this forested area.

While the forest has been designated as willow-alder and willow forest because of the species which are in the area today, this has by no means been true in the past. Such a broad river valley at this elevation would normally support a broad mixture of species from many families. Almost certainly, the ahuehuete, *Taxodium mucronatum,* would have been present in

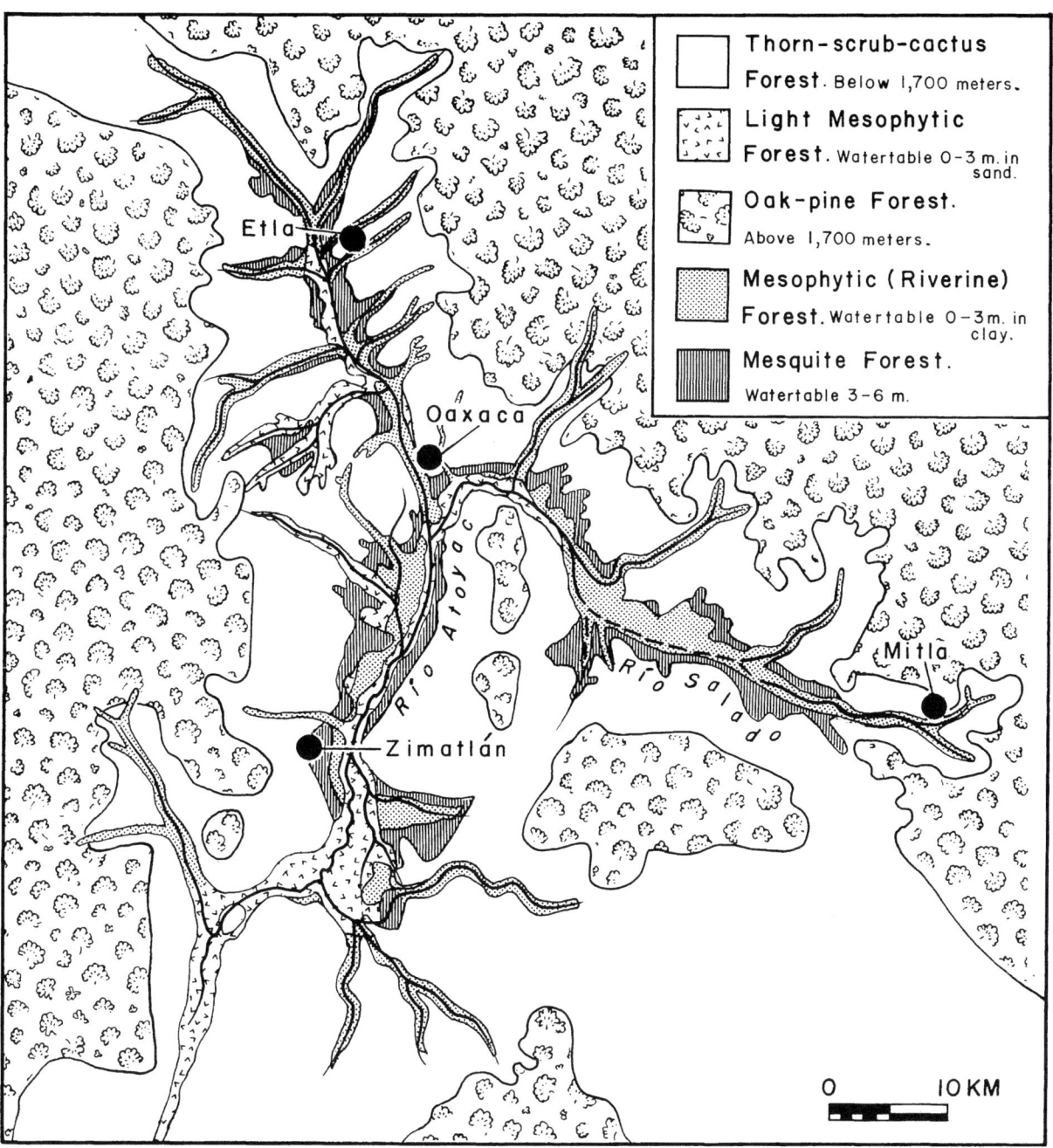

Map 2. Reconstruction of primary vegetation zones in the Valley of Oaxaca.

the areas of wet soil. At the present time, *Anona purpurea* and *Cedrela oaxacansis* are present in the quebrada forests higher on the mountainside, and would undoubtedly have been present in the forest on the valley floor. Members of the Lauraceae such as *Persea americana* are suited to such a habitat, as are many members of the genus *Ficus,* particularly strangling figs. However, the convenience of this forest for raw material, fuel, and finally the pressure for cultivable land, has resulted in the complete removal of all except scattered willow trees. In only one plot of land near Etla is there any vestige of forest. Here along a permanently flowing tributary, alder and willow form a much degraded forest, showing only stumps where other larger trees have been removed. Neither willow nor alder are considered preeminently useful, thus their persistence.

Collateral information from other areas of Mexico is difficult to find. In the first place, in the southern highlands of Mexico, the Oaxaca Valley is unique in having such a broad valley floor with an extended area of high water table. Even so, many of the valleys of this area with permanent streams and at similar elevations must have supported streamside forests. Because of human demands, these have all disappeared. Miranda says (1942), "Por lo que antecede, se comprende la impossibilidad de encontrar en estas tierras llanas un lugar suficientemente extenso y no labrado durante el tiempo necesario (siempre bastante largo) para que la asociación primitiva (climax) o una que la sustituya (subclimax) logren regenerarse." He was speaking of another area, but the facts remain the same for any area of Mexico. Perhaps a representative example of this kind of forest is that discussed by Miranda (1957) under the heading "Selva mediana y baja siempre verde" in Chiapas. A list of tree species is provided, many of which must have once grown in the Oaxaca Valley.

Another treatment, *La Vegetación de Nueva Galicia* (Rzedowski and McVaugh 1966), provides another description of forest under the name "Bosque mesófilo de montaña," much of which might once have applied to the forest of the Oaxaca Valley. Of course, both descriptions of forest associations apply to large areas of Mexico and the lists of species encompasses many more species than might have been in the valley originally, but these lists and descriptions merely provide some guide to the former richness of the Oaxaca Valley riverine forest flora (see Table 1).

At the present time, beyond the area where the water table is between 6 and 3 m below the surface of the current soil, grows a more open forest in which mesquite predominates. Prior to the development of agriculture in the Oaxaca Valley, mesquite forest must have been thickly intergrown with other leguminous trees as well as trees of Burseraceae, Malvaceae, Euphorbiaceae and others which can withstand the long dry period with a water table 3 m or more beneath the surface. Presently, the mesquite areas are characterized by heavy concentrations of prickly pear, which probably did not persist in this forest when it was much more dense. In fact, the crown density has undoubtedly been markedly changed by the removal of all of the other tree species for firewood except such persistent trees as *huizache* (*Acacia farnesiana*) and *mala mujer* (*Jatropha urens*). Thus, the heliophiles, those species requiring a large percentage of exposure to sunlight, would have been excluded from the primary forest of the mesquite area.

Again, the exact composition of the original vegetation of the mesquite zone will never be known. Not only have inroads been made here for construction material and fuel, but, with summer rainfall as high as it is in the Oaxaca Valley, these soils are eminently suitable for summer agriculture. The clearing of these relatively level valley areas was undoubtedly accomplished largely before extensive use was made of the nearby hillslopes.

Beyond the valley floor area suitable for mesquite (that is, beyond the limits of the 6 m deep water table), summer rainfall was quite adequate to maintain a good thorn-scrub forest similar to that described for the northeastern side of the Tehuacán Valley (Smith 1965). In fact, ease of distribution of plants via the Cañada de Tomellín undoubtedly had resulted in many of the same species being represented in both floras, because the elevations and the meteorological conditions are similar. Unlike the Tehuacán Val-

TABLE 1

MESOPHYLLIC VEGETATION AT SIMILAR ELEVATIONS AT LOCALITIES NORTH AND SOUTH OF THE OAXACA VALLEY

Bosque mesófilo de montaña

Dense community dominated by trees 20-40 m tall, inhabiting the mountainsides, barranca and canyon banks and other protected places at elevations between 800 and 2400 m in the middle southwest of Jalisco and adjacent regions of Nayarit, Colima and Michoacán.

Rzedowski & McVaugh 1966

Abies aff. religiosa	Perrottetia longistylis
Alchornea latifolia	Persea sp.
Carpinus caroliniana	Phoebe aff. ehrenbergii
Celtis monoica	Pinus pseudostrobus
Clethra spp.	Podocarpus aff. reichei
Clusia aff. salvinii	Prunus cortapico
Dendropanax arboreus	Prunus rhamnoides
Dipholis minutiflora	Quercus acutifolia
Fraxinus uhdei	Quercus elliptica
Gymnanthes actinostemoides	Quercus aff. insignis
Ilex brandegeana	Quercus laxa
Juglans major	Quercus planipocula
Juglans olanchana	Quercus salicifolia
Magnolia schiediana	Quercus scytophylla
Matudaea trinervia	Salix bonplandiana
Meliosma dentata	Tilia mexicana
Osmanthus americanus	Trophis mexicana
Ostrya virginiana	Zinowiewia concinna

Selva mediana y baja siempre verde

Found on mountainsides, abrupt barrancas and high valleys between 1200 and 2300 m elevation with a northwestern boundary to the east of Tonalá (Chiapas).

Miranda 1957

Ardisia tacanensis	Osmanthus americana
Billia hippocastanum	Parathesis tenuis
Cedrela tonduzii	Phoebe acuminatissima
Clethra matudai	Phoebe helicterifolia
Cleyera tacanensis	Podocarpus matudai
Conostegia volcanalis	Prunus tundelliana
Eugenia spp.	Rhamnus capraefolia
Hedyosmum mexicanum	Saurauia oreophila
Ilex sp.	Saurauia villosa
Inga sp.	Styrax glabrescens
Meliosma matudai	Symplocos chiapensis
Nectandra salicifolia	Trophis cuspidata
Olmediella betscheriana	Zinowiewia matudai
Oreopanax liebmannii	

ley, population pressure in the Oaxaca Valley has resulted in the nearly permanent removal of thorn-scrub and cactus from all parts of the Oaxaca Valley. Only in the Mitla arm of the valley, toward Guilá Naquitz Cave, are there some remnants of the original vegetational cover. Even here, it is obvious that this thorn-scrub is disturbed and, in many instances, has only recently returned to the area.

Some of the same species of Leguminosae and Burseraceae common to the mesquite forest would also have been prominent in the thorn-scrub. In fact, no one vegetational type will be found to have a clearcut boundary. Perhaps the most sharply defined boundary will be that of the forest which was once bordering the permanent streams of the Oaxaca Valley. For this forest, the permanent water table is a supporting factor whose lack would be immediately expressed by elimination of those species dependent upon it. Also, the intrusion of species from the mesquite forest area would be difficult. Many of these require bright light for germination and seedling establishment. They would be unable to succeed in the shade of the riverine forest, much less compete successfully in the more dense vegetation.

The boundaries between the mesquite vegetation and the thorn-scrub cactus vegetation and the boundaries between the thorn-scrub vegetation and the pine-oak forest are obscured by the blending of species in both formations along the point of contact. No single edaphic or climatic factor is ordinarily limiting; the most secure mark of change is often only in a change of dominant species. Even a change in dominant species may mean only a local difference in conditions which may be as easily observable as sandy soil versus clay soil, or entirely hidden from the casual observer.

It must always be emphasized that at least 5000 years of human disturbance (and probably more) have greatly altered the vegetation of Mexico. Today, only the vegetation of the most remote and inaccessible mountain ridges and deep barrancas remains somewhat like the original vegetation in these habitats. Even these refugia have often been selectively harvested for the more valuable plants. A person has only to stop to make a plant collection in vegetation which he feels is nearly original to find a pair of dark eyes observing him curiously.

IV

SUMMARY

Many factors, both meteorological and edaphic, control the species of plants present on any one part of the surface of the earth. In spite of intense efforts to understand these relationships in order to grow crops more effectively, we are still far from knowing the full parameters of the influences of moisture and soil on vegetation. This is primarily because a disturbance in any part of the plant body affects conditions in the remainder of the plant and disturbances of soil near the plant interrupt the normal balances in soil moisture. Thus, it is impossible to devise experiments which depend upon direct observations.

The most secure direct observations involve those of the present vegetational cover for the land. The Oaxaca Valley has been observed and its plants collected in an effort to understand the present distribution of vegetation. Currently, the valley floor and the gentler slopes are under intensive, active cultivation. Therefore, none of the original vegetational associations of the valley floor can be observed. The available slopes of the valley have been cultivated in the past (if they are not now cultivated), and most are now grazed. These have little plant cover which may have belonged to the original vegetation. In the dry, southeastern arm of the valley near Mitla, thorn-scrub and cactus is returning to a part of the land. While this includes a number of species which must have formed part of the original vegetational cover, this vegetation has been previously disturbed and still continues to be disturbed by human activity. The pine-oak forest on the heights overlooking the valley is more nearly like original forest, but even here at least three millenia of selective cutting and charcoal burning have modified the forest.

The current vegetation of the Oaxaca Valley is described as it appears. The only remnant of riverside forest is a small, highly culled segment along a tributary stream near Etla. The principal remaining trees are willow and alder. Some willow trees are permitted to grow along the banks of streams elsewhere. The much degraded mesquite forest is represented in the Mitla arm. Now, it is quite open and includes thickets of huizache and nopal. The thorn-scrub cactus forest is best developed near Mitla also, in the vicinity of the caves excavated by the University of Michigan. It is also represented near Tlacolula, at the site of Caballito Blanco. Finally, near the caves some remnants of oak forest are encountered. These are better seen near San Gabriel Etla and along the Guelatao road, as well as on other highlands around the valley.

However, observation of the soils and the current water table of the Oaxaca Valley, when considered in relation to elevation; the position of the valley in relation to sources of vegetation; and the vegetation of other areas of Mexico with similar attributes, provides information on the basis of which the original plant formations in the valley can be reconstructed. Unfortunately, the species composition of the associations can never be known, because untouched forest of the kind which once grew in Oaxaca Valley no longer exists anywhere in Mexico. It was either extensively harvested for desirable trees for lumber, firewood, or charcoal, or it has been completely removed to provide area for agriculture and the existing forest is second growth, sometimes regrown for four or more times. Every removal increases the probability that sensitive species are eradicated completely and only the most persistent, weedy species return. This is particularly true when an agricultural system involving slash-and-burn or milpa is used, which expands the clearing from an open area into contiguous areas as long as population pressure demands it.

The virginal vegetational associations in the Oaxaca Valley included a mesophytic forest along the Río Atoyac and its permanent tributaries, on loam and heavier soils where the water table currently is only 3 m below the surface or less. Under these conditions, water would have been available for the vegetation throughout the year. The closed canopy of evergreen trees would have excluded heliophilous species and all except those shrubs and herbaceous plants particularly adapted to shady forest conditions. Thus, beneath a canopy perhaps as much as 15 m to the lowermost branch, the forest would have been dimly lighted and open, with few obstructions other than the massive tree trunks. Except in thickets along the river, in the nearly inaccessible tree tops and at the outer margins of this riverine forest, hunting would have been less fruitful, and it may have been a forbidding place to early inhabitants of the valley.

Much of the valley along the river is now covered with a sandy soil. Whether this is the result of recent erosion or whether this was always present along the river bed is difficult to determine, but it has undoubtedly been augmented by erosion following the initiation of agriculture in the valley. On this soil, also, where the water table is 1 m or less beneath the surface, an evergreen forest of a different species composition would have prevailed. While this is dominated by residual willow at the present time, the primary forest on this soil would also have contained a mixture of many species. The canopy may not have closed as completely and the association may have included some deciduous species, because the sandy soil would have allowed more complete drying during the dry season.

Bounding the evergreen forest throughout the valley, the primary mesquite forest would have consisted of a number of deciduous species dominated by the mesquite, which normally inhabits water courses with a water table up to 6 m beneath the surface. While this formation would have included a few evergreen members, during the dry season it essentially would have become leafless. However, during the summer rainy season, the canopy would have been closed, albeit with a lighter shade than in the riverine evergreen forest. Even so, in such a fully mature forest, heliophiles would have been excluded. This kind of forest has long been exploited, because the less dense cover has meant greater ease in removal and the level land is well suited to agriculture during the rainy season. Generally, mesquite would be left for the crop of pods at the beginning of the rainy season. However, in time even the mature mesquite trees were destined to disappear, as cultivation prevented the establishment of seedlings and old age or accident gradually removed the original trees.

Between the margin of the mesquite forest and the oak-pine forest, the Oaxaca Valley was covered with a thorn-scrub cactus deciduous forest. At its finest development, this association must have had a canopy ranging between 5 and 10 m tall, depending on exposure, soil moisture, etc. Because root competition and the lack of reachable water table during the dry season from November to May would have limited the concentration of vegetation, the canopy would always have remained open. Enough of this kind of association is extant in Mexico to assure us that current observations are applicable to primary thorn-scrub cactus forest. Such changes as have occurred are largely in the herbaceous constituent during the wet season, largely because of the role of heavy grazing in eliminating propagules before they have had a chance to disseminate. While harvesting of fuel and clearing for agriculture have also made inroads, particularly in the species composition of thorn-scrub, this appears to be less serious than in other formations. Perhaps this has been the result of less intensive use due to the scanty water resources which resulted in this association in the first place.

Above the thorn-scrub forest begins the oak-pine forest on the upper slopes. Nowhere along the interface of these associations is there a sharp demarcation. Blending of elements from the two has resulted in a particularly rich resource for a hunting-gathering economy. In the Oaxaca Valley, this seems to have been intensively exploited in the Preceramic era.

The oak-pine forest has been extensively altered over the years since the first development of settlements in the Oaxaca Valley. The hunter-gatherers who occupied Guilá Naquitz Cave between 8000 and 6000 B.C. harvested quantities of piñon nuts from trees which must have grown nearby. This harvesting itself should not have had a harmful effect; more likely, it is the preferential use of pine (and piñon) charcoal as household fuel which has removed pine from the forest many times over since charcoal burning began. Even in the Early Formative period, Oaxaca villagers were using pine charcoal as a preferred fuel, and the much larger populations of later cities like Monte Albán and Mitla may have eliminated some favored pine species completely from the forests near the Oaxaca Valley. Although an extensive search and frequent inquiry was made, neither trees nor local memory of trees bearing piñones was evoked. Effect of continued disturbance on the species of oaks in the forest is more difficult to assess. So many species of oaks are normally present that the elimination of a single species would hardly be recognized or provable. Similarly, it would be difficult to assess the changes in the shrubs, herbs and all plants other than the oaks and pines. Fortunately, activities in the oak-pine forest have not been so intense that the forest has been completely eliminated. The present second growth oak-pine forest still provides abundant forest resources for the Oaxaca Valley, as well as preserving the surface of the mountains by preventing erosion on most of the highlands overlooking the valley along the northeast. Along the west, slopes are less steep and removal of the oak-pine forest has been more complete. Many times, grazing has resulted in the conversion of open areas into grassy pasturage into which the oak-pine forest may never return.

In all, the original oak-pine forest undoubtedly consisted of much larger trees spaced much further apart. The canopy would have been completely closed in areas of oak dominance, with little undergrowth except some forest herbs and ericaceous shrubs. The pine canopy would have been lighter, with a much higher light penetration resulting in somewhat more undergrowth, although the better drainage of pine areas would have limited the kinds of shrubs which might occur there.

RESUMEN EN ESPAÑOL

(por *David J. Wilson*)

Este trabajo reconstruye la vegetación original del Valle de Oaxaca antes de que fue alterada por el hombre. El Dr. C. Earle Smith, Jr. pasó más de 5 temporadas de campo en el valle investigando la vegetación actual y analizando los restos de plantas arqueológicas de cuevas secas y de sitios al aire libre.

El Valle de Oaxaca es un valle diversificado de la región montañosa donde los factores de la altura, el suelo, la lluvia, la evapotranspiración y el nivel del agua freática afectan el desarrollo de las plantas. La región del Río Atoyac (de Etla a Zaachila y hasta Ayoquesco) recibe más lluvia (500-800 mm) que la región del Río Salado de Mitla a Tlacolula (500-650 mm), y generalmente el piemontés recibe más lluvia que el fondo del valle.

Todo el Valle de Oaxaca ha sido alterado por el hombre—el fondo del valle por la agricultura, el piemontés por la agricultura y el apacentamiento del ganado, y las montañas por el apacentamiento, el desmontanamiento y la quemadura del carbón. Sin embargo, se puede reconstruir la vegetación original por (1) los pedazos de vegetación sobrevivientes en las áreas menos alteradas; (2) el conocimiento de los ambientes semejantes de otras partes de la sierra mexicana del sur; (3) los restos de plantas y polen de los sitios arqueológicos; y (4) los principios del desarrollo de las plantas en cuanto se aplican a las características fisiográficas del valle. Cualquier reconstrucción debe tomar en cuenta que la evaporación hubiera sido menor y la retención del suelo mayor antes de que se desmontara la vegetación original para la agricultura. En los tiempos precerámicos, todo el valle hubiera sido cubierto de bosque o monte bajo, sin llanos abiertos como los de hoy. Las áreas desmontadas de la actualidad se resultan de la agricultura.

Smith reconstruye las cuatro principales asociaciones vegetales del antiguo Valle de Oaxaca del modo siguiente.

1. *A las orillas de los ríos principales, un bosque mesófilo de montaña (siempre verde).* Este bosque alto, con su alta copa que sombrea la maleza y por consecuencia relativamente abierto, hubiera sido compuesto por el sauce *(Salix)*, el aliso *(Alnus)*, el ahuehuete *(Taxodium)*, el higo *(Ficus)*, la anona *(Annona)* y *Cedrela*. Este bosque se hubiera quedado dentro de la zona donde el nivel del agua freática se encuentra entre 0-3 metros de la superficie.

2. *A distancia del río, en la zona aluvial donde el nivel del agua freática se encuentra entre 3-6 metros debajo de la superficie, un matorral de mezquite.* Esta zona hubiera incluído el mezquite *(Prosopis juliflora)*, el huizache *(Acacia* spp.) y miembros de las familias Burseraceae, Malvaceae, Euphorbiaceae y Leguminosae.

3. *De la zona de nivel de agua freática de 6 metros hacia el interior del piemontés y los cerros bajos, un bosque espino-matorral-cacto (bosque bajo o monte alto espinoso).* Esta zona se conserva mejor actualmente en las cercanías de las cuevas de Mitla, a una altura de 1900 metros. Incluye los árboles como el guaje *(Leucaena)*, tepeguaje *(Cassia)* y *Acacia*, así como "la mala mujer" *(Jatropha urens)*. Tanto el maguey *(Agave)* como la *Yucca* sp. son comunes. Los cactos órganos se incluyen *Lemaireocereus*, *Myrtillocactus* y *Cephalocereus*; también son abundantes los nopales y chollas *(Opuntia* spp.).

4. *En las montañas de altura mayor, un bosque de robles y pinos.* Mientras que los robles (*Quercus* spp.) dominan la zona de altura menor, los pinos (*Pinus* spp.) se aumentanen cantidad mientras se va hacia arriba. A causa del desmontanamiento selectivo de los carboneros, el pino está desapareciendo, aunque se encuentran las semillas del piñón en los restos arqueológicos de las cuevas. Otros árboles de esta zona son la manzanita *(Arctostaphylos),* el madroño *(Amelanchier)* y *Cassia. Selaginella* es otro género típico.

REFERENCES FOR PART I

Comisión del Papaloapan, Secretaría de Recursos Hidraulicos, Estados Unidos de México.
   1955   Boletín Hidrológico 7. Mexico.
   1956   Boletín Hidrológico 8. Mexico.
   1958   Boletín Hidrológico 10. Mexico.
   1959   Boletín Hidrológico 11. Mexico.
   1960   Boletín Hidrométrico 12. Mexico.

Downes, R. G.
   1961   Soil Salinity in Non-Irrigated Arable and Pastoral Land as the Result of Unbalance of the Hydrologic Cycle. *In*: Salinity Problems in the Arid Zones. Proceedings of the Teheran Symposium, Pt. 5., pp. 105-110. UNESCO. Paris.

Flannery, Kent V. and Joyce Marcus
   1976   Evolution of the Public Building in Formative Oaxaca. *In*: Cultural Change and Continuity, Charles E. Cleland, ed., pp. 205-221. Academic Press. New York.

Flannery, Kent V. et al.
   1967   Farming Systems and Political Growth in Ancient Oaxaca. Science 158:445-454.
   1970   Preliminary Archeological Investigations in the Valley of Oaxaca, Mexico, 1966-1969. Report to the National Science Foundation and the Instituto Nacional de Antropología e Historia, Mexico. Mimeographed.

Hoover, M. D.
   1944   Effect of Removal of Forest Vegetation upon Water-Yields. Transactions of the American Geophysical Union 25:969-975.

Kirkby, Anne V. T.
   1973   The Use of Land and Water Resources in the Past and Present Valley of Oaxaca, Mexico. Prehistory and Human Ecology of the Valley of Oaxaca, Vol. 1. Memoirs of the Museum of Anthropology, University of Michigan, No. 5. Ann Arbor.

Kohler, K. O, Jr.
   1944   Land-Use and Vegetative Cover as Factors Influencing Runoff. Transactions of the American Geophysical Union 25:40-44.

Kramer, P. J. and T. T. Kozlowski
   1960   Physiology of Trees. McGraw-Hill. New York.

Lowdermilk, W. C.
   1944   Down to Earth. Transactions of the American Geophysical Union 25:194-213.

Milthorpe, F. L.
   1960   The Income and Loss of Water in Arid and Semi-Arid Zones. *In*: Plant-Water Relationships in Arid and Semi-Arid Conditions, pp. 9-36. UNESCO. Paris.

Miranda, F.
   1942   Estudios sobre la Vegetación de Mexico III. Notas generales sobre la Vegetación del S. O. del Estado de Puebla, especialmente de la Zona de Itzocan de Matamoros. Anales del Instituto de Biología 23:417-459.
   1957   Vegetación de la Vertiente del Pacifico de la Sierra Madre de Chiapas (Mexico) y sus Relaciones florísticas. Proceedings of the 8th Pacific Science Congress 4:438-543.

Paddock, John, ed.
   1966   Ancient Oaxaca. Stanford University Press. Stanford.

Penman, H. L.
   1963   Vegetation and Hydrology. Commonwealth Agricultural Bureau. Commonwealth Bureau of Plant Breeding and Genetics, Technical Communication 53. Harpenden.

Rzedowski, J. and R. McVaugh
   1966   La Vegetación de Nueva Galicia. Contributions of the University of Michigan Herbarium 9:1-123.

Schoenwetter, James
   1974   Pollen Records of Guilá Naquitz Cave. American Antiquity 39:292-303.

Smith, C. Earle, Jr.
 1965 Flora, Tehuacán Valley. Fieldiana: Botany 31(4):101-143.

Winter, Marcus C.
 1972 Tierras Largas: a Formative Community in the Valley of Oaxaca, Mexico. Ph.D. Dissertation. University of Arizona Department of Anthropology. Tucson.

Plate 1. *a.* To the north, the Oaxaca Valley floor is barely above the level of the Río Atoyac. Cultivation extends up the flanks of the valley. *b.* From Oaxaca de Juárez to the southwest, the broad valley of the Río Atoyac is nearly completely under cultivation.

Plate 2. *a.* While the Mitla arm is less well watered than other parts of the Oaxaca Valley, it is still under intensive cultivation. Part of the buildings of Preconquest Mitla appear at the center. *b.* Most of the valley is laid out in elongate agricultural plots. Only rocky prominences have never been completely cleared. *c.* The course of the Mitla river is heavily used and the current vegetation is largely weeds of the sunflower family. *d.* Sometimes along the margin of the river, willow trees are allowed to persist along with the Old World small cane, *Arundo donax*. Many of the weedy shrubs are members of the sunflower family.

Plate 3. *a.* The mesquite forest has been cleared and regrown many times. Near Mitla it is now reduced to this tangle of *Prosopis, huizache* (rt. foreground) and *nopal (Opuntia).* Inasmuch as the mesquite would form large trees if allowed to mature, many of the other plants would be eliminated or replaced. *b.* At the edge of Gheo-Shih, the vegetation included *Myrtillocactus, Jatropha, Ipomoea, Malpighia,* and *Cassia* among others. Were this left undisturbed for a long enough time, maturing trees would have canopies as much as 5 m high, but the current vegetation averages about 3 m.

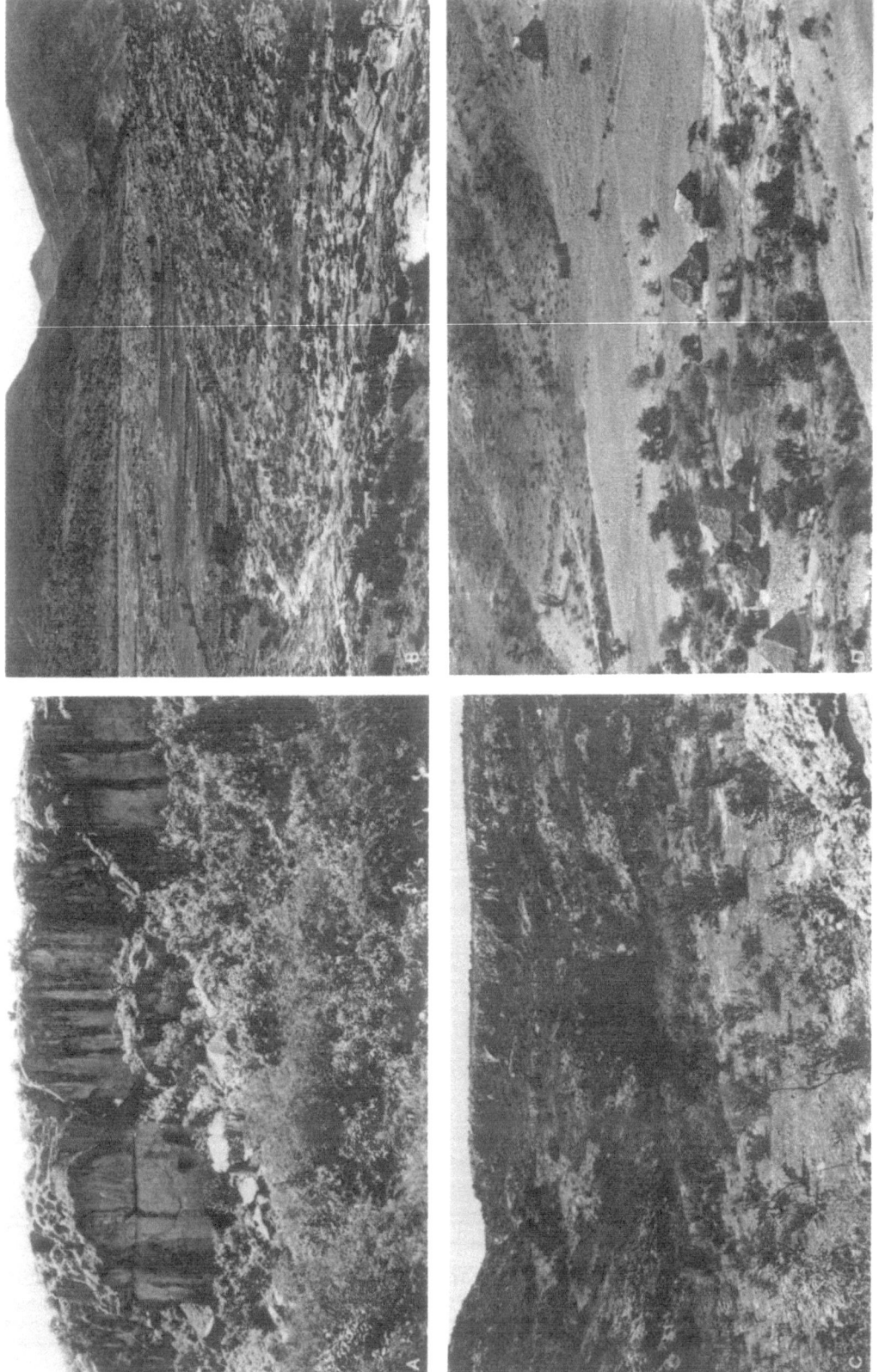

Plate 4. *a*. Thorn-scrub around Caballito Blanco has probably never been completely cleared, although it is heavily used for firewood, poles, grazing, etc. Spiny trees and shrubs include species of *Acacia, Cassia, Malpighia, Croton,* and cacti such as *Opuntia* and *Lemaireocereus*. *b*. Near Mitla, repeated clearing and cultivation has resulted in the erosion of the land to rock. While some thorn-scrub is returning, heavy grazing has resulted in a meadow-vegetation in many of these areas. In the background, trincheras hold enough soil for continued cultivation. *c*. Thorn-scrub near the ignimbrite cliffs in which are located several caves. Sparse vegetation in the foreground is due to a combination of shallow soil with restricted moisture and heavy grazing. Cacti are largely *Myrtillocactus*. *d*. Corral del Cerro lies just into the area of oak-pine forest above Mitla, but recent clearing and older clearing and pasturing have removed most of the tree cover in the vicinity.

Plate 5. *a*. Among the rocks at the level of Guilá Naquitz Cave, *Quercus impressa* is the only representative left of the oak-pine forest which must once have clothed the slope above this elevation. While numerous remains of piñon nuts were found in the cave, no pines grow in the vicinity today. *b*. Vegetation near Guilá Naquitz cave includes *Myrtillocactus* (to the right) and *Cassia polyantha* (tree to left).

Plate 6. *a.* At about 1700 m elevation, occurs the interdigitation of the thorn-scrub and the oak-pine zones. Diagonally across the center the dark trees are oak (*Quercus* sp.) with typical species of the thorn-scrub in the foreground. Cactus on the hillside is *Lemaireocereus* sp. *b.* Shrubby members of the thorn-scrub are *Jatropha, Opuntia, Lantana, Mammilaria* and *Malpighia*. Note the well-developed colonies of *Mammilaria* among the rocks.

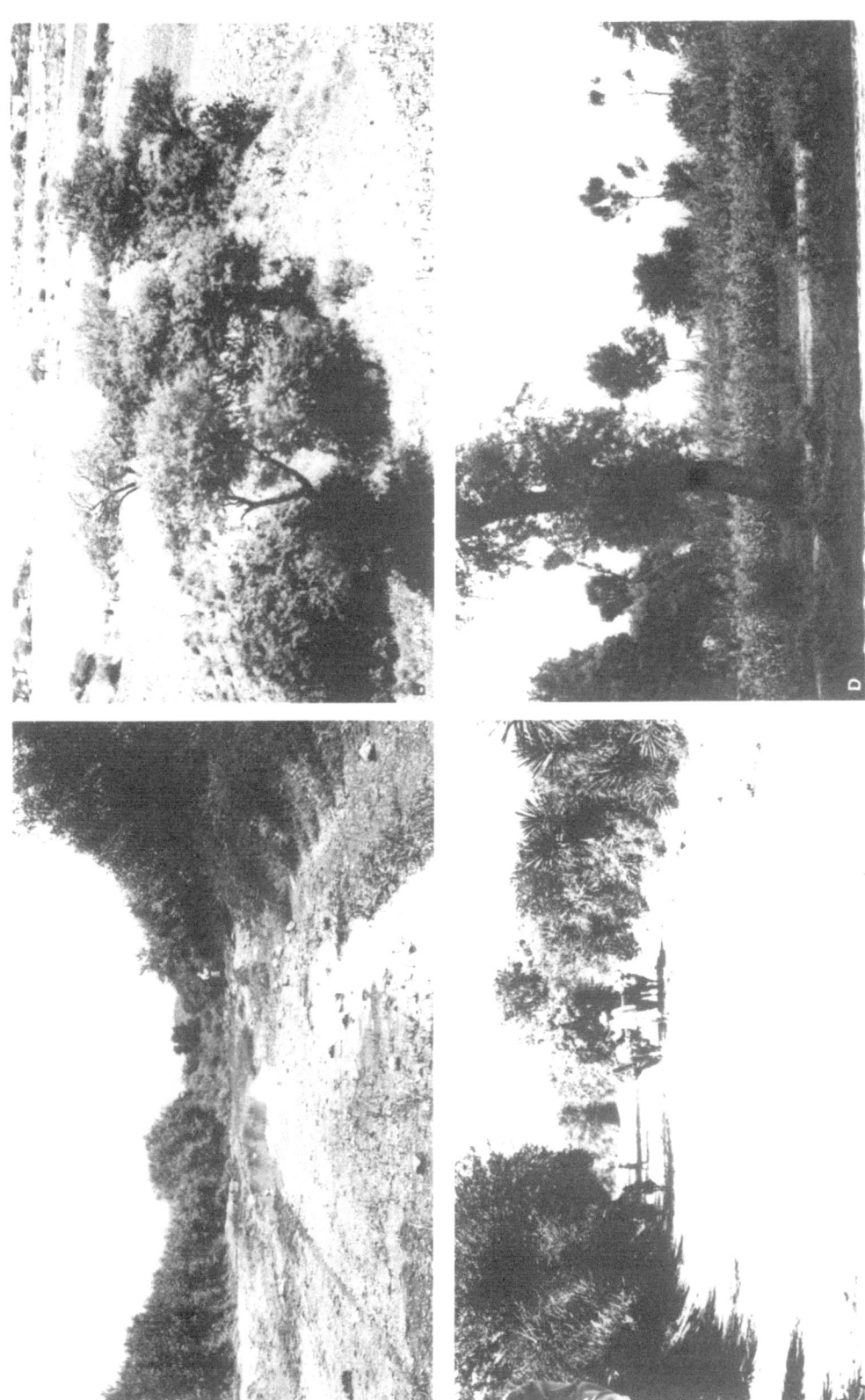

Plate 7. *a.* Hedgerows along the old Oaxaca-Tlacolula road include *Celtis*, *Prosopis*, *Schinus* (native to Peru) and *Verbesina*. These hedgerows are the only refugia available for native plants on the heavily cultivated valley floor, but they are selectively used so that they are no true indicator of the original vegetational associations. *b.* Mounds throughout the valley offer another refugium for perennial plants. These mounds at San José Mogote support mesquite and nopal among other weedy trees and shrubs, but the predominance of plants useful for their fruit is obvious: the remainder have been removed as firewood. *c.* In another hedgerow, *Agave karwinskii*, below, right, forms an impenetrable barrier. Larger trees are pirul, *Schinus molle*. At San José Mogote, isote, *Yucca*, is prominent in the hedgerows. *d.* Along the Río Atoyac some willow trees are allowed to persist, even though the fields frequently come nearly to the water's edge.

Plate 8. *a.* The only valley floor forest remnant left in 1966 was this fragment dominated by willow and alder. All of the more valuable and slower-growing trees had either been harvested by the owners or 'borrowed' by others. *b.* In the fields near Zaachila on the La Cienaga road, guamuchil *Pithecolobium dulcis*, marks the sites of old hedgerows. These trees are left because of the sweet flesh around the seeds, which is avidly sought when the trees are in fruit. *c.* The heights of these alders and willows is probably less than that of trees in primary forest on the same site, but in a valley so denuded of arboreal vegetation, they are very impressive. Enough of the mesic environment is maintained within the grove that a number of vines and shrubs of mesic habitats are found here. *d.* The hills at the north end of the Oaxaca Valley are now in various stages of usage, although they once supported a closely-grown oak-pine forest. On the pastured areas now, much of the regrowth is scrub oak.

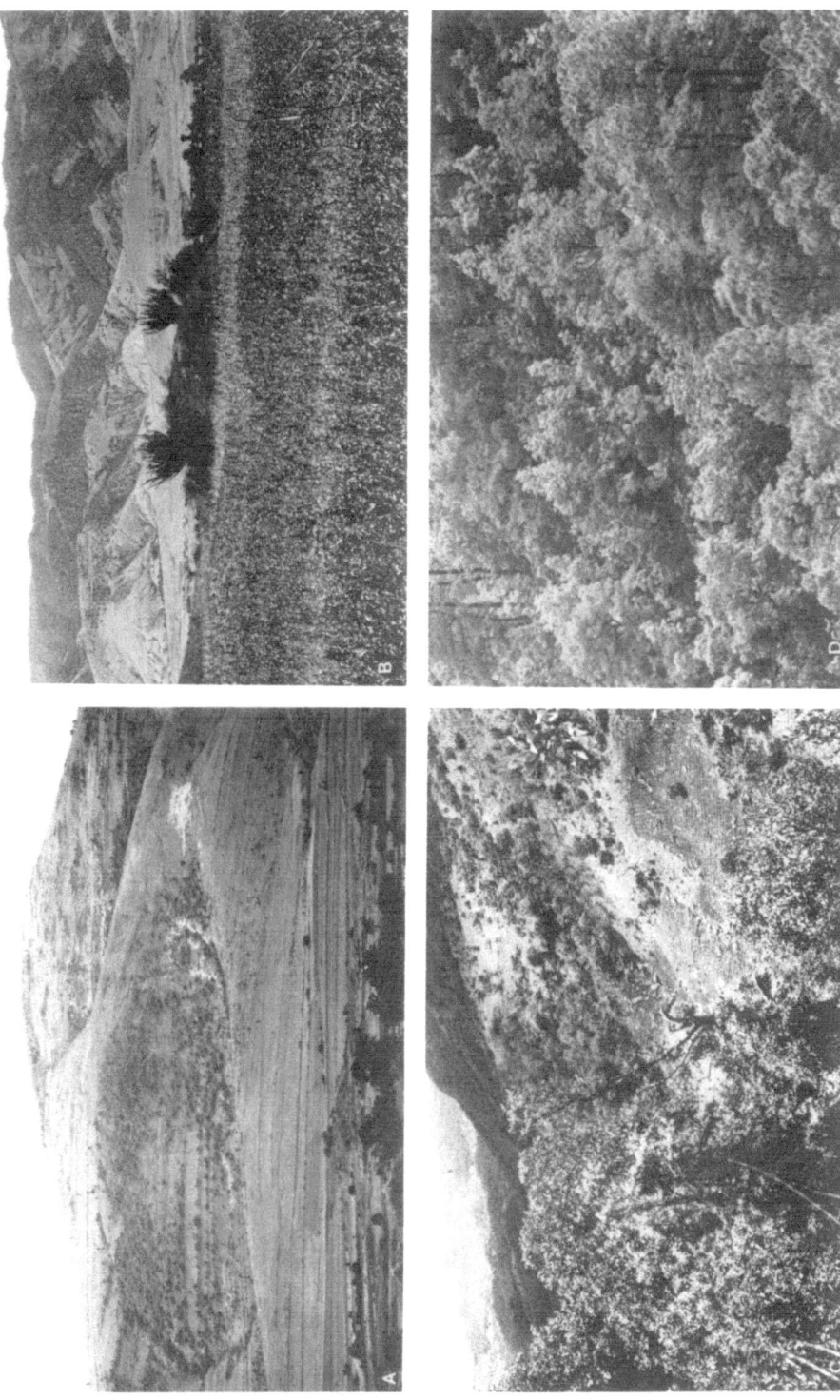

Plate 9. *a.* The valley sides immediately behind the Tierras Largas site amply illustrate the result of centuries of land use. Lines demarking property boundaries clearly show the elongate fields formerly cultivated, and the constant use for pasture has prevented the return of woody vegetation. *b.* To the southwest, the ridges are neither as high nor as steep as they are on the other side of the valley. Here clearing for fields and pastures continues, and, often, the only large trees remaining are found in the steepest quebradas. Note the mounds which here support largely *Myrtillocactus* and huizache, *Acacia farnesiana.* *c.* To the northeast above the village of San Gabriel Etla, mixed mesic forest once grew along a permanent tributary of the Río Atoyac. Higher on the barranca sides, oak-pine forest prevailed. In the foreground and on the opposite slope, a few second-growth oaks survive the repeated clearings for cultivated fields and pastures. *d.* The slopes along the road from the Oaxaca Valley to Guelatao support the best second-growth oak-pine forest left near the Valley. Here an immature area of forest has not grown sufficiently to close its canopy. As a consequence, the forest is full of shrubby undergrowth. Oaks predominate in the bottom of the barranca while pines predominate upslope. The pines appear older, because they grow more rapidly and are larger than oak trees.

Part 2

ZAPOTEC PLANT KNOWLEDGE: CLASSIFICATION, USES, AND COMMUNICATION ABOUT PLANTS IN MITLA, OAXACA, MEXICO

Frontispiece. Gathering *chipiles* while the milpa is in spikelet.

MEMOIRS OF THE MUSEUM OF ANTHROPOLOGY
UNIVERSITY OF MICHIGAN
NUMBER 10

PREHISTORY AND HUMAN ECOLOGY
OF THE VALLEY OF OAXACA

Kent V. Flannery and Richard E. Blanton, General Editors

Volume 5

Part 2:

ZAPOTEC PLANT KNOWLEDGE:
CLASSIFICATION, USES, AND COMMUNICATION
ABOUT PLANTS IN MITLA, OAXACA, MEXICO

BY ELLEN MESSER

ANN ARBOR
1978

CONTENTS

Illustrations 6
Acknowledgments 7
Linguistic Note. 7

I.	Introduction	9
II.	Methodology	17
III.	Setting	25
IV.	Systematics	41
V.	Gathering and Horticulture	77
VI.	Agriculture	89
VII.	Conclusions and Practical Applications	119
	Appendix I. Systematics	123
	Appendix II. Spanish, Zapotec, Botanical Names	127
	Resumen en Español	135
	References	137

ILLUSTRATIONS

FIGURES

1. The construction of the anthropologist's "ethno" model. 20
2. Mitla directions from the center of town 26
3. Levels of the systematic taxonomy 42
4. Dimensions of classification. 46
5. Dimensions of smell/taste 46
6. Zapotec taxonomic levels 49
7. Classifications of tomatoes 54
8. Maize colors 56
9. Maize classifications 56
10. Classifications of beans 58
11. Classifications of squash 59
12. Leaf stage classifications 59
13. Castor bean classifications 60
14. Borrowing between Spanish and Zapotec in botanical nomenclature 61
15. Morphological criteria for distinguishing plant concept categories 62
16. Use classifications of wild herbs by growth stage 64
17. Functional classifications. 65
18. Relative taxonomic levels 68
19. Mitla Zapotec categories' correspondence to botanical taxa 69
20. Edible wild plants from nonagricultural zones 77
21. Most common edible herbs from field systems 83
22. Gathering areas 84
23. Plant availability in combined agriculture and gathering 90
24. Land types 95
25. Agricultural calendar 96
26. Seasonal cycle of agriculture 99
27. *Milpa* stages, timing, cultivations. 101
28. Beans: Stage and part names 105
29. Squash: Stage and part names 106

MAPS

1. The Valley of Oaxaca area 8

PLATES

Frontispiece. Gathering *chipiles* while the *milpa* is in spikelet. 2
1a. Standing water in poorly drained land 141
1b. *Milpa* with herbs, maguey, and borders of thorny, leguminous trees. 141
2a. Gathering *chillillos (ya.bidi)* 142
2b. Corral del Cerro—Hill vegetation 142
3a. Winnowing maize 143
3b. Making tortillas in an outdoor *carrizo* shed 143
4a. Gathering herbs from the fields for animals to eat 144
4b. Planting beans in second class land 144
5a. Early sowing along the lower alluvium. 145
5b. Regular (June) sowing in the upper alluvium 145
6a. Cleaning *milpa* 146
6b. Hilling (raising) *milpa* 146
7a. First class land along the river's edge. 147
7b. Cleaning *milpa* on second class (thin) land 147
8a. The harvest 148
8b. Harvesting *guias* and green squash 148
9a. Transporting the maize by traditional oxcart 149
9b. Storing and shelling the maize 149

ACKNOWLEDGMENTS

I have many to thank for both institutional and individual support during my five years in Michigan and Mitla. My first two years of graduate study were as a National Science Foundation Trainee. My first field season in Oaxaca (1971) was supplemented by a Ford Foundation travel-study grant. My next three years of graduate research and fieldwork were as a Junior Fellow of the Michigan Society of Fellows. Without the Fellows' generous financial support and stimulating intellectual environment, I would not have had the time and impetus to pursue some of the ideas in this and future works.

In the Museum of Anthropology and Department of Anthropology at the University of Michigan, I received enthusiastic support and encouragement from my first day. Richard I. Ford was a rigorous advisor. I thank him for introducing me to ethnobotany and ecology, and constantly encouraging my progress. Kent V. Flannery also introduced me to ecology and directed me to Oaxaca. His ideas and comments both in class and in the field have always added excitement and a sense of humor to my work. Roy A. Rappaport also initially directed my thinking to ecology, then to communication theory and religion. He has been a stimulating intellect and friend. These three who served on my predoctoral candidacy and doctoral committees have had continual impact on my development in anthropology, and I thank them for their patience and advice. Also, Rogers McVaugh, Director of the University of Michigan Herbarium, was invaluable to my research, enthusiastically identifying all plant specimens and serving as the fourth member of my doctoral committee.

In Mexico, I would like to thank the Instituto Nacional de Antropología e Historia for permission to work in Oaxaca and particularly Manuel Esparza of the Oaxaca I.N.A.H. office. Also, I thank the Herbario Nacional and the Department of Forestry for permission to collect plant specimens.

I also gratefully mention those friends who helped this project along its way. Dane Harwood did some careful editing; Liz Brumfiel, Ellen Harwood, Lynn Hunt, Leonore Max, Naomi Miller, and Ann Rappaport also made suggestions. I thank them for their friendship as well as their advice. Also, I will not forget the support of my fellow Museum students.

Most of all, I thank the people of Mitla for receiving me as a member of their community. To them I dedicate this work.

LINGUISTIC NOTE

The Mitla Zapotec phonemic system as described by Briggs (1961:1-8) includes 26 consonants: fortis p, t, k, k^w, s, š, M, N, L; lenis b, d, g, g^w, z, ž, m, n, l; and neutral f, x, r, r̃, h, ʔ, w, y; and six vowels: i, e, ä, a, o, u; and two tones: high (ˊ) and low (unmarked). k^w is a fortis, labialized velar stop; g^w is a lenis labialized velar stop. š and ž are alveopalatal sibilants. ʔ denotes the glottal stop; r̃ a trilled vibrant. Consonant clusters ts and dz are designated in the text as č and ǰ respectively.

Zapotec transcriptions in the text are based on my own phonetic transcriptions in the field combined with the analysis and notation of Briggs. I noted some variation in the incidence of aspiration (h) and the voicing of consonants (e.g., š to ž) among different speakers. These variations are also affected by regular morphophonemic shifts. For example, *yahg* ("tree") before a pause becomes *yak* before voiceless consonants and *ya* before voiced consonants. The possessive of *k^wan* ("herb") is *šk^wam* before b (as in *šk^wam bäl*). *Gihš* ("wild") becomes *giš* or *giž*. I hope that these notes will help make the Zapotec a bit more comprehensible for the reader.

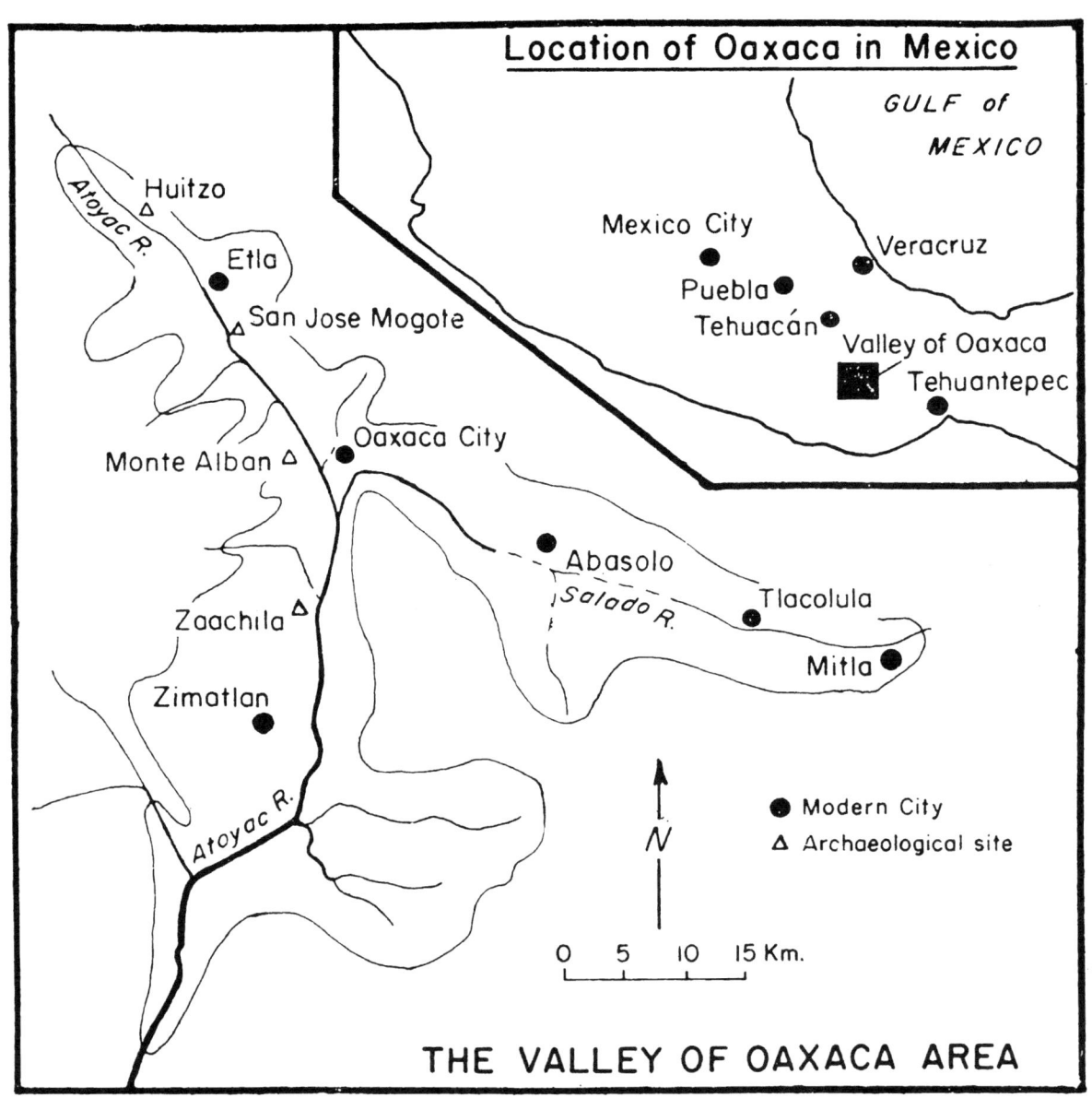

Map 1. The Valley of Oaxaca area (after Flannery et al. 1970).

I

INTRODUCTION

Mitla is a predominantly Zapotec Indian town in the southern highlands of Mexico (see Map 1). Though the human population is becoming increasingly less dependent on the local environment for subsistence, fuel, and medicine, the botanical landscape still serves as an important focus for food and thought. Annual cycles of germination, flowering, and fruiting mark the seasons, while habits of growth indicate cultural as well as natural space.

PREHISTORIC PLANT USE IN MITLA

Archeological remains indicate how plants have been used in Mitla since the arrival of human populations. In the preceramic levels of the Mitla caves, archeologists have found remains of *Agave* and other uncultivated genera, which by analogy with ethnographic examples, are assumed to have been used as food. From later sites in Mitla, pollen and desiccated or carbonized plant remains have yielded evidence of early agriculture (Flannery et al. 1970). Plant remains have provided documentation for the origins of maize-bean-squash agriculture, which has continued into the present, despite changes in potential cultigens and great changes in agricultural technology. Archeological data also provide evidence concerning early patterns of plant food gathering and processing. Though archeological evidence of medicinal plants is lacking, the 16th century Spanish chroniclers recorded an established tradition of curing with plants (del Paso y Troncoso 1905). Native herbal medicine, a tradition prevalent throughout Mexico, has been documented up to the present despite the influences of national culture and modern medicine on indigenous culture.

Given the antiquity of human habitation and plant exploitation in the Valley of Oaxaca and the importance of plants in the modern Zapotec culture, it is natural for the anthropologist to wonder which patterns of human-botanical population interactions have remained unchanged, which have changed and why they have changed. Framing and answering these questions are the major foci of this book.

The above questions are investigated both biologically and culturally, and ecological methods provide the first tool for analysis. I define an ecosystem as a system, in a spatially limited area, composed of physical factors, plant, animal, and human populations, the members of which exchange matter, energy, and information (adapted from Odum 1966). Within this larger unit, one can discriminate microenvironments, and in these smaller, spatially limited systems, one can examine biological populations in interaction to show how and where biological relationships have changed in a circumscribed area.

For the Valley of Oaxaca, pollen and paleoethnobotanical specimens from the archeological sites, current botanical communities, and contemporary ethnobotanical customs can be used to reconstruct (as completely as possible) patterns of plant use from 8500 B.C. to the present. Ideally, the human population and botanical populations can be viewed simultaneously as populations in mutual interaction within an ecosystem that undergoes development but maintains homeostasis (cf. Odum 1966) or, alternatively, evolves a new set of ecological relationships. To document ecosystemic change, the coevolution of different botanical communities responding to human cultural pressures, as well as the selective forces of other biological species and physical factors, should be examined. Unfortunately, for Mitla such a picture is incomplete. Both botanical data, showing the composition of the ecosystem at salient intervals in time, and cultural data, showing plant usage, are lacking for most of the prehistoric and ethnohistoric periods in Mitla.

ECOLOGICAL APPROACHES TO PLANT CLASSIFICATION

The ecological investigation of matter, energy, and information exchanges between plant, animal, and human populations raises general epistemological issues about the nature of knowledge such as: How is knowledge structured? How does knowledge change? Cognitively, how do people identify what is in the environment, and how do they organize this knowledge as a guide to behavior? Zapotec plant knowledge is a case study applicable to these abstract philosophical and psychological problems. Botanical ecology can be investigated not only objectively "on the ground" through plant collections, analysis of known attributes of species collected, and observations of plant communities, but also subjectively "in the minds" of the individuals interviewed.

Cultural botanical knowledge has both biological and social referents. To study the structure and evolution of knowledge about the botanical environment, consideration of both the social group that holds the knowledge and the biosphere, the subject and the object of knowledge, is necessary. Different cultures organize biological perceptions differently. Concepts of natural botanical organization and related human behaviors may change as a result of social change, ecosystemic change, or of interactions between the two. Methods must be developed for assessing cultural knowledge of the ecosystem—the principles through which people gain botanical information and organize it into culturally useful and meaningful patterns—and then these principles must be related to real botanical data.

BIOLOGICAL REFERENTS OF PLANT KNOWLEDGE

Turning first to the biological variables, cultural knowledge about plant species can be examined best in the context of entire plant communities rather than through individual plant-human population interactions. Though humans view their relationships with particular plants on an individual genus or species basis (e.g., particular species produce edible fruits at particular seasons), these individual units are rarely considered as isolated units by either the native population or the Western scientist. Rather, individual species or genera are parts of ecosystems or of species communities—such as agricultural field systems—which respond to biological and cultural stimuli in regular ways.

Though the individual species population may be an adequate unit of analysis for certain kinds of synchronic ecological studies, a more relevant variable, following Bateson (1972:451), is a "population-in-ecosystem." This unit retains a major weakness of the "population" as the unit of analysis, since ecosystems defined as closed systems of biological communities and physical environment in mutual energy and information exchange are almost impossible to delimit. Furthermore, human information flows into the system from outside of the local ecosystem and sometimes from outside of the regional system. Energy may reach the system from points far removed from the local context in the form of trade goods, commercial power, and chemical fertilizers. Similarly, energy produced in the local system may circulate far beyond the local boundaries. Finally, the human population-in-ecosystem is also very difficult to delimit because the personnel are quite mobile.

Despite these ambiguities, the concept "population-in-ecosystem" is useful because it connotes the idea that biological populations must be examined in the context of entire systems which maintain coherent structures, undergo development, or systemically undergo change (evolution). The population-in-ecosystem concept is particularly useful to this study for evaluating the origins of cultivated plants in the contexts of new field systems. It is also useful for examining native knowledge about the structure and orderly succession of plant populations and communities, such as the agriculture-fallow period-agriculture cycle of slash and burn dry farming.

There are clearly problems involved in defining and delimiting any "ecosystem" as a unit for study. However, the concept of a unit larger than a population undergoing annual and supra-annual development and evolution is necessary for the native or for the ethnobotanist describing knowledge about botanical structure and change.

The other major biological concept to be considered is that of the human population as the ecological dominant. The human population determines, to a greater or lesser degree, the composition of plant and animal communities in different environmental zones. Directly, through clearing land or felling trees for fuel, or indirectly through practices such as animal husbandry, the human population determines the quality and composition of its environment. Human populations classify and use different botanical species in different zones at different points in the plant life cycles and thereby regulate and perpetuate different species. This will be clearly shown in the sections on plant gathering, horticulture, and agriculture.

SOCIAL FACTORS AFFECTING PLANT CLASSIFICATION

Social factors affect human knowledge of botanical structure, development, and evolution. Within a human population interacting with generally the same physical-biological environment, it is *not* safe to assume that all members are perceiving the environment identically or acting towards it on the basis of the same information. While human beings of one culture share the same general ideas about classifying plants and using them, there may be real differences in perception, conception, and behavior. For instance, sociologists of knowledge such as Mannheim (1946) argue that there may be more than one "true" way to organize perceptions of and behaviors toward the natural world. Knowledge and behavior may vary according to age, sex, or occupational status. The natural categories which are culturally and individually recognized may vary with position in the social structure.

Similarly, the social context of communication is relevant to any description of plant knowledge. What constitutes a "useful" plant—a wild plant which is designated "good to eat" or "good for remedying headache"—may change as social connotations are added to biological knowledge of useful and nontoxic plants. To understand seemingly contradictory statements about plants from different members of the same population, one must look not only at the botanical but also at the social information communicated in the choice or rejection of plants for food or medicine.

Also, one must consider plant knowledge as part of the general system of natural philosophy, religion, and medicine. How much do individuals reflect on the form and substance of the *entire* natural world, of which their bodies and plants form parts, rather than on plants as isolated entities? To what degree does knowledge about plants conform to a native epistemology that gives all of culture predictability, consistency, and coherence? Who are the native philosophers? To what extent do they manipulate observations cognitively to produce order, and then to what extent do they communicate these ideas of order to the rest of the population? Zapotec data on medicine and binary classification suggest that the system of natural philosophy, as currently articulated by the most knowledgeable members of the Mitla population, falls far short of the order expressed in the natural philosophies of the Chinese (J. Needham 1956), the classical Greeks (Lloyd 1964), or the Renaissance (Wightman 1962). Nevertheless, there are Zapotec principles ordering plant life, human life, and the rest of the natural and social environment. Even though individuals' interpretations of human power to manipulate health and plants in this larger context vary, an underlying cultural order can be discerned, and the social distribution of knowledge about it discussed.

PERCEPTION AND INFORMATION PATTERNING IN PLANT CLASSIFICATION

Despite these social dimensions affecting access to plant knowledge and use of it, basic similarities in information processing can be ascertained. Zapotecs, like other people, recognize different levels of organization in the environment, and at each of these levels, they recognize salient differences which define biological units and their attributes (see Buckley 1968). People recognize taxa as individual types and as parts of larger ecosystems. Within both species and ecosystems they recognize development and sometimes evolution. Members of a culture share a certain minimum of information, principles of classification, and categories of behavior regarding plants. These botanical attitudes and practices, contrasted to those of other cultures, help define the uniqueness of the culture. Beyond this basic shared knowledge, individual knowledge varies. Some of the variation is idiosyncratic, a function of the individual's abilities and interests, but other variations are social and depend on the person's exposure to plants and ideas about plants. Both systematic social divisions of knowledge and idiosyncratic differences must be recognized and distinguished.

People are trained to recognize divisions in the landscape. Their classification scheme is predictive as well as descriptive. People expect individual taxa to appear in particular habitats with particular botanical associations. From past experiences, they expect taxa to conform temporally to seasonal cycles and spatially to certain terrains. How individuals within a culture organize and act on their perceptions of the botanical world is important in understanding the structure of plant knowledge in context with other kinds of cultural knowledge and behaviors. The description of such perceptual organization necessitates a very specialized kind of communication model.

When a person looks at a landscape, he sees many botanical relationships at once. He sees gestalt features as well as particular attributes of the landscape or of the individual taxa. One scanning of a hillside may evoke images of trees, mountain, and three kinds of mountain bushes usually associated together. The perception is not serial but simultaneous. The entire view, including the discriminations made in the mental picture of the viewer, constitutes one bit, one unit measure of information, since that view is saliently different from other possible views. The view also contains information at several different levels of organization. At each level of organization, the viewer identifies the particular unit as different from other units at the same level of organization. "Mountain" contrasts with "valley;" a "pine-oak forest" mountain landscape contrasts with other kinds of mountain landscapes; "oaks" contrast with other genera; "white oaks" contrast with other kinds of oaks. The landscape perception is mapped hierarchically at several levels by a kind of "mental scanning" which classifies the total visual event, as well as many of its constituent parts, and parts of the parts, into known categories, at each of several levels. Each category provides a recognition of difference and distinctiveness.

The information provided by a landscape is distinct from its meaning. Whereas information can be defined as the resolution of uncertainty between alternative choices within a contrast set (such as "mountain" versus "valley" landscape), meaning takes into consideration the pattern of the information (Miller 1967:3-13) and the relationship of the information to the receiver (Bateson 1972:128-156, 399-426.). A mountain landscape may be composed of pine and oak trees. The perceived differences between them are bits of information. That pine and oak trees may be cut for excellent firewood gives the landscape as well as the individual taxa additional meaning.

Plant information may be extracted and patterned in a potentially infinite number of ways (Durkheim and Mauss 1963; Bulmer 1970), but each culture chooses how information will be selected and incorporated into culturally meaningful patterns. Plants are perceived not only as parts of nature but also in cultural contexts, such as those of economics and ritual. Each individual, viewing a landscape, finds certain cultural associations, in addition to physical attributes, of the flora he identifies on the landscape. While one plant may connote bitter taste, another may bring to mind a particular ritual experience. Each association gives added meaning to a particular taxon, since meaning is derived from the *number* of contexts within which a taxon participates (Bateson 1972). Although the possible dimensions of classification—the information in a given taxon—are potentially infinite, they are culturally circumscribed into a finite number of meaningful patterns; thus meaning is culturally delimited and even further specified by the individual's awareness of and reference to the corpus of culturally meaningful patterns.

Individual Variations in Perception

Not every individual viewing the same landscape maps the visual image equivalently. Each derives slightly different information and meaning from the visual event.

Differences in perceptions of a landscape as part of plant knowledge may be analyzed as differences of both sight and insight. People must believe that they see generally the same phenomena or they would be unable to communicate. Behavior, guided by particular sets of plant classifications, must be standardized or the members of the cultural group will not relate to one another as members of the same culture, sharing certain ideas about the structure of the (botanical) world and people's relation to it. If within even one culture individuals perceive biological data differently and organize cultural data slightly differently, such differences must be minimized in the actual process of communication. Phenomenologists have argued that people share enough biological perceptions in common to communicate, and though each individual may see slightly differently, verbal communication usually renders the differences insignificant (Merleau-Ponty 1964). Different perceptions are only recognized when the communicants produce contradictory evidence. Even if two speakers do not organize exactly the same sets of perceptions into the concept "oak tree," they can communicate as long as the differing perceptions do not result in one calling the oak tree "wild apple." As long as speakers share a general cultural structure of plant classification, including plant use, and do not produce evidence of contradictory classifications in everyday speech and patterns of plant use, then differences in plant knowledge do not interfere with cultural communications about plants. Discussions of binary classifications in this volume will demonstrate further this phenomenological (common sense) model and show why individuals can comfortably communicate with others of the same culture who do not share their knowledge.

In addition to describing social contexts of communication about plants, one can also examine the bio-social contexts in which cultural and individual plant knowledge arise. The acquisition and use of plant knowledge by an individual can be described in terms of both communication theory and cognitive psychology. Cultures provide social mechanisms by which each individual develops his human cognitive procedures for organizing information contained in the environment. In addition, cultures provide social routes to knowledge which selectively train individuals to search the environment for particular signs to be used in activities such as agriculture or medicine. What an individual "sees" in the surrounding vegetation will depend on what he has been taught, what he is capable of learning, and what he chooses to learn. Similarly, the plant knowledge which one individual transmits to another is a function of these same factors.

Cultural Contexts of Information Patterning

A basic aspect of plant knowledge that all members of a culture can share is principles of organizing information. The kind of organizing principles (the structures of different classificatory schemes) can be judged along several dimensions: (1) adequacy, to account for existing data; (2) flexibility, to incorporate new data into the existing structure without undue stress to memory; (3) clarity; and (4) consistency. These characteristics of information organization are important for describing ongoing cultural as well as individual knowledge about plants.

Certain patterns of information may be more conducive to errors in transmission than are others. Miller (1967) has shown that it is not the content of the information but its "packaging" that is important. An individual may process equally well any of a series of messages of varying length; however, beyond a certain critical length, there is a great deal of "noise."

Models of Information Learning

Philosophers, as well as systems theorists, have suggested models to explain how the mind organizes data into meaningful patterns. For problem solving, there may be several ways of presenting a set of rules for arriving at conclusions or for describing processes of directed thought. Some processes are quite economical. Descartes showed how a set of rules, instead of being serially conceived, becomes linked in the memory and is conceived as a unity. The idea, rule, or symbol is packed with information but can be thought as a single unit (quoted in Miller 1967:6). Alternatively, two individuals of the same culture may set out to solve a problem, use differing sets of cultural rules, and arrive at the same solution. Both the principle of information bundling or "chunking" (Miller 1956:93, Simon 1974) and the principle of equifinality (Wilden 1972:322-323) are relevant to study of plant classification. The bits of information which an individual bundles to identify plants within a cultural classificatory scheme may be far fewer in number than those which he uses to describe the plant category verbally. Similarly, two individuals may not bundle or chunk the same information equally but may arrive at the same plant identification. "Equifinality" refers to reaching like conclusions by a number of different routes.

In addition, the concept of boundary information may help to describe the cognitive process of plant identification. Though a plant potentially contains an infinite amount of perceptible and affective information, the culture selects certain bits of information which it organizes into meaningful patterns. Within these patterns, there are certain bits of information which identify the plant and assign it to one or more classificatory schemes. One leaf can serve to identify the whole taxon; a taste of one leaf can assign that specimen to a taxonomic and a medicinal category, as well as evoke a whole series of past associations with the remedy. The concept of key bits of information located at specific points in the continuum of information potentially contained in a plant is helpful for analyzing the process of plant recognition. Psychologists have used the "key bit" concept to analyze the recognition of faces (Harmon 1973), and Bateson (1972:453) has shown that a very limited amount of information located at the boundary or outline of a figure may be necessary to delimit an object. The concept is borrowed here to suggest how people perceive efficiently and act on limited amounts of botanical information, even though they potentially perceive and conceive a great deal more.

The acquisition of perceptions and conceptions of plants can also be examined in terms of learning theory. How do people know, or think they know, about the botanical world? How does this knowledge develop? Age and social factors may encourage experimentation with certain categories of plants. Children may be integrated into the agricultural process as they grow older, learning to recognize and exploit field plants.

By listening and observing people, learn to link knowledge about the plant world to other domains of thought and behavior. They develop abstract categories through which they connect the qualities of plants to the qualities of their bodies and to other parts of the natural world. Such plant knowledge is both culturally inherited and empirical; people learn about abstract plant qualities but may not believe them or apply them until they have observed the functional attributes. Experience is a critical aspect of plant knowledge, and empirical experience and the resulting knowledge are also important for developing a larger philosophical scheme. Since interpretations of empirical experience are structured to conform to a particular cultural view of world organization, knowledge about plants is both philosophical and practical. Beliefs about plants as part of the general belief system appear in folklore and ritual; they complement the economic use of plants as food, fuel, raw construction materials, and medicines. All are dimensions of information patterned into cultural meanings and may be learned and shared differentially among members of the population.

EVOLUTION AND CHANGE IN PLANT KNOWLEDGE SYSTEMS

Beyond individual cultural organization of botanical perceptions into meaningful patterns is the development and/or change in cultural plant

INTRODUCTION

knowledge as a system. Chapter 4 demonstrates that plant knowledge is a system with form and substance. Various kinds of classifications structure plant knowledge and combine it with knowledge about other domains. Structural rules in the different classifications accommodate new information such as the form of new landscapes, new individual plants, and "new" plant attributes. Not only may the substance of the system change, so may the form. Structural rules may accommodate new information up to a certain point within traditional classificatory schemes, or they may accommodate only certain new kinds of elements. Beyond these critical limits, the system may change more radically and evolve into something new.

Changes in the botanical environment, changes in the social environment, and changes in the intellectual environment may all introduce new systems of thought about plants. One purpose of this study of Zapotec plant knowledge is to discover which aspects of the structure and content of plant knowledge are most unchanging over time. Another purpose is to see how the system of knowledge responds to changes in the biological, social, and intellectual environment.

To address these problems, we will turn to cultural and individual classificatory and economic behaviors involving plants, which ultimately connect thought, language, and communication patterns to actual food getting. The thrust of this volume will be directed toward plants which are used for food, since the domain of medicinal plants is extensively described and analyzed elsewhere (Messer n.d.). However, the significance of changing medicinal beliefs and practices for ongoing knowledge and use of flora are very important, for they form an integral part of the way people learn to think about and use plants in Mitla culture.

II

METHODOLOGY

Ethnobotanical fieldwork in Mitla, Oaxaca produced plant knowledge analyzable in three interrelatable forms: (1) Western botanical structure of plant ecology; (2) Zapotec and Spanish ideas of plant ecology; and (3) social structuring of plant knowledge. Despite the methodological difficulties in defining rigorously the local and regional ecosystems as well as the local and regional populations, I chose Mitla, a town with some known prehistory and history and with observable changes taking place in the ethnographic present, as the unit for study. The population of the town, principally Zapotec Indians, with some Spanish/mestizos, was loosely defined as the human population under study. All Indian and non-Indian residents who identified Mitla as their home were counted as members of the local population. In addition, those whose origins were from outside of Mitla but whose offspring were part of the ongoing Mitla population were counted as part of the local population since all potentially utilized the energy produced in the Mitla ecosystems and exchanged ecological information. Equally arbitrarily, the lands owned and exploited by Mitla people were defined as the ecosystems to be studied. They were divided into several different types, such as agricultural and thorn forest ecosystems, each defined principally on the basis of soil, plant cover, and type of human exploitation. Boundaries between the different types could not be rigidly defined, since the patterns of human exploitation and the resulting plant cover and soil makeup, were not strictly fixed. Within the general units, however, I analyzed the physical and biological makeups of the ecosystems in Western botanical and local Zapotec terms. After compositions of the different ecosystems were described, I examined the lines of human communication about the ecosystem. Interviews recorded how various plants in the ecosystem were manipulated and how knowledge about the potential uses of an ecosystem were spread throughout the population.

DESCRIPTION OF THE FIELD PROJECT

I worked in Mitla during May-August, 1971, and returned to live and work there June-November, 1972, May-August, 1973, and January-February, 1974. In the course of initial research, I investigated questions about the composition of agricultural field systems and of edible wild flora and, at the same time, became acquainted with the range of flora available in the local fields, hills, and gardens. From the beginning, it was obvious that not everyone shared the same knowledge about plants. Working principally with three men and three women, I noted that two of the men deferred to their wives for medicinal plant names and uses. Furthermore, two different families supplied two different sets of names and uses for certain species and more than one set of uses for them. Not everyone, even within this initial limited sample, entirely agreed upon which species were edible. In addition, when two women independently supplied conceptual classification of plants in terms of abstract hot/cold properties, their lists did not correspond exactly.

Since all of the native population observe and act in the same biological environment, I investigated cultural factors rather than natural factors to determine the bases of differences in knowledge and communications about the environment. In addition to nomenclature, I studied use classifications to demonstrate how functional plant categories guided plant exploitation for food, animal fodder, medicine, construction, and fuel.

Though I used only Spanish in the initial field season, I spoke Zapotec, the first language of most of the Indian population, along with Spanish in subsequent visits. Knowledge of the native idiom made it possible to listen to many unsolicited conversations about herbs, trees, and agriculture, and obviously made it possible to learn Zapotec as well as Spanish terms for describing plant properties and curing.

During the first season, I gathered an initial collection of plants from the different ecosystems and also learned an initial plant vocabulary, including nomenclature, growth stages, habitats, and some uses. The second field season had three principal aims. First, I wished to collect a more complete flora, to show which plants were botanically available for manipulation. Which species were available locally and which were introduced for particular uses? What potentially was the greatest amount of information which could be known, both about the botanical system as a whole and about the individual species in particular? To know objectively what species were presently observed or used in Mitla, I continued to complete a collection of local flora and introduced herbs. To gather as much knowledge as possible about individual species and entire vegetation zones, I took field trips in the valley and hills with a variety of persons: old and young, male and female. Where species could not be identified with certainty by an individual, I looked for more knowledgeable persons to identify the species and assign it a name and use. This methodology produced an extensive corpus of information about local flora, including uses.

The second major aim of the second field season was to discover how information was systematically distributed among population members, including both individual knowledge and the means by which the individual gains knowledge. I investigated the networks of communication—kinship, fictive kinship, friendship, and socioeconomic—to show how information about plants circulates through the sociocultural system. A third objective was to ascertain the different conceptual structures in which plants and plant attributes are organized, the various dimensions by which plants are known, and the ways in which new or relatively new plants are incorporated into the traditional corpus of botanical knowledge.

BOTANICAL COLLECTIONS

Botanical collections were made throughout the 1971 and 1972 field seasons by pressing plants fresh from the field between newspapers and cardboards in a wooden framed plant press. Specimens were dried either in a special drying rack in the Oaxaca Project archeological laboratory in San Felipe, Oaxaca, or they were sun dried in Mitla. At the time of collection I noted specimen habitat, plant associations, and visual characteristics such as flower or fruit color. I also recorded additional cultural information such as plant name(s), use(s), and seasonal developmental cycle with the aid of the particular guide chosen for the field trip. Cultural information, collected in the field with different guides in the presence of actual specimen in its natural context, was later used to compare plant knowledge differentially held by individuals. This information, gathered in the field context, served not only as an initial set of data about individuals' sets of knowledge about plants, but also provided a corpus of botanical data by which the local botanical ecosystems could be described. Native guides distinguished life-zone contexts in addition to individual species. In the University of Michigan Herbarium, Professor Rogers McVaugh, an expert on Mexican flora, identified the botanical collections. These identifications provided a set of botanical terms for comparing Mitla flora with the flora of other regions.

Multiple collections of each species were taken; several specimens ensured that the same botanical species were being identified, particularly where different names and uses were given by different guides. Though at first only useful plants were collected, later "nonuseful" flora were also collected to provide a more complete picture of the botanical environment, and also to provide comparative material for cross-cultural study of botanical uses.

METHODOLOGY

THE ETHNOBOTANICAL SAMPLE

To complement the information from field interviews, there were interviews in home contexts. Initially, these took several forms. In some cases, field specimens collected in their native habitat with the aid of a local guide served as exhibit material in interviews with other persons. People in their homes observed each specimen, commented on its probable field location, and gave cultural information about the plant. I then recorded this information showing the plant named in the field and the use associated with the plant so named. In a second set of cases, the part of the plant collected in the field, such as a leafy branch, was shown and the name and cultural information recorded. In a third set of cases, the name of a plant was given, and a description as well as cultural information elicited. The different interview procedures were designed to see if the same plant species were consistently associated with the same plant names and to obtain relationships of uses to the actual species and to the species' labels. In addition, the third type of interviews provided local descriptions of the distinguishing features of plant species, on which a plant, labeled by a particular name, could be recognized.

In practice, interviews often combined the various features of plant identification and cultural ascription in and out of the sight of the actual plant specimens. In the third interview type, I collected a set of cultural uses associated with the particular name in the botanical nomenclature, without showing the actual specimens. However, my offering a series of plant names usually started the process of providing more plant names and uses. The interviewee, suggesting further names and plant descriptions, often plucked fresh specimens from the local garden or vacant house lot, or pulled dried specimens from a chest or kitchen wall crack, to serve as illustrative material and supplement verbal descriptions. These interviews were largely unstructured. They began with my supplying some source material in the form of specimens or names, and the interviewee supplied the balance.

Over the course of these basically nonstructured interviews in fields and homes, I learned basic Mitla conceptual plant classifications, as well as the plants themselves. Guides described the terrain, the floral zones, the flora, and floral features. They commented on the general growth conditions of the fields and hillside flora, and the reasons why growth was attenuated in some cases. In this manner, I learned the local floral insect and animal plagues.

Guides also demonstrated and explained how individual taxa were identified. Usually they picked the plant leaf and examined the shape, texture, and structure of the plant from which it was taken. Sometimes they crumpled the leaf into a mash and smelled or examined the plant for gum or sap. In most cases, they could name the plant taxon and tell how it was used. In home interviews, in the absence of a plant specimen, I used these same identification categories: plant location, associations, leaf form, smell, flowers, sap, etc. These classificatory dimensions potentially formed the basis for a componential analysis of plant taxa and are more completely described in Chapter 4, Systematics.

In addition to general classificatory and identificatory categories, special questions were also asked to identify certain species: "Were children playing with the flowers?" "Were grasshoppers eating it?" These questions provided special identificatory associations for particular taxa and were important for identification. Such associations were salient parts of the plant knowledge necessary to economically describe and precisely locate particular floral units in the taxonomy and in the environment.

In summary, the methodological approach was to learn as much as possible about plants in Mitla Zapotec and Mitla Spanish categories. Men and women were encouraged to ask their own questions in identifying the flora and teaching me how to identify the flora. Prior to the fieldwork, I had had no formal botanical training, so I was learning to identify plants in strictly local terms.

By learning the right questions, supplied principally by one very knowledgeable woman, I internalized at least one Zapotec's view of the botanical world (Fig.1). By letting men and women ask their own questions, I could see how

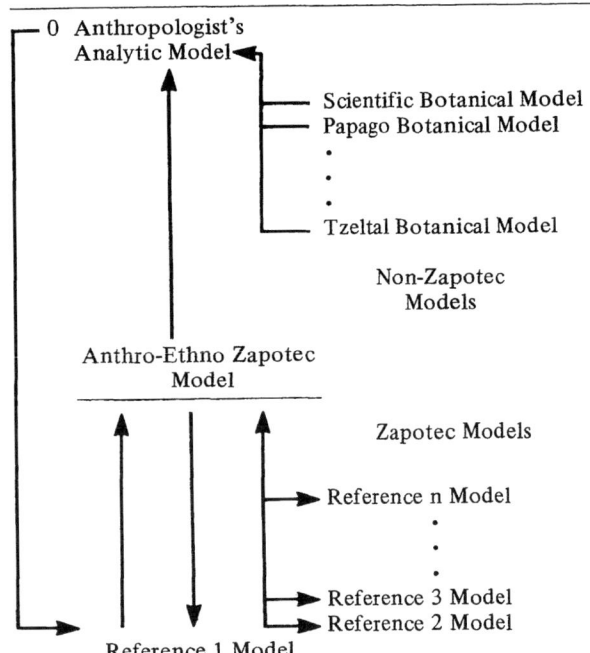

Fig. 1. The construction of the anthropologist's "ethno" model. The anthropologist enters the field with an ideal tabula rasa (0) which will be replaced by native categories of thought. In reality, the mind is not blank, but has ideas of certain possible ways to structure data (the anthropologist's analytic models). Without consciously referring to pre-existing analytic models, the anthropologist, on the basis of interviews with a very knowledgeable informant, develops a thorough idea of how the (plant) world is structured (Reference 1 Model). This is one person's assessment of the "cultural" view and becomes the anthropologist's "ethno" model, a combination of the reference model and the pre-existing analytic models in the anthropologist's mind. This first anthro-ethno (Zapotec) model is then revised and expanded, on the basis of new analytic models, and new ethno-reference models. The anthropologist recognizes that the reference models are colored by the quality of the anthro-ethno model; that is, the questions which the anthropologist uses to elicit reference models. On the basis of the anthropologist's questions, the reference models may be elaborated in new directions.

each went about systematic analysis and functional analysis of the botanical data. In gathering data on native epistemology, one discovers a people's world view in the questions people ask, rather than in their responses to an anthropologist's questions. The question frames supplied by the interviews provided not only botanical data but more general data on world organization and structuring principles.

THE ETHNOGRAPHIC SAMPLE

Once I had gained good control over the botanical data and could converse easily about it, I began to broaden my sample of acquaintances within Mitla in order to obtain data on the division of knowledge within the community and on possible systematic ways to describe this knowledge. Kinship networks, occupational associations, fictive kin (*compadrazgo*) relationships, and neighborhood ties were categories, crosscut by age and sex distinctions, that were investigated as possible communication channels for storing and spreading plant information and meaning among individuals. In broadening the ethnographic sample, I had to choose between two possible interview schedules: (1) random sampling, by working with town population lists or taking a stratified sample within randomly selected households, or (2) systematic sampling, extending out from the original population, a base group, along kinship, compadrazgo, neighborhood, and occupational lines. These could be supplemented by meetings with people on the streets and in the fields. Since one of the project aims was to investigate communication networks, I chose the systematic sampling, which provided more control over the specific questions of interest and, at the same time, provided the broadest sample of the general distribution of knowledge.

In the broader ethnographic sample, most new households were referred to me by acquaintances with whom I continued to have daily, or almost daily, contact. I interviewed within kinship networks, as young women referred me to their aunts, mothers, and mothers-in-law, and also along compadrazgo lines. I also visited sets of women who shared daily face-to-face contacts within small neighborhoods. Since I had initial contacts with more than two unrelated families within the town and made additional contacts in the agricultural fields, I reached a broad social sample of people.

In the early interviews, I noted that people structured their conversations about plants in definite ways. They lumped plants by ecological location—garden, field, and mountain—and also by usefulness in medicine or cooking. To facilitate and partly standardize interviews in 1972, I devised a systematic list of frequently mentioned plants, structuring them according to locational and use categories suggested in conversations with local people. Wherever possible, I did systematic interviews using the list as a basis. Interview time was divided between facts and thoughts about the agricultural process and information about plants useful for food or medicine. Thus, interview formats were both structured and unstructured. Unstructured interviews had the advantage of allowing the man or woman to become comfortable with me and so mention items not covered by the formal list. Structured interviews, which included a series of named plants from different botanical locations as well as a series of questions about agricultural practices, edibility of wild species, and "hot" and "cold" qualities of taxa, had the advantage of getting a number of responses from people in different social positions about the same plants and plant categories.

Interview Contexts

Interview contexts were equally important as plant name lists for providing data on the individual's plant knowledge. By observing and participating in household activities, I was able to see on which statements and beliefs about plants people acted. Without this additional ethnographic observation of plant use, there would always remain a question of determining the pragmatic relationship of the interviewees to the knowledge they demonstrated verbally in the interviews. First, did they actually know the plants about which I was asking or did they just know the names? Second, if they knew a plant use associated with a plant name, had they just heard or seen the use of the plant or did they actually use it? I tried to interview most informants on more than one occasion, both because of the nature of my questions and the problem of evaluating responses. In general, I tried to get interviews in both the home and field contexts, so I could be sure they were responding to a particular plant rather than just a particular plant label. I also asked more individualized questions to sort out some compartmentalization of knowledge. For example, in asking "Is this plant _____ eaten?" a "yes" or "no" answer was insufficient, since a person could give what she judged a culturally acceptable response (usually "no") rather than a personal response ("Yes, I eat the plant when I am in the fields.").

Observation of Herb Use

Interview contexts were also critical for investigating changing knowledge about botanical conditions and uses. Hearing what people said and then observing how they acted in agricultural and medicinal manipulations of plants often revealed contradictions between word and deed. Observing individuals' agricultural and medicinal behaviors from June 1971 through February 1974 gave me an opportunity to discern changes in views regarding agriculture and the uses of plants. Moreover, it was possible to observe development of knowledge on the parts of certain individuals. Through field interviews, I discovered what was known about field conditions and how people acted on this knowledge. I interviewed a number of people about their decisions to plant or not to plant, their choice of field preparation, their choice of seed, and their choice of labor. These were both ideological questions and economic questions. Was the *milpa* ("maize field") a value in and of itself, or merely an alternative source of maize?

In interviews I also asked questions about and observed the use of plants in curing acts and rituals. How did the set of beliefs about the healing properties of plants articulate with the general (Christian) belief system about the organization of the world? How was knowledge distributed among different persons who cured? Did they possess special knowledge? Choice of medicinal practitioners as well as medicinal herbs were included in the investigation of plant uses. In this way, I examined two levels of the decision making process on whether to use herbs in curing: (1) the level of the choice of authority, and (2) the basic level of administration of particular remedies. These procedures revealed the relationships of individuals to sources of authority, particularly traditional herbal medical authority, and the different choices of medical systems available to the population.

Further information about remedies was gathered by spending hours behind the counter of the store best known in Mitla for distribution of pharmacological remedies. Men, women, and children would come in for patent remedies such as syrups, pills, and ointments for various ailments. Here I got a chance to see how people chose remedies, the type of advice given, the alternatives they had tried, as they discussed their ailments and sought effective alternative remedies. Here people also discussed their experiences with doctors in Mitla, Oaxaca, and Tlacolula. Information about one of the two doctors practicing in Mitla was also gained during visits to the proprietor of the shop across from the road leading to the doctor's residence. People going to and from their visits to the doctor would stop off for a rest, a refreshment, and a bit of conversation, at which point they would tell a bit about themselves, their ailment, and the effectiveness of the doctor.

STRUCTURING OF THE DATA PRESENTATION AND DISCUSSION

Used in its broadest sense, the methodological approach of this ethnobotany is "ethnoscience;" there is an attempt to arrive at a cultural description which "stemmed from the material itself" (Metzger and Williams 1963). There is also some attempt to arrive at a "complete" cultural description, so that in talking about plants one is not limited to them but enters other domains of the biosphere and symbolic, conceptual, and cultural spheres. At the same time, the approach is ecological; it seeks the influence of human cultural activities on the flora, and the influence of botanical ecology on shaping or reshaping human behavioral and economic patterns. In keeping with the above methodology, which provides initial data on the Mitla ecosystem, its component parts, the cultural setting of the town in the context of the Valley of Oaxaca and the rest of Mexico, I will present in detail the ethnographic, geographic, and botanical description of the Mitla area in Chapter 3.

Then, in Chapter 4, the examination of Mitla flora from a native point of view will begin with ethnosystematics, an ethnoscientific study of the kinds and diversity of plants and of any and all relationships among them (cf. Simpson 1961). It includes the study of systematic taxonomy, the hierarchical groupings of plants based on different classes of natural relationships. The methodology here is not as rigorous as in many ethnoscientific studies, since the dimensions on which plants are distinguished were elicited in field and home contexts. The number of potential, "real" attributes on which segregates may have been formed is not discussed, but instead only those attributes used in recognizing particular plant species as conceptual entities are considered. Problems of communication structured into the nomenclatural system are presented. Data on plant growth and use are presented in Chapters 5 and 6. Chapter 5 introduces edible plants both gathered and horticultural, and Chapter 6 includes an introduction to the history of agriculture and current agricultural decision-making. Chapter 7 will provide a summary and conclusions about the changing ecosystem and the changing relationships of the Mitla population to nature.

INFLUENCE OF FIELD METHODS

Throughout field research and data collection, I developed insights into the communication of ideas about plants. Since I was working in both Spanish and Zapotec with a primarily bilingual population, I tried to collect data from monolingual Spanish speakers, to see if their categories of plant perception and plant use differed substantially from those with a Zapotec background. Also, the observation that people in working contexts often acted differently than they said they acted led me to participate more and more in the life of the community households rather than to bring informants to a field headquarters to record data. Though I was interested in the semantic contexts of plants (the meanings of the physical objects and their labels), I was equally interested in the pragmatics of plant recognition and the syntactics of linking plants with other domains, on the basis of shared symbolic qualities. This means that I have not given as great a weight to linguistics as have other ethnobotanical studies (such as Berlin, Breedlove, and Raven 1974). Instead, I have looked at plants in use—in medicinal brews and cooking pots—to observe the results of people's ideas about botanical organization.

Ideally the ecological unit of analysis for this project was the regional Mitla ecosystem or the populations analyzed in relation to the parts of this ecosystem in a constant state of development and change; practically I found this unit to be too diffuse to work with. The two parts of the natural system over which I had limited control were the agricultural system, with its composition (distinguished from the "wild" system) and the vegetation of the Mitla hills before and after firewood cutting. The latter ecosystem is not well analyzed but should be a good area in future years in which to study the influence of human cultural activities on ecosystems, both in terms of the changing availabilities of particular flora and in terms of the impact of the changing floral community on the human cultural system in local practices of heat production and curing.

III

SETTING

Mitla is located in the Valley of Oaxaca, in the southern highlands of Mexico. The valley (between 16°40′–17°20′ N latitude and 96°15′–96°55′ W longitude) has three "arms," extending in the northern, southern, and southeastern directions. The former two are drained by the upper Río Atoyac; the latter by its tributary, the Río Salado or Río Tlacolula. At the extreme end of the southeastern arm, generally agreed to be the driest, is the town of Mitla (approximately 16°55′ N latitude, 96°19′ W longitude).

The Valley of Oaxaca is part of the greater state of Oaxaca. Its capital, Oaxaca City, which stands at the central hub of the three arms of the valley, is the state's center of commerce and government and the market center for the surrounding valley and mountain towns. District centers also serve government needs for the smaller towns and villages. Within the southeastern arm of the valley, Tlacolula is district capital, and the municipal records of Mitla are deposited there. Tlacolula is also an important periodic market center, serving the mountain and valley towns in the vicinity each Sunday. On Sundays, as well as during the week, government offices handle land and social documents for the district peoples.

Mitla has *municipio* status and includes the Hacienda Xaagá, Corral del Cerro, and a few other ranchos. It is a very important town and probably has been throughout the history and prehistory of the area. Lying at one end of the Valley of Oaxaca, it connects the mountains beyond it, the Mixe region, with the valley. It also lies at the junction of the valley and the road to Tehuantepec on the sea, thus linking mountain and valley; valley and coast. Through Mitla, the distinctive products of those different zones had to pass.

PREVIOUS ANTHROPOLOGICAL WORK IN MITLA

Throughout the twentieth century the ethnographic populations as well as the ruins of Mitla have attracted the attention of anthropologists and geographers. Schmieder (1930), provided a brief account of the local environment and population in his survey of the Zapotec and Mixe regions. Elsie Clews Parsons resided in Mitla from 1929 to 1933 and recorded thorough descriptions of agricultural, medicinal, and other folk customs in her classic ethnography, *Mitla, Town of the Souls* (1936). Her corpus of geographical locations, plant names, curing rituals, and festival descriptions from forty years ago still describe accurately many features of contemporary Mitla culture. Charles Leslie, who studied Mitla twenty years later, concentrated on world view in his book, *Now We Are Civilized* (1960), and although the book is not useful for a comparative study of plant knowledge, it does provide insights into changing intellectual concerns, which affect how plants are used.

Archeological and documentary sources also provide materials for background and comparison with the current ethnobotanical study. The Mitla ruins have been excavated and reported by a number of archeologists (cf. Paddock 1966). They are important for understanding the prehistoric development and importance of the town and also its contemporary economic development through modern tourist industries. The Oaxaca Project under the direction of Kent V. Flannery has contributed insights into the development of subsistence strategies in Mitla. Remains from the preceramic dry caves as well as other excavations within the Mitla vicinity provide valuable evidence on early plant usage (Flannery et al.

1970). Anne Kirkby's *Prehistory and Human Ecology of the Valley of Oaxaca* (1973) is an important study of soil and rainfall patterns, farming practices, and crop yields throughout the valley, including Mitla.

Ethnohistoric studies, including the sixteenth century *Relaciones* (del Paso y Troncoso 1905) describe Mitla and other towns in the vicinity. William Taylor's regional study of landholding patterns in colonial Oaxaca, also provides valuable information relevant to ethnobotanical research in Mitla (see Taylor 1972).

In this chapter and those following, all descriptions are derived from personal observations and analysis, except where otherwise cited. Description concentrates on environmental and social information particularly relevant to understanding how Mitla Zapotecs know and use their plant world.

ETHNOGEOGRAPHY

In the local folklore, Mitla is described as the "highest" place on earth, and also as "the town of the souls," beneath which all of the dead congregate. All of the souls of the dead are supposed to return to Mitla on *Todos Santos,* "the Day of the Dead," November 1. Mitla customs celebrating this holiday combine Catholic ceremony with Precolumbian practices. Within the Valley of Oaxaca, the tradition of Mitla as the Town of the Dead is recognized, and Mitla, with its ruins, retains a special place in the religious, geographical, and conceptual space of the Valley of Oaxaca and the surrounding mountain regions.

Mitleños, like everyone else, distinguish features of local space by naming each of the rivers and surrounding mountains. In addition, the town is divided into *barrios,* distinguished in conceptual space by the designations high/low and up/down. Though individual streets and town areas are named, Mitleños, in conversation, more often describe a journey as "up" or "to the high side" of town; or "down" or "to the low side" of town (Fig. 2). "Down" refers to the side of town which leads into the valley. "Up" leads

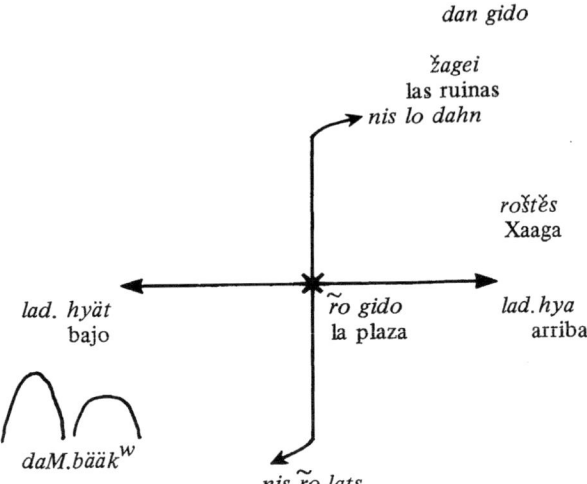

Fig. 2. Mitla Zapotec directions from the center of town.

to the ranchos of Corral del Cerro, Xaagá, and the road to the Mixe region. One may also refer in Zapotec to the sides of town by reference to the water plus the side of town: *nis lo dahn* ("mountain water"). Alternatively, the former may be glossed "valley side," beyond which are the hills of "*daM bääk^w* (*dahn/m,* "mountain") and the road leading out to the valley center. This side of town corresponds directionally to south. To the north are the *dan gido* ("church mountain"), the hills on which the ruins and the Church of San Pablo, the past and present temples of Mitla religious life, are set.

Each of the rivers is also named: the Río Tlacolula (*yeu ro?*), which flows along the southeast arm of the valley, is formed by the junction of several streams, *yeu wîh* and *yeu rošteš,* which join just to the east of *dan gido,* and *yeu r̃o. lats.* Farming locations around rivers are glossed with the same name; thus *yeu wîh* names the region of fields around the river *yeu wîh.*

People also distinguish and name areas by small bodies of water contained in them. Particularly pools of "white water" (*nis yé?t*) are noted in naming parts of the local geography.

CLIMATE

Mitla has the same wet season/dry season alternations that characterize the climate of most

SETTING

of Mexico. Low latitude and relatively high elevation (1600-1850 m) join to make the climate mild throughout the year. People complain when the temperature drops from November through February, but the occasional frosts, which cover the ground "like sugar" in the early morning, are soon melted by the rising sun. Mitla is subject to occasional tropical storms. Heavy showers may last all day long for as long as a week. Generally, however, late afternoon rains, following mornings and early afternoons of sunshine, are typical of the rainy season. Thus overall, the climate in any season is moderate, not marked by extremes of temperature, wind, or precipitation.

The rains usually begin in late April, although they may be delayed until June, and continue through September. As Anne Kirkby has noted (Kirkby 1973:15-17), rains are extremely variable, both topographically and seasonally, in the Valley of Oaxaca. Though the total precipitation in the Valley of Oaxaca ranges from 550-740 mm, with a mean annual precipitation of 631.4 mm recorded over a 40 year period in Oaxaca City, the quantity of precipitation varies in accordance with particular topographical features, so that the distribution of rainfall within small local areas is by no means uniform.

Within the valley, towns receive more or less rain depending on their topographical relationships to mountain features. Within the southeastern arm of the valley, precipitation falls off as one proceeds eastward.[1] Mitla, at the extreme eastern end of the valley, receives less plentiful rainfall on fewer days per year than towns such as Abasolo, nearer to the junction of the valley. But even within the town of Mitla, whose various sections are shielded by different mountain and hill formations, there are local differences in rainfall. On any rainy day, not all of the fields will receive equal amounts of precipitation. Short rainfalls are highly localized, and farmers heading out to their fields from the center of town where it is raining may not be surprised to find their field destinations, in hillside locations, dry.

Timing of the rains is also variable and particularly significant for agriculture. Though the Valley of Oaxaca farmers do not race against an early frost, as do maize farmers to the north in Mexico, dry farmers must still schedule their agriculture within the brief growing season provided by the rains. The pattern of the seasonal rainfall is extremely important. The heaviest rainfall occurs during June and early July; then rains usually taper off until September, when there is another precipitation peak. In the interim period—mid-July through late August—there is often a drought, or the *canícula* as it is called in Spanish. The timing and severity of these "dog days" of drought have a profound effect on cultivated plant growth, a phenomenon which will be further discussed in the section on agriculture.

NATURAL GEOGRAPHY

The Valley of Oaxaca region can be divided generally into zones of low alluvium, high alluvium, piedmont, and mountain (Flannery et al. 1967; Kirkby 1973). The Mitla terrain is quite variable, and within these divisions, each zone has its distinctive vegetation. Human activity, particularly wood cutting and animal husbandry during the twentieth century, have greatly modified the natural flora and underlying soil structure. Beginning from the river and walking toward the hills, one may describe the different vegetation as follows.

River Alluvium (1600-1700 m)

Most of the river floodplain of the Río Tlacolula (*yeu ro?*) is now cultivated in milpa systems (maize, usually with beans and squash). Thick soil along the water's edge permits two crops per

---

[1] The eastern Tlacolula Valley suffers from the most severe rainshadow effect and the highest potential evapotranspiration rates (rainfall/evapotranspiration is less than or equal to 0.26) (Kirkby 1973:17).

The phenomenon of decreasing rainfall is clearly illustrated by the progressive dryness of the rainy season vegetation as one proceeds by vehicle from the central hub of the valley (Oaxaca City) to the end of the Tlacolula arm (Mitla) along the Pan American highway. Near the origin of the trip, the vegetation along the roadside is green and lush. It progressively dries, until after Tlacolula, the view is "arid."

year if the soil is well drained. With proper drainage, this soil, fertilized by the river floodings, is the most productive in town. Where soil is thin, or water cannot drain adequately, crops may be flooded and harvests lost (Pl. 1a).

Along with corn, cane (Sp. *carrizo,* Zap. *yag. biki*) is sown. Cane does well in moist locations, and economically is very useful for construction and fuel. All of the vegetation in this zone has been affected by man. The natural plant associations include the "weed" species *Amaranthus hybridus, Chenopodium* spp., *Anoda cristata, Sida rhombifolia, Bidens pilosa, Salpianthus purpurascens* and other annuals which invade disturbed, moist areas. The zone along the river *yeu ro?* is particularly fertile since it also serves as the town dump. Thus, among the garbage, the footpaths, and the milpa, one sees associations of "weedy" species.

Mitleños refer to this land as permanently "humid terrain" (Zap. *yuh kohp*). The first crop (usually in February) is often laid in by digging small holes with a digging stick *(coa)* or small hoe and inserting seeds into the moist soil beneath. This was undoubtedly the aboriginal manner of sowing, since it demands the limited technology of digging stick and human labor.

Higher Alluvium

Above the river floodplain, soil again varies in thickness and productivity. The natural flora of this zone is mesquite *(Prosopis),* and other thorny, leguminous trees (Pl. 1b). *Mimosa* spp., *Acacia* spp., and *Prosopis laevigata* are the major trees, often intertwined with the vines of Asclepiadaceae. Herbs and shrubs such as *Solanum* spp., and *Argemone mexicana* are also well represented. Much of this land is currently in cultivation. The field systems, in addition to maize, beans, squash and sometimes maguey, include the weed associations of *Amaranthus* spp., *Chenopodium* spp., *Galinsoga parviflora, Anoda cristata,* and *Argemone mexicana.* In fields which have been left uncultivated for one or two years, weed associations will be predominantly small, thorny shrubs, as well as incipient thorny trees, such as *Acacia* and *Mimosa.* In fields left fallow for several years, the thorny shrubs usually are represented in small form, and field weeds such as *Amaranthus* have disappeared. Field borders include both trees and bushes. In addition to mesquite, the common hackberry (*Celtis* sp.), *Opuntia* spp., *Solanum* spp., *Mimosa* spp. and *Acacia* spp., there are also cultivated nut trees and cultivated guajes. Herbage includes certain species such as *Chenopodium* spp. and also a number of shrubs, *Brickellia veronicaefolia, Eupatorium espinosarum, Tournefortia volubilis, Rivina humilis, Hymenostephium guatamalense, Verbesina abscondita, Gymnosperma glutinosum* among them. Where this natural vegetation does not provide a natural impenetrable boundary against animals, *dohb serial,* a species of maguey, may be planted as a fence, or thorned branches will be laid on top of existing vegetation as a barrier against animals.

Thorn Scrub Zone (Piedmont)

The next higher elevation zone is characterized by various *Cactaceae, Agave* spp., grasses and low shrubs (Pl. 2). Though this land is also farmed, it is generally classified as "second class" agricultural land, since it does not receive yearly "river manure" through flooding. Soils may be thick or thin and the amount of rainfall becomes a critical variable for the two different soil types. Thin soil yields well in a marginal year but will be eroded by heavy waters. Thick soil will profit by heavy rainfall, but will not wet sufficiently during the marginal rainfall year.

Botanically, this zone includes *Lantana* spp., *Eupatorium espinosarium, Dodonaea, Viscosa,* and Cactaceae, among other plants. In its higher reaches, are "lilies" (Orchidaceae), which are gathered in season. *Agave* and *Jatropha* also have species well represented here. Leguminous thorn trees are also found in this vegetation zone.

In Mitla, many parts of this vegetation zone are now reduced to milpa cultivation, maguey cultivation or combined milpa/maguey cultivation, or the land is barren, except for low grasses with occasional *Ipomoea pauciflora* trees. The rocky limestone hills are almost bare, exposing the shallow soil cover to erosion by wind, sun, and water. The hills have been and continue to be heavily grazed. Though the hills have been terraced and canaled to direct the flow of water and hinder the erosion process, rainfall has been limited. Where milpa and/or maguey have been sown, fields usually support the same range of weed species as at the lower elevations.

Pine-Oak Forest (1850-2000 m)

The higher elevation forest zones are not well represented in Mitla. Most of the zones fall outside of the range of the pueblo proper, to the ranchos of Corral del Cerro and Xaagá, and beyond. In addition to pine (*Pinus teocote*) and oak (*Quercus* spp.) these zones also have quantities of *Arctostaphylos* spp., *Bursera, Jatropha, Opuntia* and various Cactaceae. Increasing demands for firewood in the growing population of Mitla have led to unparalleled exploitation of woods and probably to increased erosion at this level and down below.

Vegetation is slightly different in these mountain regions. Flowers for special festivals, such as *flor de Todos Santos,* grow well, and may be gathered and sold to the lower elevation's populace in their proper seasons. Other herbs and bushes, including *Vernonia monosis, Calea hypoleuca, Stevia* spp., *Tagetes* spp. are abundant here, though also occasionally represented at lower elevations. Farming may be carried out, but most of this zone falls outside of the Mitla pueblo area.

Ethnobotanical Zones

Mitla Zapotec vocabulary distinguishes between "hill" or "mountain" (*dahn*) and "valley" (*lats*) zones in natural geography, though they are both called *kămp* from the Spanish *campo*. Location rather than more specific vegetation zones are named when one talks about distributions of natural flora. To gather *manzan gihs* and *žob.nihd* one would have to go to "the hills" (*dahn*) or to a specific hill, such as *daM bääkw*. For locations not in the hills, but at lower elevations, one would say *ča?a lo kamp*, "I am going *al campo*."[2]

People distinguish several different kinds of soil, some common to particular locations (Zap. *yuh kohp,* Sp. *tierra de humedad,* "humid land;" Zap. *yuh dahn,* Sp. *monte,* "mountain land"). Other types are descriptions of the soil layer: thick vs. thin, black, stony, sand. These are diagrammed in the section on agriculture.

Most plants are named, and their locations, as well as their habits of growth, are known. The classification, naming, and identification procedures are detailed in Chapter 4.

ETHNOGRAPHY

Ethnic Composition

The municipio of Mitla currently has a population of approximately 4600 persons, of which the majority are Zapotec Indians. The town has some Spanish stock, particularly those who have moved down to Mitla from the outlying ranchos, Xaagá and Corral del Cerro, and others who have moved into Mitla from towns in other regions or occasionally from other towns in the Valley. The former category, rancheros, are children of those who served under the hacienda system. The latter category includes persons from several communities, such as Nejapa on the road to the coast, Mata Gallina on the road to the Mixe region, Yalálag in the Sierra Zapotec, and Santo Domingo, still part of the valley proper. Though individual life histories vary, families or individuals who came from the ranchos or other towns usually were trying to improve their economic status. Some nonlocal women had been brought in as servants in their youth, and then married in the town.[3] They are significant for

---

[2]Conversations suggested that in the past, *ča?a lo gihš* may have been the expression which designated going to the lower elevation versus higher elevation tracts of fields or woods. *Gihš* means *"del campo"* or "wild" as opposed to cultivated. *"Dahn"* is used semantically the same as *gihš*, but in contexts of distinguishing plants which grow at higher elevations.

[3]Mitleños are scattered in coastal towns and in the pueblos on the roads to the coast. They also have family ties in some of the mountain Zapotec communities. Some of this scattering may be due to the Mitleños' roles as traders.

the current study since they introduce new plants and plant knowledge from nonlocal zones. In addition, there is a colony of United States citizens living on the outskirts of town, in the area of Mitla known as the *campo de avión,* "airport," where Americans practice flying planes. These people, many of whom are missionaries, own their own land and houses. Their presence is felt in Mitla both as a proselytizing force, and as an economic sector which contributes some employment and new dimensions to social relations in the town.

Within their population, Mitleños distinguish between "*los Indios,*" the indigenous population of Mitla, "*rancheros,*" those from the ranchos, and "*los gringos,*" those from the north, including both those from other states within Mexico and those from the United States. The identity of "Indian" as opposed to "Oaxaqueño" contrasts with the self-identity expressed by those living in villages in the northern, Etla arm of the Valley of Oaxaca. Zapotec Indians, *behN dijsah,* contrast with Indians from other regions, who speak other languages. Aliens may be contrasted with Mitleños on the basis of language: *behN dijsah* are Zapotecs whereas *behN miž* are Mixes. Foreigners may be categorized on the basis of their town of origin: *behN šandyäu (Santiago)* from Matatlán or *behN dzun* from Tlacochahuaya. Since language or dialect differences also have spatial referents, the two categories of classifying foreigners overlap to some extent. Within this classificatory scheme, Mitleños and Valley Zapotec speakers are usually seen as superior to other kinds of local people. Foreign customs, particularly if they originate in the less Mexicanized mountain regions, such as the Mixe, are informally judged inferior.

Language

Local Mitleños are traditionally bilinguals, who learn and speak Mitla Zapotec in their homes and learn Spanish through school, commerce, and mass media. The exceptions to the true bilinguals are monolingual Zapotec speakers, usually elderly persons, most often women, who have had little contact with non-Mitleños in business or society.[4] There are also monolingual Spanish speakers, nonnative Mitleños with origins in the ranchos, or non-Zapotec speaking towns. Many of these adults understand Zapotec but are "afraid" to speak.[5] In addition, there are many children whose parents feel that speaking Spanish in the home is an advantage in school. These children may learn a certain amount of Zapotec listening to their elders and to their peers, but they are basically monolingual Spanish speakers. Mitleños who come from nearby valley pueblos can usually communicate with speakers of Mitla Zapotec, though the individual town dialects vary. Bilingualism and different dialects of Zapotec have relevance to communication about plants since the plant lexicon is constantly expanding (see Chapter 4).

Residential Structure

Most Mitleños live in nuclear or extended family compounds. The usual pattern for residence is patrilocal after marriage and neolocal after the son has accumulated enough capital to be able to set up his independent household. If there is family property, he may receive land as a gift either from his mother or from his father. Land and property are given and received by both males and females.

By custom, the youngest son inherits both the household and the debts of the parents and is supposed to assure them of care in their old age. Older sons must set up independent households. This process is accelerated by pressure from the

---

[4] In cases where there were almost total families of monolingual Zapotec speakers, the men of the second generation had usually learned Spanish for their work. Since schooling in the past has not been compulsory, young women could be isolated in their work at home and have little occasion to use, hence, to learn Spanish.
In one isolated case, I met an older man who had traveled all over Mexico, and had also been a bracero to the United States, but he had managed without learning Spanish!

[5] Most of the people from Xaagá, first and second generation, understood Mitla Zapotec perfectly, but spoke only Spanish. They were able to communicate in most cases with family members who spoke only Zapotec in the home, but usually made their replies in Spanish. The usual explanation for their reluctance to speak Zapotec was *Tengo verguenza,* "I am embarrassed." My lack of embarrassment was a great amusement to them.

young wife, who faces problems of adjustment and cooperation with her mother-in-law; problems of overcrowding once the young couple have one or more children; and pressure from younger brothers who want to set up their households. These pressures force young couples to organize their independent social and economic lives after an initial period of learning and adjustment to married life within the young man's parents' household.

Not all young people are fortunate enough to receive large plots of land for households and cultivation. As the numbers of children reaching adulthood increases per family, existing plots are subdivided into smaller units of both residential areas and agricultural land. Some must purchase land from other members of the community. Since there are no laws against selling land to nonmembers of the community, land has been sold to gringos from various origins. In some cases, land has been sold for the general purpose of living off the profits. Alternatively, some sell their land with particular capital investments, such as trucks, in mind. All land sales remove property from the traditional system of inheritance, and mean that less land per person will be available for the future. Changing land holding patterns thus have real effects on both short run and long run patterns of land use and the occupational structure of Mitla.

Diet

The Precolumbian agricultural staples of maize, beans, and squash continue to provide the basis of the Mitla diet. Though bread is eaten with the morning and evening "coffee," tortillas are eaten with every meal. Beans, especially Oaxaca black beans, are the most frequent *comida* ("meal"), particularly if one has a home agricultural supply. Potatoes and rice are also frequent comidas. Greens, either wild or cultivated, also provide vegetarian comidas. All dishes are spiced with different kinds of chiles, tomatoes, and other green spices such as oregano, depending on the culinary rules and tastes of the cook and her family. Condiments may either be included in the cooking process, or added in the form of *salsa* ("hot sauce") or plain chiles at the table. Salt is consumed in relatively large quantities. Lemon also accompanies particular foods, such as beef soup and squash leaves.

Supplements to protein provided by the varied combination of vegetable foods are supplied by cheese, eggs, and occasionally meat, fish, or poultry. If a family can afford meat on only one day per week, the meat meal will usually mark Sunday, as the Christian day of rest. Festivals, both calendrical and life cycle, are marked by special comidas. *Mole,* a sauce combining several different kinds of chiles with condiments and chocolate, is the festival dish par excellence, and is prepared for most baptisms, weddings, and for Todos Santos.

People buy most of their food at small shops or the central plaza marketplace in Mitla. Poultry are raised at home, purchased from neighbors, or acquired in Tlacolula or Oaxaca City's periodic markets. Pigs are similarly raised at home for festival consumption or sale. Goats and sheep are fattened by shepherds for *barbacoa* ("barbecue"); cattle are raised for meat and for milk, either on the outskirts of Mitla or in surrounding towns.

People also exploit the countryside for food—wild herbs, fruits, and insects. The red maguey worm, which grows around the roots of *Agave* is collected and prepared in salsa, as are certain wasps in the larval stage. Grasshoppers are collected in the early fall. They are toasted and eaten with chiles.

Households do not have precisely fixed meal schedules, but there is a discernible pattern. "Coffee," the first meal, consisting of a hot beverage—coffee, herb tea, *atole* (maize or occasionally oatmeal or wheat gruel), or chocolate served with bread—is prepared between 6 and 9:30 a.m., depending on the work schedule of the household members. During this time period, the woman of the household, if she is going to make tortillas, will go to the mill to grind her maize. She begins to make tortillas, a process which may take her until 11 a.m. depending on her other chores, so that there are hot tortillas for the morning meal, *almuerzo*. This meal may be hot or cold, varying in content from dry cheese and salsa, to a fresh pot of herbs, to the heated leftovers of the day before. Almuerzo can be served anywhere between 9 and 11:30. The afternoon comida, the major meal of the day, is hot, filling, and served anywhere from 2:30 to 6:00 p.m. A final evening "coffee" around 8:00 p.m. is like the morning "coffee" and completes the food for the day.

Economics

The occupational structure includes a mixed economy of subsistence farming, small scale livestock and poultry keeping, and domestic production in most households. Though many Mitleños still farm, very few households rely on agriculture as the sole source of income. Most members of the population engage to some degree in the tourist textile industry, such as primary production of cotton and wool clothing, or some aspect of distribution, wholesaling or retailing. Some employers who own spinning wheels, looms, and sewing machines, buy the raw materials, and then hire local labor to manufacture the garments. Such "entrepreneurs" usually contribute to the work effort, and in addition, coordinate distribution and sales of their products. Other employers follow the pattern of buying the raw materials and then farming out the work to individual households. These employees are paid by the piece, but the work, usually embroidery and macrame, can be done at home where it interferes less with other chores. Other employers operate with a combination of the two paid labor systems for the different aspects of production of finished garments. The majority of the work, however, is done by independent households.

The availability of cash is the main determining factor of the production arrangements of the individual. To buy a spinning wheel, standing loom, and sewing machine requires an initial outlay of money. It also involves a certain level of liquid assets to maintain production, particularly in off seasons when production must proceed but sales are few.

Marketing is the next problem. Some persons of limited resources prefer to produce the goods of others for an assured income, rather than produce independently. Others may alternate production strategies to produce their own goods during peak tourist seasons, when income is assured, and then rely on wage income from piecework during off seasons. Many Mitleños have trade arrangements with persons from Mexico City or the United States who buy their goods. Others travel to Oaxaca to sell to the stall owners of the Oaxaca City market. People also sell either wholesale or retail to buyers and tourists in other Oaxacan and Mexican markets. All of this mercantilist trade is carried on by Mitleños, in at least one of the middleman stages. Yet, there is no formation of what one would call an incipient mercantilist class. Production and distribution are divided between the members of single families or groups of kin or fictive kin. Hired labor may replace labor of nuclear family members as the scale of operation increases or the time commitments necessary for distribution increases, but the family members each contribute to the total context of production in most operations. The increase in domestic production has resulted in some growing disparities in income distribution between Mitleños. Also, home industries have meant that labor has been diverted from subsistence agriculture to alternative employments, where, in all seasons, or in some seasons, the return for effort expended is higher.[6]

In the social/political sphere, the change in occupational structure has had other repercussions. Much of the town business is now concerned with improving the saleability of Mitla manufactured goods. Within the household, the contribution of the individual members has likewise changed. Women and children are definitely economic assets for production and distribution

---

[6] So far, there is very little class consciousness among the population. There are as yet no class distinctions, only those who are more or less relatively well off as a result of their personal industry and craftiness in the business world. The major "class" distinction which has resulted from the switch to a cottage industrial economy has been the growing distinction between the peasant farmer and the other kind of worker. Mitla is really no longer a town of peasant farmers.

In 1972, a union formed, to both buy raw materials at lower costs and market finished goods at higher costs. In its initial stages, only larger operations, producing and marketing a variety of saleable textiles joined.

of goods. Though women generally do not work on the standing loom, they do take part in all other aspects of the production of cotton goods: cutting, sewing, and embroidering. Women also help tie the points of woolen and cotton garments, cut and sew the finished goods, and also produce macrame bags and belts. They also help with the marketing of goods either by journeying to periodic markets in Tlacolula or Oaxaca or points farther away or by selling locally to the tourists who come to visit the ruins.

Children also contribute to many aspects of production. Young girls embroider shirts and cloths for sale and also learn crocheting. They contribute to the macrame work in garments, bags, and belts. They are also extremely clever salespersons who hawk their wares, along with inexpensive pottery pieces and necklaces, in the town marketplace and the Mitla ruins. Hence, children are a definite economic asset in the current occupational structure.

Domestic industry has thus resulted in changing the relations of the household production unit. There are few full time agriculturalists, since men divide their time between agriculture and industry according to their land holdings, occupational interests, and work preferences. Similarly, there are few women who spend all of their time doing household chores. Rather, women take advantage of modern conveniences such as mills and stoves to release their time for production and earning cash income. Much as most men spend less time in the fields than they did in past generations, women buy more commodities and spend less time in the fields and hills for agricultural, fuel, and food gathering activities. Children also have less exposure to the countryside and more exposure to home industry.

Opportunities for working outside of Mitla are few. Wage labor is scarce, and subsistence expenses of living outside of one's own home cannibalize much of the gains made in income. Some young people go to Mexico City to seek employment, but the route of working in Oaxaca is less often mentioned. In the past, many men went to work as *braceros* in the United States, but today there are no longer work permits. Only those who purchased working papers ten years ago still regularly go north six months of the year and return to Mitla in November.

Additional occupational pursuits are trade and outside marketing. Mitla has always been a source of traders for the state of Oaxaca. Though there is no Precolumbian evidence, during the Colonial period Mitleños gathered the products of the Mixes and the Tehuantepec coast and middlemanned them through the valley and outside of the state. In more recent times, many Mitleños have made their livings buying and selling coffee in the Mixe region. With their mules or horses, Mitleños leave Mitla shortly after November 1 and return the beginning of April, in time for the planting season. More recently, much of this trade has been suspended, since highways have eliminated the need for animal travel and transport. However, in the backwoods regions, where highways have not yet penetrated, Mitleños are still active with their mules and trade activities. Moreover, Mitleños are still principals in the coffee trade, now carried on through trucking. They also middleman other products of the Mixe, such as oranges and avocados, and carry Mitla goods to the Sunday periodic market in Ayutla, the principal source of goods for the Mixes.

Mitleños are also still active in trade with the coast. There are several families of Mitleños living in Salina Cruz and engaged in trade. Older people said that many families from Mitla left during the Great Hunger of the early part of the century and have never returned. Hence, there are Mitleños scattered in various parts of Oaxaca and Mexico.

Tehuantepec, Juchitán, and Salina Cruz are famous for fruit, cheese, fish, and gold jewelry. The last item is an important source of income in the tourist industry, and Mitleños have set up several different arrangements to move goods from Juchitán to Mitla, from Mitla to Oaxaca, and from Mitla to Mexico and the rest of the world. The trade in jewelry is carried mainly by women, though men may manufacture the jewelry. Mitla women journey to Juchitán, buy lots of gold earrings and pendants, market some of the jewelry in Oaxaca, sell some in Mitla and Oaxaca, and journey to Mexico, where they sell to wholesale traders. Though the time and expense of the journeys are considerable, the profit makes the ventures worthwhile.[7]

In summary, the Mitla occupational structure is changing, removing men, women, and children from traditional agricultural occupations. Exposure to the central markets at Tlacolula and Oaxaca City as well as Mexico increases as people enter into a regional, state, national, and international economy. Most young people look forward to occupations in home crafts or commerce. Adults weigh the opportunity costs of time spent in the fields and in homemaking, since there are now alternative incomes in home industries. Finally, the traditional expenditures of *mayordomias* have been removed (see below).

Religion

San Pablo Mitla is principally Catholic. The rituals and beliefs of the people are a combination of Spanish Roman Catholicism and Zapotec folk traditions. Though people are not familiar with non-Mexican varieties of Roman Catholicism, they describe their own practices as partly "Indian customs," particularly the set of beliefs and rituals associated with Todos Santos, which has been combined with a traditional folk festival celebrating the return of the dead to Mitla. The pervasiveness of the pre-Hispanic religion is also seen in the layout of the town. Though the traditional Spanish colonial town pattern was church, municipal building, and school arranged around a central market plaza, the church of San Pablo is located in the hills to the north of the plaza, the location of the famous ruins of Mitla. A folk history explains that San Pablo wanted to go to his natural "home" by the "temple" of the ruins, and eventually, the people built his permanent home there.

Protestantism is proselytized by visiting preachers, new converts, and Americans, many of whom are from the Wycliffe Bible Institute Summer Institute of Linguistics. Mitleños break away from Catholicism to leave the saints, the display, ritual, expense, drinking, and corruption which they associate with the Catholic church. Conversion is a movement toward faith and away from an unsatisfactory spiritual and social life. Protestantism presents a conflict, since Mitla social relationships are still set by the formal ties of godparentship or compadrazgo. At baptism, confirmation, and marriage, the individual is sponsored by godparents, usually a married couple, and these godparents then become fictive kin, *compadre* and *comadre* with the biological parents. Compadres are extremely important, since many social activities are determined by compadrazgo relations, as well as by real kinship ties. One's compadre and comadre may be solicited for advice and aid during times of trouble. In particular, the godparents of one's children may be important in meeting daily crises of everyday life if no real kin are accessible. Often, neighbors formalize their ties by sponsoring each others' children during principal life events, or leading the neighbors' children to the altar of a nonlocal church during a festival away from home. Thus, Protestantism disrupts traditional social relationships with their attendant economic and social ties.

Movement away from the Catholic church also eliminates the festivities and celebrations of the Mitla calendar. The annual cycle is punctuated by Catholic Saints' day celebrations, some of which, like Our Lady of Carmen in July and San Pablo in January, are important parts of the town ceremonial year. The relative paucity of display of the Protestant Church is probably felt most keenly on All Saints Day, November 1, when all Catholic households prepare elaborate displays on their altars and exchange visits and food with both kin and fictive kin. Protestantism also affects the use of local decorative and medicinal plants. Elaborate ornamental floral displays to honor saints as well as the use of plants to counteract witchcraft, "fright," etc. may be curtailed.

For Catholics, the elimination of the com-

---

[7] Alternatively, the traders from Juchitán may come to Oaxaca with the jewelry, and save the Mitla women the trip to the coast, but this arrangement is rarer. One enterprising Mitla woman has now begun her own jewelry workshop, and is producing her own goldwork in Mitla for immediate sale, thus saving middleman costs.

pulsory mayordomo system has also greatly changed their lives. In the early 1950s, there was a general agreement by the town council and presidente that mayordomías should henceforth be voluntary festivals sponsored by individuals fulfilling promises to the church. Prior to this, Mitleños were forced to sponsor large festivals at critical times in their economic lives. The mandatory expenses both exhausted one's capital and indebted one within the system of *guelaguetza*, the traditional system of borrowing and exchanging goods and labor within the community. Each household still holds a guelaguetza account book in which are written all of the debts and credits incurred at particular festivals, but the chance to incur extensive debts in fulfilling social obligations is now mainly restricted to weddings.

For the individual, religion may or may not provide an organizing structure and world view for life. Though some believers articulated their conception of a world created and organized by God and then perverted by man and his evil ways, many individuals expressed skepticism in their individual beliefs. Each Catholic household has an altarplace in the main living room. The altar is decorated with fresh flowers and sometimes plastic ornaments; it serves as a shelf where all fresh fruits and sometimes other foods are temporarily placed and is also the location for burning tapers and incense to God and the saints. Incense is still used for fumigating the household from evil and for visits to the cemetery, which is also well supplied with fresh flowers. Agriculturalists constantly refer to God and the saints in their supplications for rains and a good season. (Religious persons definitely saw a connection between evil youths who did not have faith or respect for their elders and the poor agricultural seasons which the farmers had been suffering.) For their personal life events and crises, all Catholics arranged their lives through the traditional Mitla Catholic pattern of compadrazgo relationships, Catholic ritual, and home festival.

For ritual curing, which is still performed along with Western medicine, belief in God and the saints is considered a necessary prerequisite for both the curer and the patient. Appeals are usually made to Catholic saints, ritual burning of incense is construed within the Catholic ritual system, and procedures often involve the manipulation of Catholic symbols, such as the cross, in talismans and in physical massage.

Even though certain curing practices might be viewed as falling outside the normal range of Roman Catholic behaviors—the possibly syncretistic elements of the curing paraphernalia and ritual, such as the burning of copal, addressing the four corners of the room (and world), and beating the victim of illness with sanctified palm—the ritual participants describe their customs and belief as Catholic. Even those ritual practitioners who might be classified as "witch doctors" by Western scientists (or their local neighbors) rely on the priest to bless all of their paraphernalia and on the saints to give them curing powers.

In summary, Mitla is still a Catholic town, San Pablo Mitla. Since the elimination of the mayordomo system, religion is no longer a means of discouraging economic progress and leveling economic and social distinctions between citizens. Catholicism is still an important part of the expressed identity of Mitleños. For older people, it may still provide a general world view through which nature and people are seen participating in some sort of divine plan. Where such belief is lacking, Catholic ceremony still provides a force for organizing one's social life and meeting the exigencies of social intercourse and disease.

Socioeconomic Organization

Municipally and economically, Mitla is tied into the business of the southeastern arm of the valley, through Tlacolula offices and the Sunday periodic market and to the state, through Oaxaca City. Mitleños purchase seed, animals, cloth and other raw materials at Tlacolula and Oaxaca. The textile business also takes them outside of the region to Mexico City and other states. Transportation is primarily by long distance bus, though other kinds of goods are transported by trucks, many of which are owned by local citizenry.

In addition to the movement of Mitleños to different regions of Oaxaca in their trading activities and to Mexico and beyond in their commerce, other regions, the state, and the nation also penetrate into the local sphere. Products from the Mixe region and the Isthmus reach Mitla by bus, truck, and private car. Though commerce has been facilitated by the introduction of modern motor vehicles and highways, the current trade patterns only expand on an older pattern, which included distribution of goods by means of beasts of burden. Mitla, in the colonial sources, is noted as a town of traders (del Paso y Troncoso 1905). The ancient pattern of bringing goods from the valley to the coastal and mountain regions of the state of Oaxaca continues. In addition, Mitla is a central location to which traders from other regions come to sell their goods. Vendors from the Mixe and the coast middleman their goods in Mitla. Some of the goods are transported by bus or truck; others are transported by tumpline loads, with the human being the beast of burden, as in pre-Hispanic times. Though the roads and the buses exist, not everyone can afford to use such modern conveniences.[8] In addition to agricultural products, including coffee, avocados, oranges, and fruits in season, Mitla receives woven goods from the Mixe regions, sandals and embroidered shirts from the Yalálag area of the Sierra Zapotec, and fish, cheese, and gold jewelry from the coast. Many of the traders now deal directly with the personnel at the marketplaces of Tlacolula and Oaxaca City. For the small trader, however, Mitla is still the selling point for small quantities of agricultural produce and small home-manufactured goods such as leather thongs, brooms, and ropes. In sum, Mitla is less important as a central marketplace for the valley system, than for trade in small items for people coming to the valley to sell their goods. On the other hand, Mitla traders continue to go into other regions of the state, to buy goods for resale within the valley system and beyond. Through such trading contacts, Mitla participates in an intraregional and interregional system of exchange of goods and information. In the process of traveling and receiving travelers, Mitleños have been exposed to the land, customs, resources, and economies of a wide number of areas. As a result, persons from widely dispersed communities can claim social ties with persons from Mitla. Also, the traditional knowledge of many areas has been circulated through Mitla. Though Mitla has rich local customs and her own local resources, the community is by no means isolated, and probably never has been.

Links with Mexican National Culture

Currently, Mitla is being more closely integrated into the nation socially as well as economically. The increased speed and scale of transport communications link Mitla more firmly with the state and national economy, while government programs, particularly schools, create ties between Mitla citizenry and the Mexican state. Though in the past many children went to school only long enough to master functional literacy and arithmetic, today most children obtain compulsory education provided by the Mexican government[9] through the sixth grade. Parents encourage their children to complete at least a sixth grade education, in the hope that the children will find good employment when they are older. Children of families who have the financial means and interest commute by bus to continue their educations at secondary schools in Tlacolula or Oaxaca. Some go on to a *preparatorio* (similar to undergraduate college in the United States) and finally to a university for a career.

In school children learn Spanish, reading, writing, basic arithmetic, history, geography, science, and crafts. Some teachers also instruct their students in basic principles of hygiene and nutrition, information that children can introduce into

---

[8] The trip from the Mixe to the valley takes four days with a moderate load, according to a traveller carrying *huipiles*. He did not think that with the busfare (8 pesos = $.64 from Ayutla to Mitla) his trip would be worthwhile.

[9] Many of the males with whom I talked had completed one to three grades of primary education. They had learned to read and write before quitting school to work either in the fields or for wage labor. Many of the older women had never even completed this much schooling.

their homes.[10] The knowledge carried home by children from the classroom may have practical effects in their households, as adults act on the information about vitamins and nutrients discussed in the schools. Even those who had never attended school conversed about vitamins and nutrients found in vegetables and grains, nutritional wisdom which they had heard from school children.[11]

Hygienic and nutritional information are also passed on from the national government to the pueblo through extension workers. During 1972 and 1973, a government nurse distributed new kinds of food to Xaagá and Corral del Cerro, and instructed the mothers of the ranchos how to prepare unfamiliar items such as soy products and dried milk. In addition, a social worker in charge of "household improvements" oversaw the digging of latrines to replace the open ground refuse area in some households. There was also a government program, carried out by teenage girls in the town, about infant nutrition. The young girls visited different households with illustrative materials to educate young mothers and impress upon them the need to give their babies strained, hygienic foods, in addition to breast milk. One government teacher, supervising young girls in sewing and cooking classes, also distributed seeds for home vegetable gardens. Thus, government programs, as administered by several teachers, were quite diverse.[12]

In addition to these government workers (women who lived in the town and held classes or women who visited Mitla, among other towns, to distribute goods and information) government health programs inoculated children against tetanus, typhoid, smallpox, polio, measles, and tuberculosis. Loudspeakers in Mitla and radio announcements loudly publicize the dates of the health services. In addition to these communication media, informal kinship, compadrazgo, and neighborhood networks spread news about inoculations against disease, government health services in Oaxaca, and the free government health clinic in San Felipe (near Oaxaca City).

The government also provides services in agriculture, food aid, and general civic improvements. Though agricultural programs have not made a great impact on the Mitla traditional agriculture, some farmers do try the experimental seeds distributed by the government. On a small scale, seeds for garden crops, such as sorghum, sunflower, and vegetables, originating from the government, have been distributed informally through social networks.[13] On an environmental scale, the government has sponsored work projects, such as a dam to the northeast of the town center, to prevent flooding and provide irrigation waters. In addition, the government sponsored the building of a series of canals in the Mitla hills, to channel water to the fields and, at the same time, to prevent erosion. Neither has significantly affected agricultural practices, however.[14]

Though people complain about the lack of aid from the national government, they received government stores of grains, and occasionally fruits and vegetables, during a period of food shortages and rising food prices in 1973. After the drought and meager harvest of the 1972 agricultural season, staple food prices jumped thirty to forty percent. The government brought in maize at low cost,[15] temporarily preventing

---

[10] For example, children were taught to drink only purified water, and some parents found the information being disseminated—that well water or tap water was unsafe to drink—both disturbing and disruptive.

[11] One woman said that as an orphan, she had not been able to attend school, but had listened to her patron's children talk about nutrients when they returned from school.

[12] The teachers received introduction and access to the town through a *presidente* in charge of town committees. I was fortunate to be learning about herbs from the president of the town committee and was able to meet these young Mexican "teachers" whenever they visited, and learn about their programs.

[13] One woman introduced sunflower, sorghum, and several vegetables and herbs to her economic contacts in Xaagá and Corral del Cerro, as well as Mitla.

[14] The canals were not serviceable in 1972. Since there was a drought, they could not channel water which was not available. They fell into disrepair. In 1973, following a week of heavy rains, the dam broke under the pressure of the water. It had been built of stone set in concrete, with earthen ramparts forming the major part of the structure. One farmer had been working his fields with canal water channeled from the dam, but his efforts were negated when the dam broke.

[15] Government maize could be purchased at 1.10 pesos per kilo versus 1.50-1.60, the going rate for *maíz criollo*, the local variety. Problems arose in distribution. Deliveries were not always regular, and quantities not always sufficient. Finally, a five kilogram limit per adult per distribution day was set.

further price increases and immediate grain shortages. They also occasionally provided beans and vegetables, at lower than market prices. When low price government grain stores were not available in Mitla, some local people went to the government *bodega* ("storehouse") near Tlacolula and purchased low cost grain there. Such government food distribution policies serve to further integrate Mitla into the state and national economy.

Also influential for the development of the town have been the national improvements of basic services: water, electricity, telegraph, postal service, and regional roads. Individual households have installed running water and electricity. Running water for drinking, washing, and garden irrigation greatly reduces the energy and time expenditure devoted to food, household, and garden preparation. It releases household members, particularly women, from the burdensome chore of drawing water; people no longer rely on limited quantities of water for their activities.

Electricity has probably been of even greater significance for changing work patterns. First, most grain mills are electrically powered,[16] and the resulting relief of women from the chore of grinding maize has significantly altered their occupational roles. Where previously their whole day might be spent in preparing tortillas, comida, and a few other chores, women now spend less time in food preparation activities and devote their time and energy to more economically remunerative pursuits.

Electric lights have also meant that people can more easily work at night. During two major power failures and minor power failures in 1973 people managed to work by candlelight or kerosene lantern, but with difficulty. Electricity is also very important for home industry. The growth of the cotton shirt industry has been facilitated by electric-motor-powered sewing machines. Though many households can afford only foot power, electricity is critical for the efficiency of larger operations. Production was halted during the 1972 power failures. Finally, electricity at night has affected folk beliefs by eliminating the darkness and whatever potential evil it may harbor. For some local persons witches went out with the electric light, a change which has affected cosmological beliefs as well as curing ceremonies and herbal medicine.

Other basic services—specifically telegraph, postal services, and regional roads—have greatly facilitated communication between Mitla and the other states and regions of Mexico. Business and commerce have been expanded and expedited on the basis of these improved communications. Distant goods and information now move into and out of Mitla with much greater speed and frequency. The variety and quality of life have been affected by new foods, medicines, consumer goods, and ideas which affect traditional diet, medicine, and consumer practices.

The mass media have had other effects on traditional Mitla. Improved literacy keeps people in touch with the rest of the nation. The radio, a treasured possession in almost every household, plays constantly, accompanying people in their chores, meals, and major employment. In addition to music, the radio provides news about the rest of the world and the state of the economy.

Finally, tourists affect the character of Mitla. Tourists both supply a market for the burgeoning domestic industries of Mitla and provide indicators of tastes and practices from greater Mexico and the United States. Tourists provide not only economic material but cultural ideas, which local people can then use for amusement or change.

In summary, Mitla is tied into the rest of the valley and surrounding regions through trade, the periodic market system, and government. With improved transportational, oral, and written communications facilities, Mitla receives new information and goods, and greater quantities of them, than ever before. Improved communication with those outside of traditional Mitla affects the knowledge and decisions of the current popula-

---

[16]During 1973, there were two major power failures which affected Mitla; one for five days, one for seven. At the onset of the first failure, only one miller had a power source other than electricity. As a result, all meal life was disrupted and women did not get their maize ground until 11 a.m.–1 p.m. On subsequent mornings, the women began going to the mill at 2 a.m. to assure some return to their normal daily schedule. By the end of the second power failure, two more millers had acquired nonelectrically powered mills. The situation showed how dependent people have become on the convenience of electricity.

tion. In this setting, the traditional system of agriculture can now be presented and analyzed.

To comprehend the way people communicate about plants one must first understand their language as it is associated with plants. For this purpose, the following chapter introduces the nomenclature and taxonomy of plants as discussed by Mitla Zapotecs.

IV

SYSTEMATICS

All people classify, organizing their world into meaningful categories so that its component parts may be systematically conceived, discussed, and used. Anthropologists have been particularly interested in native classificatory principles for both intellectual and practical reasons. Native classificatory principles have been viewed as keys to basic categories of human thought or, at least, the basic structuring principles underlying particular cultures (Lévi-Strauss 1966). As a special case, folk taxonomies—classifications that group folk segregates on the basis of hierarchic inclusion—have been viewed as possible keys to the structure of lexicons, human language, and ultimately the human mind (Berlin 1970). Folk classifications should be able to show how different cultures recognize and code similarities and differences in their environment. For the anthropologist, studies of folk classifications should lead to a better understanding of human behavior in particular cultural and natural environments (e.g., Fowler 1977).

PLANT CLASSIFICATION STUDIES IN ANTHROPOLOGY

Plant classifications, particularly plant taxonomies, comprise an important corpus of data for anthropologists searching for cultural principles through which natives divide up the natural world and regulate behavior toward it (Conklin 1954; Berlin et al. 1974). Ethnoscientists, or "linguistic anthropologists," who seek " ... through interview, observation, and when possible experiment to discover some part of the system of meanings by which people organize the world" (Kay 1970:19), have developed rigorous methodologies, including question-answer frames and plant card sorting techniques. Using terms the natives supply for higher and lower categories of plants, they have attempted to describe the semantic domain of plants among different cultures, in order to ultimately discover semantic universals (Berlin 1970:15) and linkages between human information processing, conceptual thought, and human behavior,

> ... arriving at the cognitive system, or systems, employed by people as a device for classifying their environment, evaluating various states of that environment, predicting what the outcomes of various behavioral possibilities open to them will have on that environment and ultimately, selecting a course of action. (Kay 1970:29)

Ecological anthropologists foresee folk classification studies leading to "more complete and thorough description of the relationships of native peoples to their environment" (Fowler 1977:243). Ecological archaeologists hope that studies of contemporary functional plant classifications may provide insights into the distribution of plant genera in antiquity (Flannery et al. 1970). Quite distant from these goals are the aims of cognitive anthropologists and psychologists, who hope that the study of plant classificatory activities will show them the different kinds of concepts and criteria people use to structure various domains of thought (e.g., Price-Williams 1962) and the patterns by which children learn about a taxonomically structured domain, such as plants (e.g., Stross 1973).

Though folk classifications may be functional, abstract, ritual, or other, folk botanical studies in the past have largely concentrated on systematic taxonomies based on morphological features. Using the method of componential analysis to discover the binary distinctions by which people discriminate between two folk segregates, anthropologists have rigorously examined the logic of folk taxonomic and nomenclatural systems and the relationships between these and have compared the structure and content of particular folk botanical classification systems with folk botanies in other cultures and with systematic botany. Recent botanical systematic studies suggest that all folk and modern botanical classifications share certain features (Berlin et al. 1968, 1973, 1974). First, all plants can be hierarchically grouped and named at one of several levels; in folk systems these levels include: unique beginner ("plant"), life form ("tree," "herb," etc.) generic, specific, and varietal (Fig. 3). Each taxonomic level becomes progressively more precise as one moves down the hierarchy from "plant," the most general category. In addition, plants in folk taxonomies may be sorted into "covert categories"—unnamed groupings between the named levels of the taxonomic hierarchy.

Using this scheme, Berlin and others have proposed a number of generalities about Tzeltal folk botany based on their fieldwork among the Tzeltal Indians of Chiapas, Mexico which invite comparison and discussion. First, they have argued that folk and Linnaean botanical taxa are largely congruent, i.e., that folk and scientific botanical taxonomies are structured by equivalent logic and largely map onto one another. They have suggested that economically useful plants receive consideration at greater taxonomic depth than less economically useful plants and are named at a lower level in the taxonomic-nomenclatural tree, and this sometimes accounts for overdifferentiation or underdifferentiation by Western botanical standards (Berlin et al. 1966). Second, they have proposed that the Tzeltal rules for naming plants at the generic and specific levels are largely comparable with the binomial rules of nomenclature used in modern scientific botany and that most taxa are named to the generic or specific level (1973). Where correspondences are not clearly evident, one may look for and find "covert" conceptual categories which show how natives are grouping plants taxonomically, even in the absence of labels (Berlin et al. 1968, 1973).

The botanical systematics studies so far cited have concentrated on the elicitation of folk systematic taxonomies, using the technique of componential analysis to discover the salient differences between forms. Are these aims and methods, however, the most useful ways for learning all that people know and think about

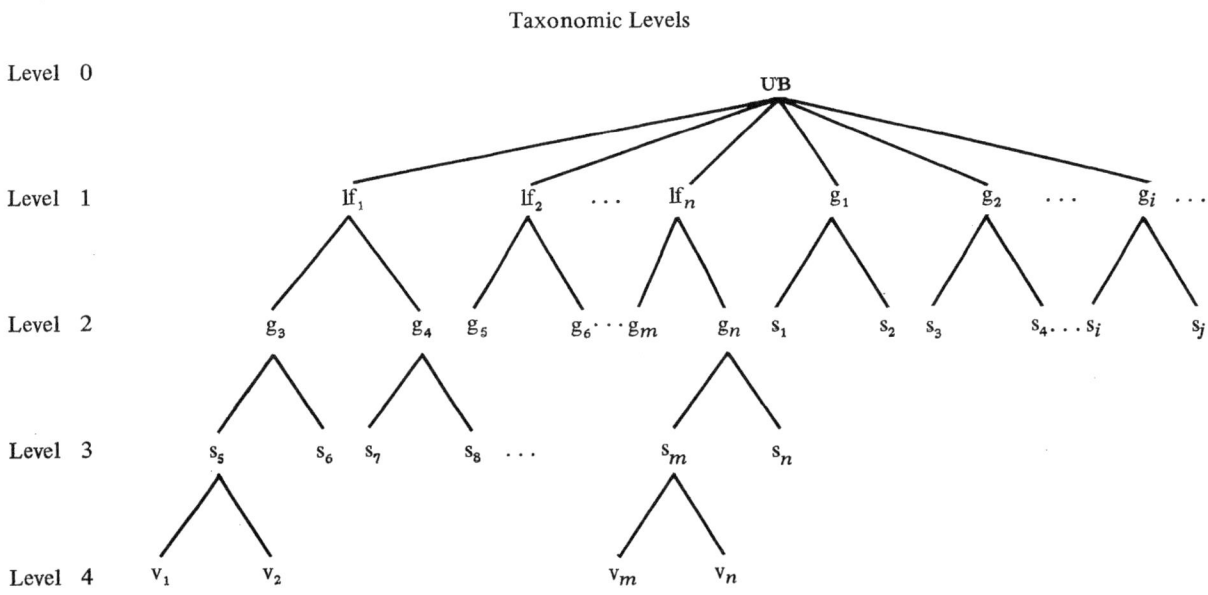

Fig. 3. Schematic relationship of the five universal ethnobiological taxonomic categories and their relative hierarchic levels in an idealized folk taxonomy. **UB**, unique beginner; **lf**, life form; **g**, generic, **s**, specific; **v**, varietal (redrawn from Berlin, Breedlove, and Raven 1974:26).

plants? What do plant labels mean in different contexts? Conklin (1962) has shown that the number of different responses which are "correct" to the question, "What is this (chile pepper plant) called?" in Hanunóo depends on the knowledge of the speakers and the context of identification and naming. Multiple levels within systematic taxonomies as well as alternative classificatory schemes exist, and the use of particular terms in real speech contexts (as opposed to experimental elicitation contexts) can be analyzed as part of the greater cultural communication system.

Finally, folk classifications of plants potentially provide very important data through which basic perceptual and cognitive processes (how conceptual thinking develops in children and in cultures) can be discovered. Plants may provide literal as well as figurative material for arguments about the relative abilities of natives to think "abstractly" (cf. Cole and Scribner 1974:"Trees in Search of a Forest"). Complementarily, psychological theories of cognitive development, cognitive variability, perception, and conceptualization supply a framework through which to view the nature of plant concept categorization and plant concept learning.

MITLA ZAPOTEC PLANT CLASSIFICATION

As part of their cultural heritage and training, Mitla Zapotecs, like other people, learn to classify, identify, and name plants. They recognize individual unit categories on the basis of selected features. These units, called "plant concept categories" in the discussion to follow, refer to the whole plant entity, and take into account the development of particular taxa. People learn to sort specimens (mentally or physically) into plant concept categories even though the specimens may be missing some or most of their mature parts. Most, but not all, plant concept categories are named, and the conceptual processes of naming and identification may be inseparable in many cases.

This study will begin by introducing the botanical world available to the native Mitleño and by showing how distinctions are made within it. Following the presentation of local classificatory, taxonomic, and nomenclatural procedures, I shall discuss the implications of classificatory procedures for communication of information about plants. The term "systematic taxonomy" will be used in a very strict sense to refer to the hierarchical classification which distinguishes groupings at the life form and lower levels within the taxonomy. This taxonomy will then be contrasted with other kinds of classifications (growth stage, functional categories) to show how people can select information from one or another classification to correctly identify and use flora. In describing the Mitla Zapotec flora, I will emphasize the properties by which plants are identified in the field or in speech rather than the sum of properties which potentially exist in a plant form. All data derives from plant collecting field trips or other participant observation activities, rather than from carefully structured and experimental interview procedures. The presentation of data will begin with a brief description of the social-economic botanical setting. Then, the discussion will follow a standard botanical format to cover the topics of Zapotec folk botanical description, taxonomy, and nomenclature, and delineate apparent differences between folk and Western botanical taxonomy and nomenclature. Next, alternative classificatory schemes will be presented along with further discussion of the differences between Mitleño and Western botanical classification. Implications of the Zapotec folk botanical data for general questions of concept learning and communication about plants comprise the final discussion.

SETTING

Mitla folk botany considers mainly plants of Mitla and the surrounding vicinity, the plants most frequently encountered and most commonly used in ordinary activities. Both men and women recognize that the flora of Mitla is distinct from the flora of other areas. Many Mitleños travel to other regions for business (traveling merchants), for pleasure or out of piety (usually fiesta attendance). In their travels, they become more or less familiar with the flora of other localities. If they have kin or compadrazgo relations in distant towns, they may enter milpas and walk through countryside for the avowed purpose of learning about the local plants, both classes and uses.

The fresh and dried plants of other areas reach Mitla in a number of ways. With the advent of modern highways between the coast and Mitla, and the mountains (Mixe region) and Mitla, economically useful plants are transported with ease from one region to the next. They may be brought by friends and relatives or by traveling herbalists or herbal entrepreneurs.

In addition to the oral exchange of knowledge and the physical transfer of specimens, information on plant food and herbal medicine is also transmitted through books. Children learn about plants and nutrition to a limited extent in school and pass on this knowledge to adults. Medicinal herbals are very popular. Even persons who are barely literate can refer to the pictures and names of plants in herbals and use these as additional sources of botanical knowledge or as substitutes for traditional knowledge. In some cases, where herbal distributors publish their own herbals, the new medicinal herbs may quickly become sought for relief of particular ailments.

Locally, one is not trained specifically in plant use or systematics, but one receives training as part of normal development in the local culture. Child, youth, or adult may learn about plants through participating in agricultural activities or accompanying parents, friends, or relatives to gather edible herbs or fruits or medicinal plants. Excursions to cut or gather fuel, watch domestic animals, wash clothes or bathe in the white water pools and mountain streams, or pleasure outings all bring Mitleños close to plants in nature. In the home, the Mitleño also sees herbs in the kitchen and herbs and trees in the garden. He may note the difference in the flora near the river, where he dumps the garbage or the contrast of vegetation between the hills and valley. Men may have a better knowledge of the hillside vegetation since women are often kept close to the house, but during the course of the year, a great many plants are introduced into the home. Flowers decorate the altar, herbs are collected to prepare remedies for illness, spices and vegetables are brought for meals, and special wild fruits and flowers mark particular seasons and holidays. From all of these experiences, one learns about a plant—the botanical object—its characteristics of growth, its seasonality, its divisions into parts, and its names.

DESCRIPTION

Western botanical classification is codified in books. Species defined with reference to particular type specimens are described on the basis of selected taxonomic characters. Botanists identify their filed specimens with reference to a descriptive key, enumerating the features relevant for identification. The unknown specimen is identified on the basis of the fit between the unknown's characteristics and the description presented in the key. When the plant is identified with a species description in a key, it is also identified by the name applied to that description, with an understanding of where that plant fits in the taxonomy. In contrast, the ethnobotanist (either native or anthropologist) looks at a specimen and takes note of certain descriptive characteristics, identifying a particular specimen as a member of a conceptual ("identity") category of plants, usually named. He may *then* analyze why he chose one method or another to arrive at the decision. What makes this plant identity category different from other plant identity categories, and what features figure in the decision to assign the particular specimen to a particular category, is largely an unconscious process of thought. The ethnobotanist at the end of the identification may be able to indicate certain factors which influenced his decision, but there may be more than one route to the identification and this may depend on the individual classifier.

The local taxonomic system clearly classifies plants as the same or different, but with little apparent use of a mental key. Instead, persons make reference to a "type" specimen, a plant concept category existing in the mind, which is made up of several characteristics, some visual, some chemical, some conceptual. Classifications are not made on the basis of a single set of criteria but on various sets of features. This type specimen may exist at any taxonomic level below that of primary life form. Each field specimen is sorted into categories on the basis of the primary type specimen image, classified, and sometimes named on the basis of anatomical parts, color, scent, and ecology.

PLANT PARTS

Particular physical features go into constructing the type concept category (see Fig. 4). One can talk about the root (Zap. *guh*, Sp. *raiz*), its thickness, its characteristics of shallow or deep growth in the soil. In certain cases, the root is necessary for type classification and specimen identification. One excavates the *camote* of *gu-žehl*[1] to see if the small tuber is present, and one can identify the plant on the basis of the root, or better, the taste of the root. The thick deep root of *škʷan tst* is distinctive; it is excavated for identification and use. Taste of the root is also used as a classificatory and identification procedure. *Gu-žehl* is sweet, and may be identified by taste in the absence of vegetative parts.

Habits of stem growth are also diagnostic features. The stem may be with "thorns" (Zap. *ya-geč*, Sp. *espina*) or "smooth" (Zap. *xžol*, Sp. *liso*). Color of the stem may be green (most herbs in Zapotec are *nŏl*, "white") or colored (e.g., Zap. *bitia? morad*, "purple" or *geč niz*, described as "blue" in Zapotec). Plants may also be contrasted according to habits of stem growth. Thus, there are two classes of *yahn;* one grows extended along the ground, the other upright.

Leaf color, texture, outline, and arrangement are also critical features for certain Zapotec identifications. Leaves may be "big" or "thin" (*škʷan-ĵehb ro?, škʷan-ĵehb lăs*); "toothed" (*balak tsun*) or not; "sticky" (*kʷan-ȋgid*) or not. Gross size of the leaf and whether it can be peeled (as in the case of *mostaza* [*Nicotiana*]) may also be identifying characteristics. Moisture is another dimension of leaves, (*dzědz* is "wet;" *nis* is "water") as contrasted with other leaves. Leaf color is also an important distinction. Red and white classes of *guladz* (*quintonil*) are distinguished. Juice—milky, colored, or colorless—may also be a diagnostic feature. *Binya* is distinguishable by its milky juice, *geč niz* by its yellow juice, and *suzi* by its sap, which is colorless to red.

Chemical characteristics are also distinctive for identification. Leaves may smell odorless, sweet, bitter, foul or delicious. *Salb nŏl* smells "sweet" (*niž*); *yerba maestra*, "bitter" (*La*); *giht lahn*, "foul" (*lahn*). Taste is also a dimension for perceptual classification, in some cases, but not always, overlapping with smell. For example, a sure identification procedure for *kʷan ghihb* (*cacahuatón*) is to masticate the leaf, which releases its extremely bitter essence. The odorless leaf may be a plant specimen otherwise denuded of classificatory features.

Flowers (*gi*) are an integral part of the concept category describing each segregate. Flowers may be noted, when present, by their size, composition, color(s), and odor. *Yäb dahn* with large flowers is contrasted with *yäb gihš* with smaller flowers. *Gi togol kʷa?č* is distinguished from *gi togol*, a plant with similar leaf form and smell but with a different flower. Colors of flowers are noted and may be distinctive features for particular taxa. *Lahk* with lavender flowers is considered superior to *lahk kuněf* with white flowers and a less vivid odor. Flower odor may also be a dimension for discriminating between species whose flowers otherwise appear equivalent. For example, the flower and vegetative parts of *manzaniy neš* is "sweet" while the identical looking flower of *manzaniy La* is "bitter."

Plants having flowers described by one or more criteria of difference may nevertheless be placed in the same class or even called by the same name. Colors of *lo gid gai* vary; some flowers are yellow with dark centers, others are red with yellow centers, but this is not considered sufficient reason to give the segregates separate names.

---

[1] Zapotec names will ordinarily be used in the discussions on systematics and nomenclature. Spanish names follow in parentheses where they illustrate the same taxonomic points, or where they supply a Spanish common name which is used in further discussions in the text. Spanish names (e.g., *mostaza*) are used in the text, where the Zapotec label is a phonetic modification of the Spanish, i.e., the same Spanish term is used in Spanish and Zapotec. Appendix 2 lists the Latin scientific equivalents for local labels used in the text.

PLANT PART	PERCEPTIBLE ATTRIBUTES	TAXONOMIC LEVEL	NOMENCLATURE
ROOT	form	supra-generic	guh ("tuber")
	taste	generic	gu.žehl
	color	specific	guh nŏl, guh morad
STEM	form	supra-generic	ya geč ("thorn")
	color	generic	geč niz (chicalote)
	growth characteristics	specific	yahn
LEAF	form	generic	škʷan.ǰehb ("espanto herb")
	size	specific	škʷan.ǰehb roʔ, škʷan.ǰehb lăs
	color	specific	guladz nŏl, guladz morad
	moisture	generic	dzědz
	taste	generic	cacahuatón
	smell	generic	monstranza
JUICE	consistency	generic	binya
	color	generic	geč.niz
FLOWER	form	generic	gi.togol
		specific	gi.togol, gi.togol kʷaʔč
	smell	specific	gi.lakh, gi.lakh kuněf
FRUIT	form, season	generic	biruʔn manzan.giš
		specific	bidz lats
	color	varietal	bidz lats nŏl, bidz lats šynă

Fig. 4. Perceptible attributes that distinguish named classes at different taxonomic levels.

ODOR OR TASTE	SABOR	R̃LYA	EXAMPLES	USE
"sweet"	dulce	neš	manzaniy neš	Medicinal tea
"delicious," "tasty"	sabroso	níž	škʷan ǰehb roʔ	Medicinal drink
"foul," "stinking"	feo	lahn	giht lahn	Not eaten
"bitter"	amargo	La	manzaniy La	Medicinal drink
"spicy"	picante	nayan	gin (chile)	Condiment
"no taste"		žet nak	nis	Water

Fig. 5. Dimensions of smell/taste.

A slight contrast is the plant concept category labeled *geč niz*. Some of the specimens have white flowers, and others yellow, but both are usually assigned to the same category. However, some people do distinguish between the white flower, believed to be efficacious for earache and the yellow flower, classed as nonefficacious. This example suggests a potential for subclasses to be distinguished at the species level on the basis of flower color and usefulness.

Another case is the use of flower descriptions to distinguish between genera labeled identically but conceived as different plant concept categories. For example, the long tubular form of *mostaza* (*Nicotiana glauca*) contrasts with its small round flowered form (*Brassica nigra*). These two plant concept categories are distinguished as taxa, but labeled the same. To avoid confusion, speakers note the form, color, petals, and centers of the flowers in addition to the name, *mostaza*, when referring to the plant. (The assignment of one name to more than one taxon, will be further discussed below.)[2]

More important, flowers are seasonal markers, both for the life cycles of particular species and for the yearly cycle. People expect particular species to follow a seasonal round. When species fail to conform to the expectations, people comment that they are "out of season." For example, *ya-geč beh* ("mesquite") is expected to flower during the dry season (February) and develop fruits which are ripe in late July. During the drought of 1972, mesquite was blooming in September, and people commented that *el tiempo está cambiando,* "the climate (season) is changing." When the mesquite did not bloom at its usual time, there was a feeling that there was something wrong, a feeling exacerbated by the milpa-killing drought. *Lya* (*guajes*) are classed by their time of flower and fruits. The August blooming *guajes* are followed by January fruits, *Lya kureš* ("dry season/*cuaresma*/*guajes*"). The flowers presage the fruits of the dry season, as contrasted with *Lya gusgih* ("wet season *guajes*"). Similarly, the flowers of the organ cactus, *yag bidz žob,* are seasonal plant markers, as are their fruits, which appear in the spring.

Fruits are also segregate markers and seasonal indicators. Size, shape, color, and seasonal relationship to flower are noted. In addition to the above examples of mesquite and *guajes*, there are fruits of *manzan gihš* in September, *žob nihd* also in September, and *ya geč čahd* in August. *Manzan gihš,* a tree in the hills surrounding Mitla has distinctive red wood and yellow fruit. Golden when ripe, the fruits cling to the trees, and turn brown when drying. *Žob nihd* is identified by the blue/black fruit and by the tree's close association with *manzan gihš.* The two fruits are usually gathered simultaneously. The yellow fruits of *ya geč čehd* (*rompecapa*) are classified by some people as edible. Since the thorn trees line many of the paths to the fields of Mitla, the species is well known, and the fruit often eaten by people, especially children, in the campo.

Though there was some mention of "male" vs. "female" plants, this is not a common axis for discrimination among trees or herbs. The *pirú*, called *ya luỹ* in Zapotec, was the most commonly noted tree, but the distinction of male was applied to the fruiting state (red fruits) and female to the flowering stage (white flowers). There was no distinction among trees by sex, and only one young girl specifically mentioned that she sought the leaves of male trees to treat women and female trees to treat men. Older, more trusted women said that the leaves of any *pirú* would serve equally well in a remedy.[3]

ECOLOGY

Though most systematic botanists rely on morphological features in classifying plants, locations and associations are integral parts of a Zapotec plant identification. Those aspects of plant ecology which are contained in a descriptive note below a taxonomic key entry are part of the taxonomic procedure in Mitla classifications. *Dahn* or *gihš* ("mountain" or "countryside") species are distinguished from those which look like these but which are located and usually sown within the pueblo. For example, *ya luỹ dahn* ("mountain *pirú*," *pirú del monte*) is distinguished from the common type, located within the pueblo. *Yäb gihš* is used to distinguish the field herb, *acahual,* from *yäb,* the cultivated sunflower, if both are present in a field.

There were no species on which controlled studies could be made of artificial distinctions of "cultivated" versus "uncultivated" types of the

---

[2] This particular case is complicated by the fact that one subsequent speaker distinguished the two by name and function—the former, *mostas gihš* the latter *mostas štil* (Sp. *mostaza de Castilla*) of which "You eat the leaves and seeds."

[3] Elsie Clews Parsons mentions at least two tree classes distinguished by sex: the *pirú* tree, distinguished as "the woman," when "with flowers" and "the man" when "with fruits" (1936:9). This corresponds to the single report in the current data. Parsons also mentions *mala mujer,* considered the female of *chichicasle.* Though she does not supply identifications, she notes that the root of the latter is ground and taken for gonorrhea, while three leaves of the former are made into a tea, and taken to stop excessive menstrual flow (1936:124-125). Thus, it appears that formerly, some medicinal plants were classified according to "sex," and one treated disorders of the sexual parts by matching plants to the afflicted part of the same sex.

same plant. *Mostaza* (*Brassica nigra*) does appear occasionally as a field herb, but it is not cultivated, so only one type is noted. There are no representatives of the wild ancestor of maize. *Giht lahn*, a feral squash, is named "stinking squash" and recognized as related to, but different from, cultivated squash on the basis of leaves, flowers, and fruits.

Since there is a constant alternation between sown and unsown gathering of some species, there is no confusion that the species in the home garden are other than the species in the fields. Home grown varieties may be bigger, but they are not different in kind from the wild plants gathered nearby. For example, *Lya yodz* (*chapiche*) may be gathered in the countryside or hills or purchased in the market. The market specimens are larger, and the seeds of the purple flowers may be saved to sow in one's own garden. However, they are the same species as the herb named *chapiche* which one can gather near Mitla. The seeds of larger specimens of the wild herb may be saved and sown in the garden also.

Bityuš giž ("husk tomatoes") are mainly purchased in the market. However, the plants also grow wild in the fields, and the fruits of these individuals are equally savored in sauces. If young, vigorous plants are found along the sides of fields or in fields, some enterprising women uproot these "weeds" to transplant into their gardens. There is no question that they are all *bityuš giž*, though "large" (*ro?*) and "thin" (*lǎs*) varieties can also be distinguished.

DESCRIPTION FOR IDENTIFICATION

Plant descriptions include a variety of features, but not all are necessary for the taxonomy or for identification. The following four examples show the features which were noted in distinguishing each taxon, as well as other palpable attributes which could have been noted.

1. The plant grows over fields even in the dry season. The flower is yellow or white. The leaves and the entire plant look blue.

The plant was *geč niz*, and the man giving me the description did not know its Spanish name, *chicalote*. The features were sufficient for his identification, and he expected the anthropologist to know to which plant he was referring on the basis of this description. Apart from the description, which was adequate to define the plant, he later added that the plant was thorny (hence the name *geč*) and when broken produced a yellow juice. The juice is applied to the eyes when they are red, sore, and hurt. Thus, the plant has a functional classification as a medicinal herb.

2. A very small plant in milpas or the edges of fields which extends over the ground. Sometimes it has a reddish appearance, particularly when there is little moisture. It has white flowers.

This plant was the common stomach remedy, *biyušit* (*billushíto*), boiled for stomachache, particularly *empacho* ("indigestion"). The plant has very small leaves and no characteristic odor, except when boiled in tea. It is classified as "hot" and used to treat "cold" stomachaches; this is again a functional classification.

3. The plant is small, and grows in the hills. The leaf is a little bit like the leaf of beans or another plant which has similar leaves but a purple flower. There is a pink flower in July and August. The plant has a *camotito* (size shown by touching thumb to forefinger or by digging out the root).

This plant was *gu-žehl* (*camotito*). The identity in the field is usually established, in the absence of the distinctive flower, by digging out the root. The root may be tasted for certain identification, since it is nontoxic and sweet.

4. *Pirú del monte*. The tree looks just like the *pirú* tree which is all over the pueblo, but this class grows only in the mountains. It is dangerous. People say that if one stands in the shade of the tree, one will break out in pimples and swell up.

Ya luỹ dahn was not collected, since the leaves were considered dangerous. By all appearances, it is equal to the pueblo variety.

These descriptions give an idea of the limited

number of details that may be used to successfully delimit a plant class. Descriptions assume some knowledge of flora of the area, and often descriptions are used to identify some part of the botanical environment which has been recognized but not named or used by the person receiving the communication. Plants may be recognized through examination of the leaves, stems, growth, associations, etc., but pure description or comparison of a specimen with a verbal description is rarely used. As a substitute for, or in addition to a description, an actual specimen may be brought to touch, examine, and identify, and the contexts and uses described. Alternatively, contexts and uses may be described, and the recipient of the information may be brought to a specimen at a later date. Not all Mitleños are equally trained in plant identification, but an observant person has the opportunity to learn, purely by oral tradition and teaching, if he has the desire and interest to learn the natural flora. Since a leaf or branch or the entire plant if small may be collected without much trouble, one can go to an authority for a plant identification and not worry about a detailed mental taxonomic key at all.

TAXONOMY: THE HIERARCHY OF ORGANIZATION

The natural relationships between plants are constructed by careful observation of shared characteristics of growth, leaf form, and scent, flowers, and fruits. Mitla Zapotec distinguishes the contrast between plants, *yahg* (*plantas*) and other living things—"animals" (Zap. *mahn,* Sp. *animales*) and "people" (Zap. *behN,* Sp. *gente*) (see Fig. 6). The term *yahg* denotes both "plant," as a general category, and trees and shrubs as "woody plants," a "primary life form" (by Berlin et al.)

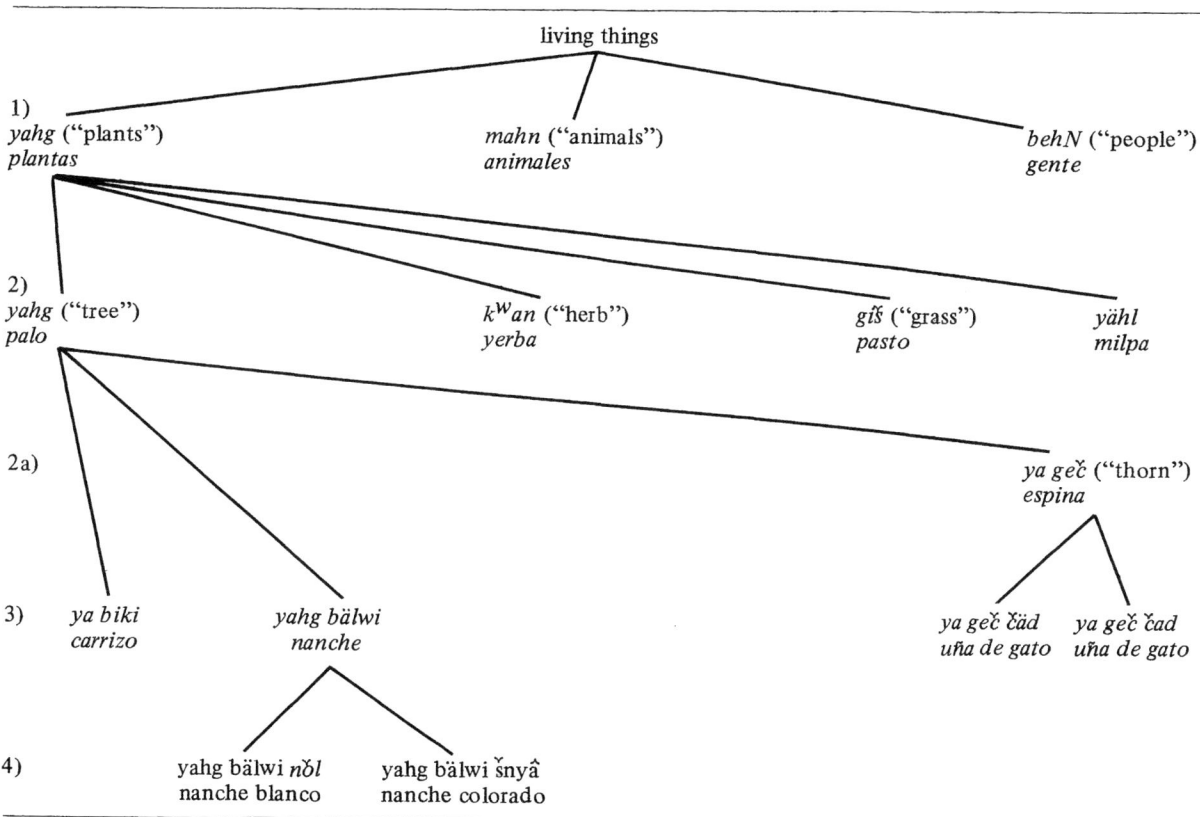

Fig. 6. Taxonomic levels. 1) Unique beginner (polysemous at level 2); 2) Life form; 2a) Named category ("thorn trees," for instance) between life form and generic; 3) Generic (shown for "trees" only); 4) Specific.

Yahg is used in naming most trees and can be translated into Spanish and English as *palo* ("tree") as in the case of *yak pin* ("pine tree"), *ya banú* ("*pájaro bobo* tree"), *yak tsin* ("oak tree"). It is also used to denote the woody plant part of shrubs, bushes, and vines. The Spanish term *una mata* ("a bush") of beans, squash, milkweed vine will all be glossed *yahg* in Zapotec. In addition, any dry, vegetative form suitable for firewood is glossed *yahg*. Thus, *yahg* is polysemous: it designates several related categories including plant, tree, bush, and firewood.

K^wan, *giš*, and *yähl* are other plant primary life forms. K^wan denotes a plant with a green, non-woody stem (*hierba*, "herb"). It refers to all green plants of small growth with distinguishable leaves. Field weeds are generally glossed k^wan, when there is no need to distinguish among them. When one goes out to clean fields of unsown vegetation, one cleans out k^wan, (which include the particular genera *manzaniy*, *yäb*, etc.). The green leaves and stems of bushes are also glossed k^wan as in k^wan *ya?* ("squash leaves"), or *šk^wam bäl* ("snake herb"). The plants would be glossed *yak k^wan ya?* and *yak šk^wam bäl* respectively, though the terminology is rarely used.

K^wan also denotes three functional categories of plants: "medicinal herbs," "herbs which people eat," and "herbs which animals eat." One cures with k^wan ("herbal medicines") as opposed to other classes of remedies, such as pills or injections. For a meal, one may prepare k^wan ("pot herbs") including *guladz*, *lakh*, etc., as opposed to another class of comida such as beans or rice. When one goes out to gather food for animals, one gathers k^wan (which include *guladz*, *yäb*, and *manzaniy*) from the fields, without specifying the types of herbs. Thus, animals feed on k^wan as opposed to *nopales* or maize. If one buys k^wan ("herbs") to feed animals, this denotes alfalfa, the principal fodder crop of the region. Thus, k^wan has meaning as a general life form contrasted with *yahg* ("woody plants") and other life forms to be discussed below, and denotes the green herbaceous parts as contrasted with the woody parts of certain bushes. These life form referents of k^wan then have cultural connotations, which could be called k^wan use categories. To the extent that these categories are also general plant use categories, k^wan also functions as a more general term for "plant." Thus, most women described my ethnobotanical study as *estúd k^wan*, "the study of herbs."

The third life form category—*giš* ("grass," *pasto*)—denotes plants with a blade leaf versus broad leaf morphology. There are several types of "grasses" distinguished, often on the basis of inflorescence. *Giš* may also denote all small vegetation, with nearly indistinguishable leaves. Thus, one can call the very small vegetative growth in one's maize field *giš*, describing the appearance of the field.

Though species may predominantly exhibit one life form and may be classed as either *yahg*, k^wan, or *giš*, these terms may also serve as life cycle markers. During its life span, a single plant may belong to more than one life form category. For example, the field weed *yäb*, may be glossed *giš* when one of a number of very low herbs in a field, k^wan when larger and full leaved, and *yahg* when large, dry, and suitable for fuel at the end of the rainy season. In general, these three labels indicating plant life form also denote principal stages of plant growth. They succinctly describe the stage of weed growth in agricultural fields or elsewhere, and linguistically mark the points in the agricultural cycle where cleaning of fields should occur.

In summary, plant life form markers carry a great deal of information outside of the systematic taxonomy. They denote life stages, functional classes, and general descriptions of particular herbs and vegetation areas. The choice of *yahg*, k^wan, or *giš* is a judgment of context as well as of gross morphological form. A Zapotec who completely identifies a specimen to one life form category is succinctly supplying the information that term carries for that particular identification context. Identifying the specimen below the life form category might be less useful in some functional contexts—such as ascertaining the state of agricultural fields and the need to clean them—or unsolicited and unnecessary, as in a description of the kind of medicine (herbal) being used to treat an illness. A Zapotec may have more information about a specimen and be able to assign it to a generic or specific class, but he may choose a life form label principally for its additional meaning—the contexts outside of the systematic taxonomy—for which it supplies important information.

Two additional life form markers should be mentioned. An additional category label used by some Zapotecs is *behúk* from the Spanish loan word *bejuco,* "vine." It identifies any twining plant which cannot be more precisely named. Since most vines in Mitla can always be named at the generic level, the term is rarely used. People say the term is primarily used in the mountains, where many unnamed vines are employed for binding wood in construction. *Behúk,* in contrast to other life form labels, does not naturally form part of generic and specific labels. Furthermore, vines can be correctly identified as an alternative life form, *yahg.* In sum, not all Mitleños use *behúk,* a Spanish loan word, to talk about their local flora.

Maize, the most important agricultural staple food plant, comprises a final life form, and is set apart in the taxonomy. The plant is called *yähl,* the seed *žob. Yähl* is never prefixed by *yahg* and never discussed as another "grass."[4] Both *yähl* and the Spanish equivalent *milpa* refer to either the single maize plant or a field of maize plants. Thus, the plant of exceptional cultural value is also set apart linguistically.

Taxonomy and Nomenclature below the
Primary Life Form Level

Plants are grouped and named more precisely to as many as three levels below principal life form ("generic," "specific," and "varietal" according to Berlin et al.). These groups, delimited by visual, olfactory, and taste attributes, form the *plant concept categories,* or "folk segregates" (cf. Conklin 1954:23) of the systematic taxonomy. The cultural classification provides names for individual botanical categories at one or more levels in the folk taxonomy depending on the other plants in the environment with which it can be compared and from which it should be discriminated for practical purposes. People select terms from one or another level in the folk taxonomy according to their own botanical knowledge and the purpose for which they are naming a particular plant.

In the life form category *yahg* are several distinctive morphological forms—*dohb* (*maguey*), *bia* (*nopales*), *yag bidz* (*órgano*)—as well as other kinds of "trees." Each of these terms denotes a plant class and may be used to name a single member belonging to that class. For more precise information, the categories are subdivided on the basis of particular species characteristics, such as habitat, color of the flowers and fruits, timing of the flowers and fruits, and particular leaf or stem form. There are two cultivated classes of maguey distinguished on the basis of their succulent stem form and functional characteristics: *dohb gih* (for mezcal production) and *dohb neph* (for pulque production). Often planted in the same field, the two are easily distinguished by the wider *pencas* ("leaves") and blue color of the latter. Wild magueys also have distinctive penca forms and distinctive functions. The pencas of *dohb pasm* are prepared and used medicinally, while the pencas of *dohb dahn* are prepared for the manufacture of rope. There are at least three cultivated and two wild types of *bia* (*nopales*) each distinguished by the distinctive form of the succulent stem. For example, *bia saʔ* is easily distinguished from *bia bäz,* since the former has a narrow, small stem, the latter a large, paddle-shaped whitish stem. The edible form of wild nopal, *bia kʷiot,* is distinguishable from the nonedible class, *bia čiv,* by fewer spines. These nopal forms may also be individually distinguished, in season, by their fruit, *biruʔn* (*tuna*).

There is also a group of named "thorn trees" (*ya-geč*), subclasses of which may be distinguished by leaf form, thorn form, flower or fruit. They are a single named grouping but people note that the plant classes *ya-geč čihd, ya-geč čahd,* and *ya-gečbeh* are more similar to each other on the basis of flowers and fruits than *ya-geččehd.* The former three are podbearing with flowers. The last ("hackberry") is a thorny bush lining milpa boundaries and roads which produces edible berries in season.

Other named groupings below the life form

---

[4]Maize is really a grass, but is never named as such. It also receives special linguistic treatment.

level are based on fruit form. Plants with berry-like fruits (*žob*) tomato-like fruits (*bityuš*) or milkweed pods (*binyah*) form named categories conceived at the next lower level in the taxonomy.

Below the life-form/fruit-form level fall the bulk of the terminal taxa-plant classes below which no further named subdivisions can be made. This level which seems to combine Bulmer's (1970) concept of the specieme and Berlin's (1972) concept of the generic includes plant classes, which are

1. the minimal, naturally occurring units defined on the basis of multiple characters and formed by observation of 'objective regularities' and discontinuities in nature. (Bulmer 1970: 1072)
2. more or less consciously thought of as the smallest groupings requiring distinctive names. (Berlin 1972:55; cf. Bartlett 1940)

With the exceptions cited above, most of the plant conceptual categories at this specieme or generic level are not directly preceded by any *systematic* mid-level category within the taxonomic nomenclature, though there may be functional category groupings at upper levels. Almost all are named (they are thought to require names, even if the lexicon does not provide them with any) though names do not always provide a good guide to absolute or relative taxonomic status.

Below this basic level are subdivisions based on finer criteria of discrimination. These criteria range from overall differences between conceptual plant categories otherwise judged to be (and named as) similar; to leaf size, flower color or odor differences; variations in fruit season, color, or taste; to location and habitat. These finer levels in taxonomy Berlin et al. have called species and varieties, following the modern botanical usage. In the Mitla Zapotec botanical lexicon, there are no grasses discriminated to these levels, though there are numerous species of trees and herbs as well as varieties of the major economic plants, including maize. There seems to be a preference for binomial names at both the species and varietal level; this fact, combined with the information that many generic-specieme names are also binomial, means that binomial nomenclature is not a good index of taxonomic status. Many potential species and varieties which can be described are not labeled; others are labeled only in particular speech contexts. The linkages between naming and taxonomy are complicated, and one cannot infer from a name that a phylogenetic or morphological relationship between plants is perceived or from lack of a name that one is not. Similarly, one cannot assume that a difference not coded is a category not noted, since not all conceptual categories are labeled.

In some cases, names do provide an adequate guide to taxonomic status. Plants which share similar features of morphology are grouped together as one genus, and then sorted at the next lower level of the taxonomy by color, location, or some other salient feature. For example, *salb gohts* (called *salvia amarillo* in Spanish, and "yellow salvia" in English) and *salb nŏl* (*salvia blanco*, "white salvia") are two plants with similar leaf morphology and sweet smell distinguished by habits of growth and flowers in season. Flower color codes the distinct species. *Bälwih šnyâ* (*nanche colorado*, "red *nanche*") and *bälwih nŏl* (*nanche blanco*, "white *nanche*") code two fruit trees producing of comparable form and function (the boiled bark of each forms part of a remedy drunk for dysentery), one with red, one with white fruits. *Guladz morad* and *guladz nŏl* ("purple" and "white" pigweed respectively), *žiht morad* and *žiht nŏl* ("purple" and "white" onions), and *guh morad* and *guh nŏl* ("purple" and "white" *camote*) are further examples of colors describing leaf, corm, and tuber that distinguish related species in named genera.

The taxonomic nomenclature also provides in depth flexibility when real plants to be used for specific cultural ends fall somewhere in between the ideal conceptual categories. For example, *bitia? nŏl* ("white *epazote*") has green leaves and stems. *Bitia? morad* ("purple *epazote*") has purple stems and purple venation. However, many plants fall somewhere in between the absolute categories, which leads some women to call their specimens *bitia? mediomorad* or *bitia medionŏl* ("half purple" or "half white" *epazote*). In Spanish, one may similarly describe the specimens as *medioblanco* or *mediomorado*. These three contrast with other kinds of *epazote*, such as *bitia? zä?* ("green corn" *epazote*), which is a separate species used to flavor green corn gruel and never to flavor beans or other dishes, as are the other three. Though white *epazote* is always preferred for cooking, one can substitute half white or, as a last resort, purple to flavor a pot of beans. By contrast, one would never substitute *bitiaʔ zäʔ*, which is only used to flavor green corn gruel.

Smell/taste is another dimension for coding related species within single genera. Two cultivated *manzanillas*, *manzaniy neš* (*manzanilla dulce*, "sweet *manzanilla*") and *manzaniy La* (*manzanilla amarga*, "bitter *manzanilla*") are plant categories sharing similar morphological features, which are distinguished and named according to taste.

Distinctions of location also create and name related species within genera. *Yäb* (*girasol*, "sunflower") and *yäb gihš* (*acahual*) leaves are called "identical" and so share the same name. Ordinarily they are both labeled *yäb*, but to distinguish between them in a field, the latter adds the modifier "wild." Two kinds of pepper tree are recognized and distinguished by locational modifier: *ya luǰ* (*pirú*) which grows in the pueblo) and *ya luǰ dahn* (*pirú del monte*, "mountain" *pirú*) which looks identical to the local species. *Anis*, *bala šoh* (*yerba santa*), *pitiona*, *romero*, *lechuga*, *lya* (*guaje*), *rábano*, *šiǰ* (*chipíl*), and *žiht* are further examples of Mitla Zapotec and Spanish genera which have species distinguished and labeled by location (and, by extension, cultivated/uncultivated status).

Size of either leaf or fruit is another means for distinguishing and labeling related species. There is *škʷan ǰehb roʔ* (*yerba de espanto, espinosilla*, "big, fright [curing] herb") and *škʷan ǰehb las* (*yerba de espanto de noche, yerba de espanto delgado*, ("thin, fright [curing] herb"). There are "big" and "small" *miltomates*, *bityuš giž roʔ* and *bityuš giž las*, and "big" and "thin" black beans (Zap. *bisya roʔ* and *bisya las*, Sp. *frijol grueso* and *frijol delgado*), though these can be considered varieties within species rather than species within genera. In all of the above cases, salient differences between related concept categories are both noted and coded in the nomenclature.

By contrast, taxonomic linkages are not always related linguistically. Some genera, definitely recognized as speciemes, have no known names.

These include *Boerhaavia coccinea,* a well-known herb succinctly described according to habits of growth, flower form and color, and function as well as more recently introduced plants, like certain weed species which agriculturalists recognize as different from other weeds but for which they have no names.

In addition, there are plants for which taxonomic linkages are not clearly evident in the nomenclature. Among the fruit trees, two producing almost identical edible fruit are both labeled *bälwih* and distinguished by color (see above). However, *bälwih* also includes a third binomial category, *bälwih bäz*, which designates similar fruits and leaves but is more dissimilar to the former two than the former two are to each other. *Bälwih* thus divides into two speciemes, the first, or "type" *bälwih* being the class which includes trees with edible white or red fruits. The second is the class with inedible fruits. Unless one knows the flora in advance, one cannot learn this taxonomic distinction from the nomenclature. Alternatively, *bälwih* can be analyzed so as to illustrate one of Berlin's (1972) hypotheses about the growth of botanical nomenclature. In that paper, he proposed a progression from generic categories and names, to generic names with modifiers, the latter of which arise in order to differentiate related species within a genus. In that process, the type species for the generic category is at first unmarked relative to the other species which are marked. Later, as the nomenclature grows, this type species is also marked, according to the dimension of non-type species contrast.

In this case, *balwih šnyâ* can be viewed as the type species of the category *bälwih*. Another generic category labeled *bälwih bäz* was named alongside of it. Finally, in fruiting season, white fruiting *bälwih nǒl* were differentiated from the red fruiting trees, which came to be labeled *bälwih šnyâ*, which was at first unmarked, but later labeled red using the same dimension of non-type species contrast. In brief, the plant categories labeled *bälwih* can be manipulated to fit Berlin's scheme. However, for the Mitla Zapotec the most significant characteristic of the plants, known from the taxonomic nomenclature as well as from natural botanical relationships, are the two speciemes, and the different colored fruits of the type specieme in season. Taxonomic relationships and the names employed are always relative to the other floral materials being contrasted in a particular context.

Analogously, there are three kinds of "milkweed" (*binya*), of which two are vines and one shrublike. The former two form a natural contrast set, *binya kače⁊* and *binya xžol* differentiating between the "horned," edible fruit of the former and the "smooth," inedible fruit of the latter. Together, they comprise one specieme that contrasts with the third concept category, *binya bä⁊kʷ* ("dog's milkweed"). This is a separate specieme producing inedible fruits. Again, the taxonomic relationships and levels of contrast among the three would not be distinguishable simply from the nomenclature, since the names indicate that they are all equivalently related. A third example of this phenomenon is the category *bitia⁊* (*epazote*), cited above, within which there are two speciemes.

The opposite situation, where relationships are noted in the taxonomy but divorced from the nomenclature, also arises. The best example is the category *bityuš* ("tomatoes"), a generic or suprageneric label for a number of botanical genera within the family Solanaceae, all of which are grouped together in the folk taxonomy because they bear tomato-like fruit. However, one concept category definitely classified with other *bityuš* in the taxonomy, but not labeled *bityuš* in the nomenclature is *lobidzun* (*ojo de venado*, "deer's eye"). Anyone describing the plant begins by noting its tomato-like fruit and the close similarity between leaves and fruits of this plant and *bityus bä⁊kʷ*, its closest relative. Correspondingly, *bityuš bä⁊kʷ* is described as more like *lobidzun* than like any other *bityuš*. Yet, *lobidzun*, conceptually a tomato, is not labeled as such (Fig. 7).

From these examples, two general points can be made. First, not all taxonomic relationships noted in description are coded in the nomenclature. Second, some of the problems of discovering taxonomic relationships from the nomenclature are probably related to the ongoing changes in the flora, taxonomy, and nomenclature with which the Mitla Zapotec deals. New genera and species are constantly recognized and named as new plants or uses for plants arise to be classified. Plant concept categories' ranks and names in the taxonomy are not absolute but are always relative to the amount of botanical information a Mitla Zapotec has. The numbers of species he can differentiate and name within a given genus will vary according to his knowledge of the local flora and current state of the taxonomic nomenclature.

Alternatively, the relationship between plants, taxonomy, and names can be examined in cultural communication contexts. Naming a plant to the generic rather than specific level may be a contextual decision rather than an indicator of the limited amount of information a speaker has about a specimen. The speaker will usually not provide more taxonomic information than he judges necessary for a given communication. Much as he

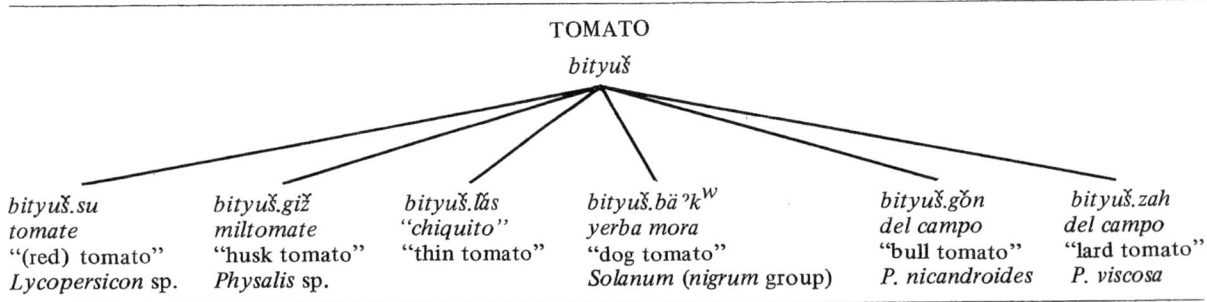

Fig. 7. Kinds of tomatoes. All *bityuš* are in the family Solanaceae and produce tomato-like fruits. Yet, *lo.bidzun* (*Saracha procumbens*) is not *named* as a "kind of tomato" though it is always said to be "like *bityuš.bä⁊kʷ*."

will use the life form label k^wan to describe the general herbage of a field rather than the individual genera or species, he will use the generic *manzaníy* to denote that he is feeding *manzaníy* rather than *yäb* to his poultry. He could further differentiate between *manzaníy gihš*, the "wild" *manzaníy* of the field from the cultivated *manzaníy* of his garden but for his message, the generic *manzaníy* supplies sufficient information. The context—herbs which are "food for animals"—distinguishes which class of *manzaníy* he means. By contrast, were he to tell what garden remedy he was drinking for stomachache, he would have to distinguish between *manzaníy neš* ("sweet" *manzaníy*) and *manzaníy La* ("bitter" *manzaníy*) since no label at a higher level in the taxonomy would clearly indicate which species he had selected. Similarly, *yäb* denotes not only three classes of common field weeds but also the cultivated sunflower. For most purposes, such as feeding herbs to animals, *yäb* clearly denotes which class of herbs is being discussed. Only in the rare instances where sunflowers are also part of the conversation is it necessary to distinguish "wild" *yäb gihš* from other kinds of *yäb*. Below the generic form *yäb*, three uncultivated specifics may also be distinguished: *yäb gid-gai* ("cock's" *yäb*), *yäb dahn* ("mountain" *yäb*), and *yäb gihš* ("wild" *yäb*). These forms are commonly distinguished only when plants are mature with flowers, on which the distinctions are based.

The class of herbs used in curing the folk illness, *ǰehb* (*espanto*, "fright" resulting in soul loss) provides a further illustration of how generic and specific names are used selectively. The generic label *šk^{w}an ǰehb* (*yerba de espanto*) potentially includes four different species of *espanto* herb, though not everyone recognizes the same plants by the same names. The most frequently used species grows on the higher hills around Mitla but not in the lower elevation zones. If someone is using *šk^{w}an ǰehb*, it is usually this herb (*Loeselia mexicana*), which is also named *espinosilla* in Spanish. Ordinarily, this generic label is sufficient. However, if someone wants to emphasize it is the "real" *espanto* herb (*la mera espinosilla*) which contrasts with *šk^{w}an ǰehb las* ("thin [leaf] *espanto* herb"), *šk^{w}an ǰehb yäl* ("night *espanto* herb") or *šk^{w}an ǰehb cruz* ("cross *espanto* herb"), one will label the first *šk^{w}an ǰehb ro?* ("big *espanto* herb"), a name which notes its large(r) leaves, and identifies it as the "type" *espanto* herb, rather than any of the other species. The species distinctions are necessary when one is collecting herbs for different "species" of *espanto* (curing ceremonies). In this example, as in the former two, the taxonomic nomenclature presents generic labels to which modifiers can be selectively added when species distinctions are necessary.

Classification of Principal Cultigens

All the foregoing examples show the adaptability and flexibility of the taxonomic nomenclature in grouping similarities and differences in the botanical domain. Names are provided at higher and lower levels of the taxonomy to clearly identify specimens for cultural use, and speakers can manipulate the taxonomic system to provide just enough information in a plant name to put it in its proper place. Most of the examples of splitting similar categories have involved useful plants. This suggests that the rules for forming and naming taxonomic categories to greater depth are applied as the cultural importance of particular plant categories demands finer discriminations for use. So far, we have dealt principally with wild plants. We turn now to the principal cultigens— maize, beans, and squash—the primary products of Mitla's field system, to show how they illustrate the same principles of taxonomic and nomenclatural thought as other plants. Because of the diversity of recognized varieites of each, they also provide a body of data for analyzing the potential complexities of the taxonomic hierarchy.

MAIZE

Maize is of extraordinary cultural value for the Mitleño. In addition to providing the staple food of the diet, maize cultivation is a major cultural activity (see Chapter 6). All parts of the maize plant serve, either directly or indirectly, as a food energy source.

Maize has been cultivated for at least 7000 years in the Mitla environment. In local folklore, the antiquity of maize cultivation, as well as the contemporary cultural focus on maize cultivation are noteworthy. Both indigenous culture heroes and Catholic saints participate in the discovery and cultivation of maize. Maize is the only plant to receive such extensive treatment in the current Mitla folklore. In addition, maize functions in certain curing rituals and divination. Purple maize seeds are part of the *susto* curing ceremony—they are mixed with water and sometimes cacao to form a beverage drunk by the victim of "magical fright." People also use the grains to (try to) remove warts. Maize grains are also cast in certain divination practices.

Classifications of maize take into account, at an upper level, seed origins and life cycles, and, at a lower level, grain color. Conceptually, maize is divided into two general categories: *maíz criollo* and *maíz híbrido*. The former has large, thick kernels; the latter, thin kernels. Maíz criollo is considered superior for all purposes. It is the indigenous maize of Mitla and the Valley of Oaxaca. Thin maize is sold by the government and by *comerciantes*. It is said to come from the Isthmus or from somewhere else outside of the valley. Given the choice of maíz criollo, people will not eat any other class of maize. They will buy thin maize for their animals, since it is usually substantially cheaper (10 to 20 centavos less per kilogram) than maíz criollo. Only maíz criollo is planted in the milpas of Mitla, an aspect of maize in Zapotec culture discussed in more detail in Chapter 6.

The maize plant is distinctive in its parts, the relations between its parts, and in its growth habits. Though the very young plant looks like the seedling of one of many grasses, it develops into a plant with a unique kind of leaf, cane, spikelet, and seedcase. Zapotec labels for the different parts indicate some of the similarities of maize with other plants. The roots (*lodäh*) are labeled the same; the cane (*niht*) is labeled the same as the sugar cane. (Some people say that this is because the tender sweet maize cane can be sucked like sugar cane, but sugar cane is not indigenous.) Maize leaves are labeled *lahg* rather than *balak*, the label used in talking about leaves of *yahg* and *kʷan*, which have a different structural appearance. The spikelet is labeled *doh*, the green corn *zä?*, and the ripe ear *niz*. The unique set of terms applied to maize not only identifies the outstanding morphological features of the maize plant but also the stages in the maize life cycle. An additional distinction of the maize plant vocabulary is the naming of the grain, *žob*, apart from the ear, *niz*, and apart from the plant name, *yähl*. *Yähl* denotes both the individual maize plant and the collection of maize plants in one field. The Spanish term *milpa* is used equivalently to discuss the whole field or the individual plant in the field. Other Spanish terms have domains of meaning congruent with the Zapotec terms: *žob* (*maíz*), *niz* (*mazorca*), *zä?* (*elote*), and *doh* (*espiga*).

Though maize seeds and plants are distinguished as local versus nonlocal types, and three- versus four-month varieties, a principal classificatory dimension is seed color (Figs. 8, 9). Ears are labeled by their predominant color—white, yellow,

ENGLISH	SPANISH	ZAPOTEC
White	blanco	žob nŏl
Yellow	amarillo	žob ižats
Red	colorado	žob bäldohb
Blue, purple, black	morado / negrito	žob nàgâ

Fig. 8. Maize colors.

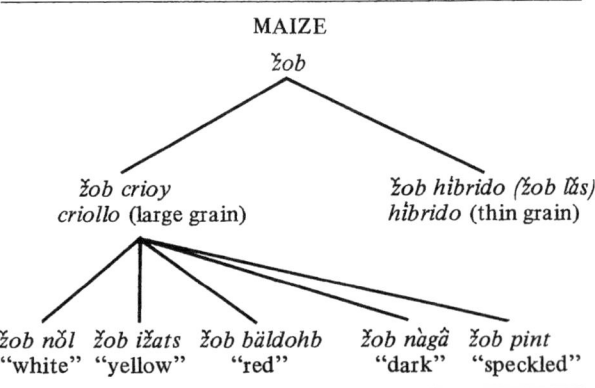

Fig. 9. Maize classifications.

SYSTEMATICS

red, or dark (blue, purple, or black).[5] If colors are mixed, the ear is called *pinto*. Fields are usually sown in one color seed, predominantly white, though yellow or a combination of colors (*pinto*) may also be sown (see Chapter 6).

The color terminology used to discuss varieties of maize is descriptively rich. Today the Zapotec color lexicon is heavily mixed with Spanish loan words, such as *verd* (*verde*, "green"), *sul* (*azul*, "blue"), *morad* (*morado*, "purple"). Yet, the descriptions of maize color preserve some of the variety of the Zapotec color lexicon (see Fig. 8).

Color terminology is of particular interest since some of the lexicon are "secondary" rather than "core" color terms (Berlin and Kay 1969). In Zapotec, there are several terms for white, yet exclusively *nŏl* is used when talking about maize.[6] *Ižats*, not *gohts*, is used to describe "yellow," since the former is brighter and more accurately describes the color. "Red" is coded by *bäldohb* which means "maguey worm." The insect, a dull red color, lives in the roots of maguey and is highly prized as a food item. Its color rather than the basic red color term, *šnyâ*, is used to describe maize kernels. Finally, *nàgǎ* which codes "dark" as opposed to "green" is the usual descriptive modifier for dark kernels. Sometimes people say *žob morad* ("purple") or less frequently *žob yâs* ("black"), but *nàgǎ* was the correct usage for most persons.

It is interesting to contrast these terms with the Spanish modifiers for the same maize varieties. There is nothing noteworthy about the selection of *blanco* to talk about white maize or *amarillo* to talk about yellow, but as is typical throughout Mexico, *colorado* is used rather than *rojo*. Dark maize may be described as *negrito*, a diminutive form of "black" or as *morado* or *moradito*, "purple." American Indians of the Southwest talk about "blue" Indian corn, but this is not the traditional usage in Mexico.

The color lexicon selected to describe maize can be usefully discussed in the total cultural context. First, the choices made in Zapotec to code maize colors more closely correspond to the actual perceptions of those colors than the core color lexicon for yellow and red. Maize has been the focus of careful cultural scrutiny, and labels have been thoughtfully applied in traditional usage. Second, the lumping of black and purple into the category *nàgǎ* shows that for cultural purposes, there is no difference between these colors. Though differences in these dark colors may be *perceived*, and talked about in Spanish and Spanish-modified Zapotec, there is no *conceptual* difference between them for purposes of maize classification and use. The category labels are clear, even if there appears to be some color variation within the categories. Culturally significant differences are coded; nonsignificant differences are ignored linguistically.

Overall, the four color maize classifications may be viewed as a cosmological as well as a biological scheme (cf. Messer 1976). The Zapotec cosmology ancient and present, includes a cornered universe with each of the four cardinal directions being marked by color, among other items. Maize, the most sacred and important of all plants, with its four colors, provides an ever present set of materials for constantly reiterating this world order. These colors exemplify how Zapotecs divide up the natural world, both in speech and in matters of practical agricultural behavior. The color labels reduce some of the variations noted in nature to four terms rich in meaning for the greater cosmological scheme.

In summary, the classification of maize takes into consideration the overall shape and place of origin of the grain at an upper level in the taxonomy. Below this, grain is classified by color and, for field contexts, by growing time. The color lexicon uses some color terms with limited semantic fields. Thus, the color lexicon applied to maize gives the maize taxonomy a particular richness. In addition, terms for the parts of the maize plant are almost exclusively limited to maize, as are the recognized stages of growth.

---

[5] The current valuations of the different varieties of maize correspond quite closely to those mentioned in Parsons (1936:52). Blue-black maize, though it matured early, did not keep. Yellow sold for more than black, but less than white, which then, as now, was the preferred color.

[6] There are two basic morphemes which denote "white": *nŏl* and *nakits*. The former is used exclusively when talking about the white color of maize, or thunderhead clouds. Either term may be used when referring to clothing, depending on the brightness of the white color.

Maize is set apart from other plants both in cultural practice and in language.[7]

BEANS

Beans, all *Phaseolus vulgaris,* are classified primarily by color, (e.g., white, black, speckled), but also at times by size (big or thin) and by named variety (*pelón,* a taxon which produces thin black beans on a low bush) (see Fig. 10). Beans which are sown in the milpa, "big" black beans, are also glossed "milpa beans." Snap beans, the green, unripe specimens of any of the dry beans, are glossed "green beans" (*bisya ya?*) in Zapotec, in contrast to dry beans. Beans are always named by a binomial, one term of which is the generic term for "bean," *bisya,* the second of which is the modifier which distinguishes the bean species or variety from all others within the contrast set at the lowest possible level in the taxonomy. Thus "black beans," *bisya yâs,* are never referred to at the generic level in the taxonomy but are always *bisya ro?* ("big beans") or *bisya lǎs* ("thin beans"). Beans are named to one of these basic types, after which the town of origin may be added for more detailed information. The additional information is not taxonomic but practical—batches of beans originating in particular towns are preferred since they "taste better" and "cook faster." Thus, beans are taxonomically classed to species (by color) and to variety (by size, if the beans are black). All in all, any other information is descriptive modification. Only cultivated beans are classified as *bisya.* The two wild beans in the area, *Phaseolus atropurpureus* and *P. heterophyllus* are described as "like beans" but they are not labeled "wild beans" (*bisya gihš*) nor are they used "like beans." The former is an unlabeled category and not used, the latter, labeled *gužehl,* has an edible tuber labeled in the name-form.

SQUASH

Squashes, cucurbits, are similarly named as binomials. The different conceptual categories can be distinguished by habits of growth, fruits, and seeds (see Fig. 11). The fruits are eaten both in their immature and mature forms, and the leaves, tips, buds, and flowers of *giht gec* supply additional elements in the native diet. In addition, all produce seeds which are edible after they are washed and toasted. *Apodanthera aspera,* an uncultivated cucurbit, is labeled *giht lahn* in Zapotec and *calabaza amarga* in Spanish. On the basis of its morphological form and edible seeds, it is a "squash" with the added characteristic that the fruit is "stinking" (Zapotec) or "bitter" (Spanish). *Chayote* (*Sechium edule*) is also classified in the nomenclature as a kind of "squash," *gihttia?p,* within which two types, one with "prickly" (*gec*) one with "smooth" (*xžol*) surface are distinguished.

Stages of growth are also important for describing and classifying the edible plant parts, the leaves and the squashes. "Green squashes" (*giht řen*) are an early delicacy of the agricultural year. They are often eaten along with the tender leaves of the squash plant. The older leaves are discarded when preparing the leaves as a pot herb. Hence, the classification and maturity of the

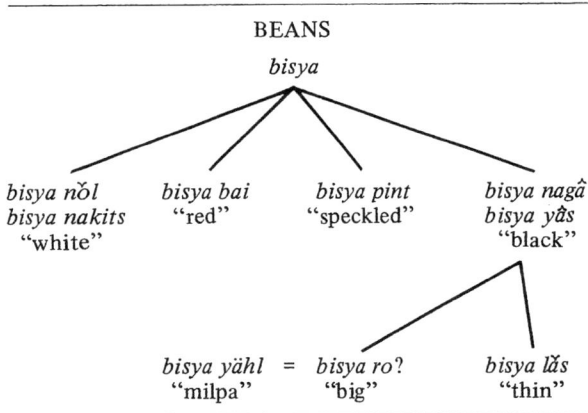

Fig. 10. Classification of beans.

[7]Wheat and sorghum are not principal cultigens in the contemporary Zapotec fields. Sorghum (Sp. *sorgo*) is usually glossed *žob yâs,* "black maize," and fed to animals. It was never mentioned as food for humans. Wheat, *trigo* (Spanish) was eaten by humans. The sorghum example suggests that the category *žob,* maize, may be elevated to a superordinate category of "maize-like grains," which include *žob, maíz,* the principal generic category, and other maize-like grains. Wheat is sufficiently different in plant and grain appearance, and also, of great enough economic importance, to have entered the taxonomic system with its Spanish name. There was also some tendency to call sorghum *maíz sorgo* in Spanish, thus showing the same taxonomic and nomenclatural principles in both Spanish and Zapotec.

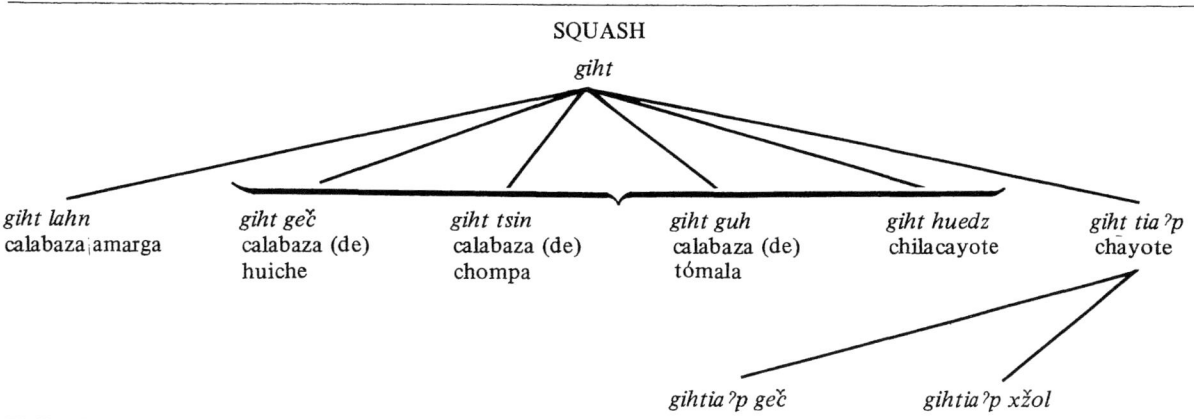

Fig. 11. Classification of squash.

squash fruits and leaves are very important information when using the individual plant parts for food.

OTHER FIELD PLANTS

Castor beans (*Ricinus communis*), though not a staple or even a major commercial crop, are also functionally and taxonomically interesting. They are grown occasionally in milpas, but more often in home gardens. There are two recognized classes: *šnyâ*, (*colorado*, "red") and *nŏl* (*blanco*, "white"). Bark and seedcase color determine the classification. In addition, there may be reference to the color of the leaves. This can be confusing, since one plant may have both red and green leaves. In the tender stage, the leaves of the red castor bean plant may be red but may dry later to green. The plant can also be described according to growth stage—either *ya?* ("green," "fresh") or *bidz* ("dry," "old"). (These terminologies add further confusion to the English speaker in that the "red" plant may be at a "green" stage of growth.)

Since medicinally, particular kinds of castor bean leaves are classed for particular "hot" or "cold" remedies, it is important to know how to distinguish among them. The castor bean leaf, *balak baláp*, may be described as *nŏl* or *šnyâ*, the reference coming from the *tree* to which it is attached, rather than the color of the leaf out of context. Each leaf may be further described as *ya?* or *bidz* depending on whether it is fresh and moist, or old and dry. Within the category of "fresh" (*ya?*) leaves, there is a further distinction of "tender" leaves (*řen*) versus "ripe" leaves (*gùyahĺ*). These distinctions about the state of living leaves can be categorically made for all plants. Within the category of *balak řeni* ("leaves which are tender"), there may again be a return to distinctions of color, as tender leaves may be *nŏl* ("white") or *šnyâ* ("red"). In the tender stage, when leaves are used medicinally, the colors are distinctive of the species varieties (Figs. 12, 13).

Other Features of Names

Almost all plants are named so that they may be easily identified, but bilingualism complicates what would otherwise be a simple one-to-one plant naming procedure. Mitleños know plants by a combination of both Spanish and Zapotec names. Since new plants names are continually being introduced, the nomenclature is in the process of

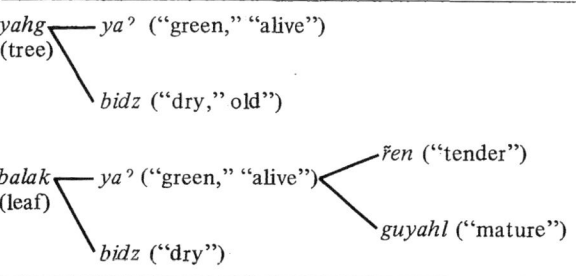

Fig. 12. Leaf growth stage classification.

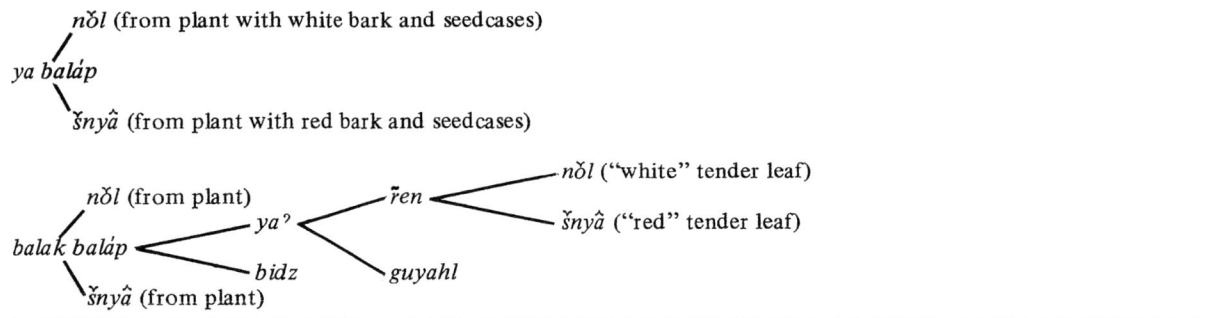

Fig. 13. Classifications of castor beans, *baláp*. One uses the tender castor bean leaf for headache and stomachache applications. There are two classes of castor bean plant; one with green stems and seedcases, one with red. Though the red castor bean plant many have mature green leaves, in the tender stage in which the leaves are used, the colors are distinctive of the species varieties.

constant change.[8] With the introduction of European plants, a whole set of flora and names had to be absorbed into the taxonomic and nomenclatural systems. This required that the names of some of the local plants be shifted in order to group similar indigenous and introduced taxa together. In some cases, Zapotec names were extended to describe Spanish taxa. In others, Spanish names were added to the Zapotec vocabulary (Fig. 14). Most, but not all, introduced plants have names which are Zapotec renderings of Spanish lexemes. *Manzanilla, yerba dulce, ruda, romero, naranja, pino, eucalipto, col, zanahoria, mostaza, oregano, pimiento, clavo,* and *comino* are just a few of the commonly used plants which retain Spanish names in Zapotec usage. At the present time, the terminological system is a mixture of Spanish names used by Spanish and bilingual speakers, Spanish names used in conjunction with Spanish modifiers, and Zapotec names. To further confuse the linguist, many of the Spanish names are borrowed from other Indian languages, principally Nahuatl. For example, common Spanish plant names like *sempolsuchet, mesquite,* and *chepiche* (*chapiche*) all derive from Nahuatl (cf. Reko 1919; Martínez 1959 for further examples). At present, it is probably impossible to sort out which names are post-Conquest and which are late pre-Conquest, when Nahuatl speakers intruded into the Valley of Oaxaca.

Names change—they may go out of use or be replaced by other names. Some of the variation is individual idiolect; other is more widespread. An example of the former are three names applied to the fruit of *Arctostaphylos polifolia*. The fruit was usually called *žob-nihd*, but I also heard it called *žob-niz* and *žob-nigʷ*. The first name was distinguished as the "correct" name by women who had heard it called all three. The second name was attributed to not learning the *name* of the plant correctly; the third to not learning the identity category of the plant. *Žob nigʷ* correctly referred to the botanical category *Cordia curassavica*, which also produces small fruits in the same season as *žob-nihd*. These are examples of two kinds of individual variations which are labeled as "mistakes" by reference informants.

More widespread variation and potential changes in nomenclature are brought about by the bilingual situation and by the numbers of sources of information presenting variant names for the same plants. For example, the botanical species *Selaginella pallescens* may be called either *siempre viva* or *doradía* (both names are used in Zapotec discussions, also). *Calea hypoleuca* may be called *škʷam bižeh, škʷan gihb,* or *cacahuatón* in a Zapotec conversation. In this manner, the use of common names for some plants varies and

---

[8] For example, one woman, noting a weed with milky sap, (*Euphorbia heterophylla* L.) identified and described the taxon as a relatively new introduction to the field system, though she could not *name* it.

SYSTEMATICS

ZAPOTEC	SPANISH	COMMENTS
gi.togol	*togoles*	Spanish has borrowed the Zapotec plant names
škʷam bäldohb	*beldobes*	of these indigenous species.
gi.lahk	*gilakes*	
manzaniy neš	*manzanilla dulce*	Zapotec incorporates the Spanish names, but
lečug gihš	*lechuga del campo*	uses Zapotec modifiers for these introduced
yak pin	*pinocote*	species.
mostas	*mostaza*	Zapotec has adopted the Spanish names of
maNzaN	*manzana*	these introduced species.
fresn	*fresno*	
žob.štil	*granada*	Zapotecs have invented terms for these
bäč.štil	*yerba buena*	introduced species.
baláp	*higuerilla (grilla)*	

Fig. 14. Borrowing between Spanish and Zapotec in botanical nomenclature.

probably changes statistically with frequency of use over time. Names also change as the plants go out of use. Thus, the *guaje*-producing tree, *Cassia polyantha* is currently glossed *Lya giš* or *Lya čiv* ("wild" or "goat" *guaje*), the second obviously a post-Hispanic label. Within the current nomenclature, *Lya giš* can also label *Lysiloma divaricata*, a "wild," edible *guaje*, in contrast to *Cassia polyantha*, a "wild" *guaje*, currently classified as nonedible.

Names for single concept categories also vary in some instances according to the plant part being sought. For example, *guzehd*, the root of *Mentzelia hispida* is required for a medicinal beverage, never *kʷan r̃gihd* ("sticky herb") which is the name for the entire concept category with "sticky" leaves. Similarly, when one seeks the tender inflorescence of the maguey in order to make *tortillas de maguey*, one looks for *ya gohdz*, the stalk of maguey, rather than *dohb*, the maguey plant. These examples of synonymy (using more than one label for a single taxon) add clarification rather than confusion to the native system. Use context and plant concept category are both sorted out in a single label. Where it is not clear from a label which part of a plant is being sought, people often name plants by the plant part, e.g., *balak banú* (*pájaro bobo* leaf) rather than *ya banú* (*pájaro bobo* tree) when the leaf is sought for a toothache remedy.

Name etymologies may also add to the understanding of the significance of certain plants. Though most Zapotec names were described as "names, no more," if names have meanings outside of the plant lexicon, they may point to some perceptible features (as in the descriptive names cited above) or some functional value of the plants.

Some plant names denote the most economically useful organ of the plant at the generic level. This is true for both wild and cultivated taxa. *Yak manzan giš* and *yahg žob nihd* are names which refer to the edible fruits, like the cultivated trees, *yahg naraž* ("orange tree") or *yak Limón* ("lime tree"). *Guni* and *gužehl* are uncultivated hillside species with edible tubers, while *gu nŏl* ("white") and *gu morad* ("purple") refer to two species of *camote* ("sweet potato"). In each case the prefix *gu* ("tuber") points to the economically useful part of the plant. By contrast, the economically useful part of the plant may be named apart from label which describes the whole plant as a concept category. In the examples cited above, the edible inflorescence of the maguey is glossed *ya gohdz* (*quiote*), but the maguey plant is called *dohb*. *Guzehd* (*Mentzelia hispida*) is also named *kʷan r̃gid*. *Guzehd* refers to the *camote*, which is shaved and prepared as a medicinal beverage. The plant may be called by that name or *kʷan r̃gid* ("sticky leaves").

Below the generic level, the particular form of the fruit may be the distinguishing feature for both classification and nomenclature. *Guajes* are classified by the time of year at which they are available, either *Lya kureš* ("dry season *guajes*") or *Lya gusgih* ("wet season *guajes*"). Among the succulents, the fruits of *yahg bidz* distinguish one species from another. For *nopales,* however, the succulent stems, not the fruits are the features of contrast. In this case, all fruits are glossed *biruʔn* (Fig. 15).

Flowers, particularly if they have an important cultural role, can also be the salient part for the plant name. *Gi saʔ* (*flor de fandango,* "wedding flower") refers to the entire plant, in or out of the flowering stage. As the name suggests, it is ritually important at weddings. *Gi togol* (*flor de los difuntos,* "flower of the [Day of the] Dead") is the generic name for *Tagetes* spp., which bloom in late October through early November and are used to decorate house altars during the All Souls' Day holiday season (ca. November 1). Many Spanish speakers call the flowers *togoles,* an example of Spanish borrowing a Zapotec name. In each of these cases, the flower name denotes the entire plant, though the leaves of both plants are used medicinally (*gisaʔ* as a tea for hangover; *gitogol* as an external remedy for hives).

Since it is not always clear from a label which *part* of a plant is being solicited for a particular purpose, people often name plants by parts in addition to labels. For remedies involving plant leaves, *balak,* (*hoja,* "leaf") precedes the plant label. Thus, one seeks *balak banú* (*pájaro bobo* leaf) not *yan banú* (*pájaro bobo* tree) as a remedy for headache. Similarly, one uses *guzehd,* not $k^w an\ \tilde{\imath} gid$ as a remedy for pimples. For hangover, one drinks tea of *balak gi saʔ*. For accurate communication, it may be necessary to specify whether it is the plant root, leaf, juice, inner bark, gum, or tender tips which are used in a remedy. This is information supplementary to the name itself.

Plant names, however, may reveal additional cultural significance attached to the plants. Already mentioned was the socio-religious role of *gi saʔ* the "wedding flower." *Šk^{w}an gusahn, k^{w}an zahn* ("family herb") is taken as an infusion to promote fertility or clean out the afterbirth. The Spanish have again borrowed this Zapotec name. *Šk^{w}an tst* ("throat herb") is prepared as a remedy for infants' sore throat. *Šk^{w}an ǰehb* (*yerba de*

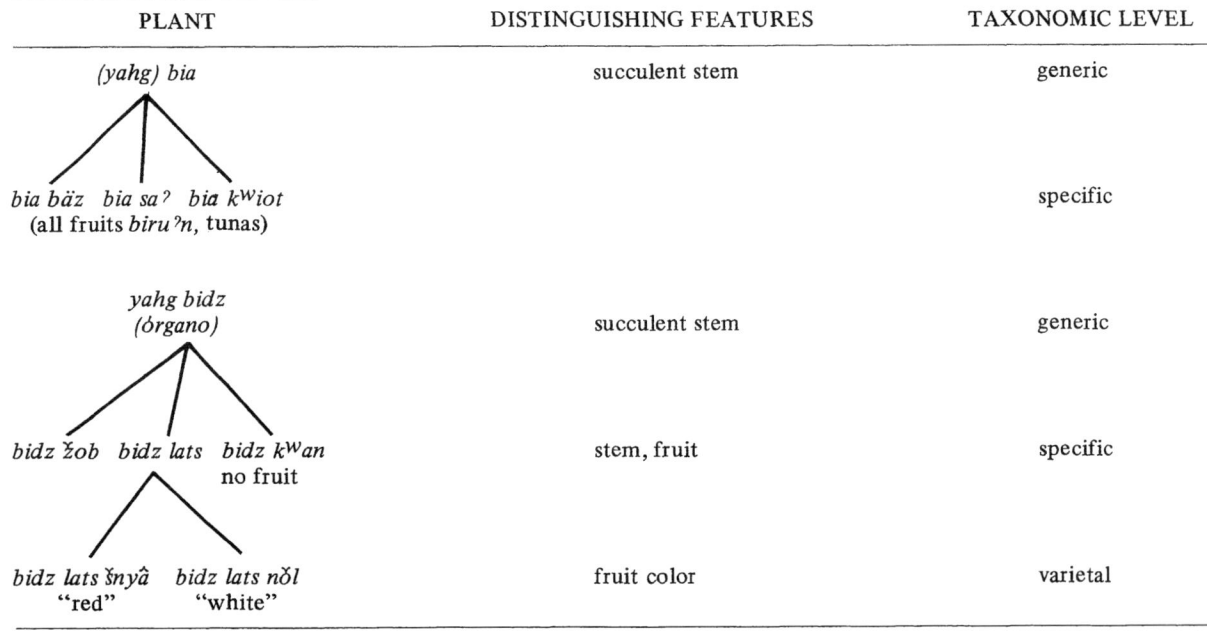

Fig. 15. Morphological criteria for distinguishing plant concept categories.

espanto, espanto herb) is drunk in the curing ceremony for *espanto* ("magical fright"). It is also called *espinosilla* in Spanish, a reference to its spiny appearance.

Certain herb names carry additional metaphorical connotations of their particular cultural contexts. For example, *gi togol* is both a seasonal and religious marker. *Togol* is both "a dead person" and "the Day of the Dead." The flower is a constant reminder of the season, which is agriculturally the harvest season and religiously Todos Santos (*togol*). *Balak binij̃ bido* (*toloache*, "elf leaf") is a leaf used to wrap sprains. In gathering the leaves, one tosses thirteen stones to the plant and calls forth its spirit: one "buys" the herb from the earth, and asks that the remedy be effective. Though one person said that any herb must be purchased with this ritual, all others specified that the small ritual of purchase is used only when dealing with the "elf" plant. These examples all show that nonperceptual cultural criteria, as well as perceptual, are used in naming plants. The names often point to the functional or metaphorical significance of the taxa.

In discussing the symbolic value of names, it is by no means clear that names do any more than point to the cultural purpose toward which the plants are put. The intrinsic healing virtue of an herb is known by tradition, and not in any way associated with a magical quality transmitted to the herb by its name. On the other hand, it is probably not accidental that the plant named "elf leaf" which is the one plant which one "buys" from the earth is *Datura meteloides*, a pharmacologically active, very potent hallucinogen, which, though not used to alter the mind in Mitla medicinal practice, is known by them to be toxic and to have such properties.

In summary, the names of herbs and trees have symbolic value for describing the environment, the seasons, the holidays, and certain medicinal practices. The symbolic value of maize names for establishing the order of the cosmology has also been noted. Clearly, plants, with their names, are important for the ongoing persistence of the cultural scheme of things. In practical matters, names enable people to choose useful plants for the right contexts with very few mistakes and in particular cases, provide added cosmological meanings either in general or in particular matters of health. Having treated briefly the systematic taxonomy and nomenclature, we turn now to some of the alternative classificatory schemes which are used in Mitla to divide up and utilize the plant world.

OTHER CLASSIFICATORY SCHEMES

While knowing the identities and names of plant concept categories is an important first step to using the local flora, functional, plant part, and life stage classifications are also necessary for the native grouping plants for cultural activities. If you gave a Mitla Zapotec a collection of plants (e.g. five edible herbs from the milpa) and asked him to explain how these plants are similar, he could organize them in many ways. He might say they were all $k^w an$, i.e., members of the same taxonomic category. Alternatively, he could say they were the same because they all grow in the same location—the milpa. They might all be the same because they were at the same life stage (e.g., "young and tender") or in the same functional category (e.g., "edible herbs"). We will look now at some of these classifications.

Stages of Growth

Plants can be named to growth stage in addition to taxonomic conceptual category. Growth stage information is important for the description of life cycles of particular taxa and often for assigning taxa to functional categories.

Herbs and trees are named to the "baby" or "tender" stage (Zap. *bäz, r̃eni;* Sp. *chiquito, tiernito*). This initial period of growth is followed by a "riper" or "more mature" stage (Zap. *aguyahlni;* Sp. *macizo maduro*). The last stage is "fully mature" or "dry" (Zap. *nabidzni;* Sp. *seco*). The same terminology is applied to all cultivated and noncultivated herbs. For edible herbs, the stage name modification is of functional significance. For example, one eats *guladz* when it is "tender" (*r̃eni*) but not when it is "riper" (*aguyahlni*). Figure 16 shows the stages at which

HERB	GROWTH STAGE WHEN EDIBLE FOR HUMANS	GROWTH STAGE WHEN EDIBLE FOR ANIMALS
Amaranthus hybridus	tender	large, mature
Anoda cristata	tender	large, with seeds
Crotalaria pumila	tender/mature	-------
Galinsoga parviflora	tender/mature	large, with seeds
Portulaca oleracea	tender/with flowers	large

Fig. 16. Use classifications of wild herbs by growth stage.

the different edible herbs are preferably consumed. Alternatively, the life form may be used to indicate stage of growth.

In addition, leaves are classified as "fresh" (*ya?*), "mature" (*aguyahlni*), "dark" (*nagã*), or "dry" (*nabidzni*). This set of terms, which codes for the stage of maturity of the leaf, also provides significant information about the leaf for use in functional contexts.

Choosing a term from the systematic taxonomy may not supply complete information about the specimen without the addition of life stage or leaf stage modifiers. This is particularly true for certain "edible" herbs (eaten only during the "tender" stage of growth), "edible" fruits (eaten only when fully mature—e.g., *bityuš bä?kʷ*), and "medicinal" plants (prepared only in the "green" stage—e.g., *ya biki ya?*).

Thus, it is clear that plant names alone often do not sufficiently identify specimens for use. The growth stage vocabulary is necessary to use the taxonomy precisely. As shown by the example of castor bean plants, growth stage may affect systematic taxonomic judgments and the precise use of medicinal plants. For edible plants as well, growth stage vocabulary more exactly communicates whether or not the named specimen is a tender candidate for the cooking pot.

Functional Classifications

In addition to grouping plants by systematic taxonomy and growth stage classifications, Mitla Zapotecs also group plants into use categories. When communicating about plants, one works back and forth between the alternative schemes of classification, providing the right amount of information so that a plant can be identified and used. The domain of economic botany, as other anthropologists have shown, can be split up in many different ways (e.g., Fowler and Leland 1967; Perchonock and Werner 1969). In Mitla Zapotec, the basic use classifications, in some cases polysemous with the basic life form terms, are filled by plant conceptual categories defined at lower levels within the systematic taxonomy and additional growth stage information. The use classifications, in turn with their defining attributes, affect the systematic taxonomy at all levels.

At the life form level, the morphological-growth stage-use classification of a plant affects its inclusion in one or another of the three main classes. Life form terms cannot or should not be considered without taking into account the functional implications of the terms *yahg*, *kʷan*, and *giš*. Below the life form level, named trees are ranked according to their different fire producing and construction qualities; edible fruit producing trees form another functional category. Edible versus inedible fodder (thorn) grasses are differentiated from other grasses, as are the class of grasses (unidentified) which produce edible root nodules in the fall. More highly differentiated are the herbs, which can be broadly separated into four functional categories: "herbs which people eat," "medicinal herbs," "herbs which animals eat" and herbs of "no use." Individual plant conceptual categories may fill more than one of these categories at different points in its life. For example, *Amaranthus* sp., cited above, is edible for humans when young and tender; edible for animals when older.

In discussing the relationship between the functional and the systematic taxonomies, two principal features stand out. First, the plant attributes on which the functional category is based are often different than those which define the systematic category. Nevertheless, since these functional features are part of the plant conceptual category, they *may* be used to define the systematic category as well. In this manner, functional attributes affect systematic taxonomy.

Second, the functional classification is hierarchically structured, much like the systematic taxonomy. Thus, included in the "life form" herb are three functional types which can be further subdivided along a number of dimensions. "Medicinal herbs" show particularly the hierarchical grouping of herbs along at least two dimensions: illness category and hot-cold quality (Fig. 17). Briefly, illness categories are classified according to location of pain (headache, stomachache, etc.), quality of pain (*aire* or *pasmo*), and/or supernatural dimension (e.g., Zap. *ǰehb*, Sp. *espanto*, "magical fright;" Zap. *biže?*, Sp. *ojo*, "evil eye"). Particular plants are known by tradition to be good for treating these named symptoms and ailments. These categories are also crosscut by the hot-cold dimension, which refers to the intrinsic quality of "heating" or "cooling" which all living and some nonliving things possess (cf. Foster 1953). Illnesses make the human body, which is normally in a state of relative hot-cold balance, either predominantly hot or cold. One purpose of medicinal herbs is to correct that imbalance; one medicates a hot or cold illness by introducing herbs of the opposite quality (Fig. 17).

All medicinal herbs possess some relative hot-cold and particular illness curing qualities. Such qualities are known by tradition, by curing information coded in names, and by other perceptible attributes, particularly taste/smell. In general, "sweet" plants are classified as "hot." They are also thought to be "good for curing cold stomachache." By contrast, "bitter" plants are often classified as "cold" and are thought to be "good for curing (hot) aroused bile." Plants with the same chemical (smell/taste) properties tend to be grouped together in medicinal categories, a practice which on the one hand expands the pharmacopoeia systematically, but as discussed in the next section, can also lead to confusion.

Other attributes defining plant classes as appropriate for medicinal contexts are less easily described. Though Arabic and Renaissance physicians developed a hot-cold humoral medical classification system which described degrees of hot-cold quality to herbs and other elements of the pharmacopoeia, Zapotec folk practitioners and botanists do not share such precise standards and information. They use the hot-cold dimension to describe one other measure by which the plant

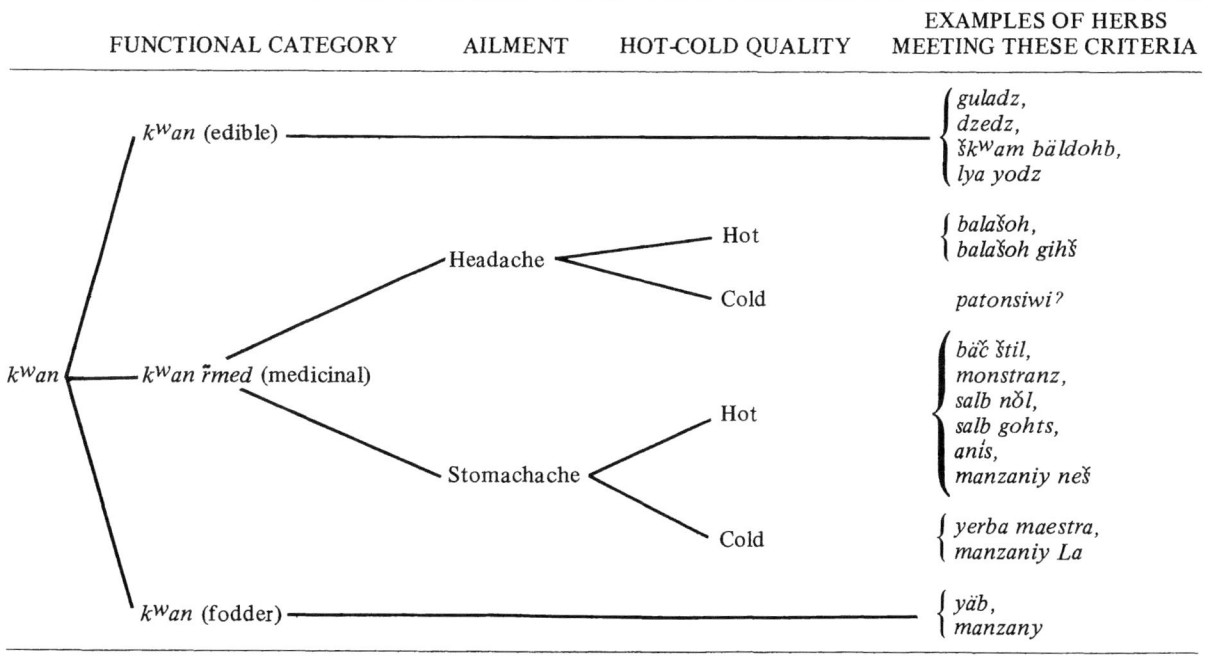

Fig. 17. Functional classifications of herbs.

world may be ordered and related to nonbotanical domains including the human body. There is disagreement among speakers about the absolute and relative hot-cold qualities of many items; and all quantitative comparisons are precise only to the extent that some items are "very" hot or "very" cold.[9]

As is the case with systematic taxonomic classifications, contexts structure the demand for information which is supplied by the choice of a plant, or a plant name. For example, "a plant good for headache" is, obviously, a demand for a member of a set of plants good for relieving headache. The membership of this class is (to some extent) common cultural knowledge. A request for "a plant good for headache *de pasmo*" (a class of headache), demands a member from a subset of this class of all plants "good for headache." The more precise demand for "a plant good for headache *de pasmo de frio*" makes the demand more precise and further narrows the subset from which a selection will be made. Thus, the superordinate class, "plants good for headache" is subdivided into a logical hierarchy of categories, much like the relationship of plants in the systematic taxonomy. Plants belong to the former hierarchy by virtue of a shared characteristic—an abstract quality which makes them "good for headache." At the lower levels of the taxonomy, they are further classified in that they possess some more precise abstract quality which makes them "good for headache" of a particular kind.

To summarize, both systematic and functional classifications in Mitla Zapotec ethnobotany share the same principles of organization. Terms are hierarchically organized to show significant similarities and differences, and as both the flora and the criteria for functional or systematic classification change, the biological concept categories are continually reexamined and regrouped. In addition, functional classifications complement systematic judgments and affect systematic taxonomic nomenclature in two ways. First, considerations of function affect the taxonomic depth of the systematic classification. Second, plants which are the same may be named the same, which can lead to "mistakes." These points will be further taken up in the following section, which compares modern scientific and Mitla Zapotec botany.

A COMPARISON OF THE FOLK AND MODERN SYSTEMS OF (BOTANICAL) THOUGHT

Comparing modern scientific and Mitla folk botanical nomenclature raises two general issues. First, are principles of classification and naming the same? Do they produce the same conceptual categories and relationships between categories? Second, are people who use the folk botanical system able to communicate without mistakes? Can they add and subtract plants from their cultural repertoire on the basis of their logical scheme? What is the potential for confusion, expansion, or contraction?

---

[9] In Islamic medicine and in Renaissance Europe, hot-cold qualities were apparently more standardized, and items were measured for their "degrees" of heat or cold, wetness or dryness. To those using the classificatory system, these attributes were "real" and objectively quantifiable, though modern physicians and botanists cannot clarify them further.

Levey noted that wine was classified as dry and hot in the second degree in his translations of seventh through ninth century medical texts. He also noted that most Arabic synoptic medical works from the ninth through twelfth centuries included drugs, named with synonyms in two or more languages, Galenic nature *and grade* (emphasis mine) and preparation, therapeutic value, and uses (1966:13). The information about nature and degree of Galenic humors undoubtedly conveyed quite specific information to physicians of the Islamic world.

Similarly, the physicans and herbalists of Renaissance Europe identified and classified plants on the basis of chemical and therapeutic criteria which are somewhat mysterious to the modern botanist and physician. Nehemiah Grew analyzed all plant tastes into ten basic elements which could be present in graded strengths in different plants. He also spoke of " 'green pods' of a certain species of clematis as being hot in the tenth degree," clearly an entry in a recognized pharmaceutical code for contemporary (seventeenth century) physicians (Arber 1953b:328).

Such precision contrasts with the lack of precision in most folk botanical hot-cold systems. People in a given society share the classifications for only a limited number of items, beyond which classifications vary according to the individual's inherited knowledge or classificatory judgment of hot-cold signs. For example, in one Peruvian village, Mazess found that there were only two items on which there was 100% agreement as to "heating" or "cooling" quality—black chunya (freeze-dried potatoes) which everyone agreed were "cold," and a kind of earth, used as a condiment, which everyone agreed was "hot" (Mazess 1968). See Messer (1975) for a more comprehensive discussion of both hot-cold and other medicinal plant topics.

Classification and Naming

Both native and modern scientists recognize plants as natural conceptual categories, almost all of which are named. Whether one calls these "plant types" (Conklin 1954), "speciemes" (Bulmer 1970) or "generics" (Berlin 1972) they exist. Both native and modern botanists also arrange plants hierarchically into taxonomies. They rank plants relative to one another on the basis of shared features and the principle of hierarchic inclusion. In the modern botanical system all plants at the species level are uniquely, binomially named. Finally, both systems constantly undergo regular change in taxonomy, classification principles, and nomenclature as actual plant populations and criteria by which to define them change (cf. Conklin 1954:163).

Beyond these similarities are also important differences. The folk and modern botanist have different classificatory aims. The Mitla Zapotec desires to identify and name the flora around him. It is part of an intellectual pursuit—to see how flora are interrelated and grow—to know what is there and how to describe it. But classification is also a practical pursuit, an effort to make fine enough discriminations that one can use flora to its utmost potential and not make mistakes in putting plants in their proper places. The folk botanist classifies plants on the basis of gross morphological features, ecological location, chemical properties, functional features, etc. At times he names equivalently plants with the same use even if they are clearly different plant concept categories, if defined morphologically. There is a general preference for binomial labels at the specieme and lower levels, and names are not a good index of taxonomic status.

By contrast, modern scientific botany tries to fit plant conceptual categories into a world floral scheme. It draws phylogenetic relations to show evolutionary linkages between plants. Classification is based chiefly on reproductive parts rather than additional functional, ecological, or other characteristics. Each plant concept category at the specific level is assigned a unique binomial name and different plant categories are never given the same name, nor are the same plant categories named differently (except where individual botanists show different taxonomic judgment). Finally, genetic relationships between genera and species are discoverable through the taxonomic nomenclature.

Given the differences, it is not surprising that Mitla Zapotec plant categories do not always correspond to botanical genera/species although they, too, are logical classes, hierarchically ordered. Some Mitla Zapotec plant classes are more differentiated, as with certain important economic plants, like maize. Some are less differentiated, like the "grasses," where, although individual types may be recognized, they are unimportant and so not named. More than one plant concept category good for the same purpose (in this case animal fodder), though distinct, may be named the same. Culturally salient categories are generally named to a lower taxonomic level than less important plants (see Berlin et al. 1966). This means that Mitla Zapotec speciemes correspond to botanical varieties through supra-generics, not simply genus or species.

The limited number of flora with which the Zapotecs deal as well as the functional and ecological attributes which are used to distinguish among them also contribute to the lack of correspondence between scientific and Zapotec named botanical categories. Figure 18 displays a selected group of Mitla Zapotec taxa distinguished at more than one level in the taxonomy. It shows that in some cases (*baláp, bitia?*) Zapotec speciemes subdivide botanical species; in others (*šk^{w}an ǰehb*) major categories and their subdivisions correspond exactly to botanical genus/species relationships (though the Mitla Zapotec category names are based on functional, not simply morphological criteria), and in still others (*bälwi, bityuš, giht),* the Mitla Zapotec recognize related genera within modern botanical families in their nomenclature. In yet others, *balašoh,* plants related by gross morphological leaf form or medicinal function but not closely related according to modern botany are named the same.

Finally, the problem of determining absolute rank within the Mitla Zapotec taxonomic nomenclature (a problem compounded by the existence of covert categories and resemblances or distinc-

MITLA ZAPOTEC TERM	CORRESPONDING SCIENTIFIC BOTANICAL NAME	ANALYSIS
baláp — baláp nŏl / baláp šnyâ	Ricinus communis L.	A single botanical species is divided into two contrasting folk species on the basis of "white" (nŏl) versus "red" (šnyâ) leaf color. This distinction is then used to contrast (1) hot-cold qualities and (2) remedies of the distinct categories.
bitia? — (x) — bitia? nŏl / bitia? medio-morad / bitia? morad / bitia? zä?	Chenopodium ambrosioides L.	Two botanical species within the genus Chenopodium are recognized as two principal speciemes. The latter is a spice used to prepare green corn gruel. The former is subdivided into three classes on the basis of color. The color distinction is used to sort prefered "white" (nŏl) versus less-prefered "purple" (morad) leaves for cooking; less powerful, versus more powerful intestinal worm medicine.
škwan ǰehb — škwan ǰehb ro? / škwan jehb lás	Loeselia mexicana (Lam.) Brand in Engl. / Loeselia caerulea (Cav.) G. Don	Two species of the botanical genus Loeselia are grouped on the basis of similar form and function and distinguished into two folk species on the basis of leaf size and function.
giht — giht huedz / giht geč / giht lahn / giht tia?p	Cucurbita pepo L. / Cucurbita pepo L. / Apodanthera aspera Cogn. / Sechium edule L.	The botanical family Cucurbitaceae is divided into different classes of "squashes." The first two are cultivated, the third wild but with edible seeds. The fourth is a vine which produces edible vegetable pears.
bälwi — (x) — bälwi nŏl / bälwi šnyâ / bälwi bäz	Malpighia sp. / Bunchosia montana Juss.	Two genera of botanical family Malpighiaceae are recognized as two principal speciemes. The latter has no use. The former is subdivided into two classes on the basis of color. The "red" (šnya) fruits are the type class and more common than the "white" (nŏl). The bark of either is boiled into a remedy for dysentery.
bityuš — bityuš bä?kw / bityuš gŏn / bityuš gihš / bityuš lahn / bityuš su / bityuš zah	Solanum (nigrum group) / Physalis nicandroides Schlecht. / Physalis sp. / Passiflora foetida L. / Lycopersicon sp. / Physalis viscosa L.	One subset of the botanical family Solanaceae is divided into different classes of "tomatoes" with various uses.
bala šoh — bala šoh / bala šoh gihš	Piper sp. / Marsdenia mexicana Decne.	Two unrelated botanical species are grouped together on the basis of gross leaf morphology and function; They are separated according to habitat—cultivated versus wild (gihš).

Fig. 18. Relative taxonomic levels.

tions that are noted but not named) destroys the possibility of forming a consistent equation between Zapotec and modern botanical taxonomic nomenclature. The problem of sorting absolute and relative ranks within the categories bälwih, bityuš and others have already been treated at length above and will not be repeated here. The taxonomic and nomenclatural data can be sorted in more than one way to relate speciemes as generics, suprageneric, and species. The natural variability of the flora, as well as the flexibility of the cultural classification and naming procedures complicate the translation from folk to modern botany.

The above lead to the more general question of mid-level taxonomic categories. Berlin et al. have noted the relative paucity of mid-level categories between level of life form and generic in native taxonomic systems. They have suggested that where such categories exist, they are unlabeled, "covert" categories whose psychological reality may be hard to establish (Berlin et al. 1972, 1973). Other anthropologists have agreed that such categories exist, though they have not always concurred that they are unlabeled. For example, Brown (1974), responding to Berlin, noted that certain mid-level groupings, such as those based on function, may not only exist but may be labeled, though not within the systematic taxonomy.

The Mitla Zapotec data presents several different insights on this controversy. First, as in the examples just cited, certain "family" level taxa may in fact be present *and* labeled if one cares to sort the taxonomic nomenclature into such a construction. The Mitla Zapotec suprageneric *bityuš* and *giht* both label several genera within the scientific families as well as several genera within the Mitla Zapotec botanical nomenclature.

Other examples of mid-level conceptual groupings analogous to portions of scientific family taxa can be found in the domain of medicinal plants. For example, several plants in the category defined by "sweet" smell/taste and the medicinal property "good (for curing) stomachache" come from the family Verbenaceae (Fig. 19). This mid-level taxonomic grouping found in the Mitla Zapotec functional classification, corresponds to one portion of a modern botanical family Verbenaceae. Both group plants on the basis of their own, but obviously related, versions of biochemical systematics.

Thus, mid-level groupings, which may or may not be "covert" can be discovered both in systematic and in functional taxonomies. In general, Berlin et al.'s scheme, though useful for talking about relative levels in the taxonomy, complicates rather than simplifies the logic of many portions of the native hierarchy in which taxonomic rank is relative to other items being classified within a particular portion of the taxonomy. The Mitla Zapotec taxonomy produces a set of logically consistent relations between

MODERN BOTANICAL NAME	MITLA ZAPOTEC NAME
Family: Verbenaceae	Medicinal Category: Stomachache Cure
Aloysia triphylla (L'Her.) Britton	cedrón
Lippia alba (Mill.) N.E. Brown	salb nŏl
Lippia graveolens H. B. K.	pitión
Lantana spp.*	žob.leh*
Family: Labiatae	Medicinal Category: Stomachache Cure
Mentha rotundifolia Huds.	monstranz
Mentha sp.	bäč štil
Origanum vulgare L.	orégano
Satureia mexicana (Benth.) Briq.	wăs

*When mistakenly identified as salb on the basis of sweet smell/taste, the leaves were reported to be good for curing stomachache.

Fig. 19. Mitla Zapotec functional (medicinal) categories and their correspondence to modern botanical family taxa.

plants which must be recognized and used but that do not necessarily correspond to the demands and structures of the scientific system based on morphological form and reproductive characters. Finally, one should add that even in the scientific system, there is by no means complete agreement about the "natural" phylogenetic relationships between plants. How much more complicated is the native system, which seeks to relate plants along multiple dimensions!

Homonymy and Synonymy

Mitla Zapotec classification also contrasts with scientific taxonomy in that homonymy (one label designates more than one plant concept category) and synonymy (one plant concept category is designated by more than one label) are permitted. These are impossible in the canons of the scientific system, where every plant category is uniquely named. Though at times a single specimen may be assigned to two different categories, this is due to differences in taxonomic judgment rather than to inherent properties of the taxonomy.

In Mitla Zapotec, most plants have unique

Zapotec names. Though some, like *Calea hypoleuca*, have more than one herbal designation and others, like maguey, are given more than one name depending on the plant part stressed, these are exceptions rather than the rule. However, the situation is immediately complicated by the bilingual situation; most plants have at least one unique Spanish as well as Zapotec name. The situation is further complicated by the movement of plants and plant information between towns; through this process names may change botanical referents. Fieldwork in San Sebastián Abasolo, another Valley Zapotec town, in 1971, showed Zapotec names for common field herbs were not completely shared, while a brief plant collecting trip in the vicinity of Nochixtlán in the same year showed substantial variations in common Spanish herb names. Thus, names appear to be in constant interchange and flux, a subject demanding more intensive investigation.

In addition to these sources of nomenclatural variation, the logic of using the taxonomic system to communicate information about plants also encourages certain forms of homonymy and synonymy. One form of homonymy results from using names polysemously (at two different levels of contrast). As cited above, the life form *kʷan* may be used in place of a unique name at a lower level of contrast; and the generic name *yäb* may be used in place of any of the precise terms subsumed under that category. When there is additional contextual information, these usages are not sources of confusion for native speakers, who extract information from the context of plant naming. Ambiguities or misunderstanding are avoided by simply selecting the correct name at the next lower of contrast or supplying a modifier (such as growth stage) at the same level of contrast. In some cases, the selective use of modifiers gives more information than the systematic names alone, since the use taxonomy demands practical information as well as conceptual.

More troublesome is the second form of homonymy, where the same name is applied to unrelated taxonomic classes, though again, if the speaker provides further description to clearly identify which plant class he means, mistakes can be avoided. For example, *siempre viva* labels two distant plant classes: *Selaginella pallescens* and *Rumfordia floribunda*. When a knowledgeable woman was given a remedy which used *siempre viva*, she thought to ask whether her teacher meant "the green kind, which grows in the rocks in the hills" or "the tree which grows in the garden?" They may both be called *siempre viva*, though they have no traits in common. She learned that this particular cure (for *nervios*, "nerves") involved the former class, called *gisedz* in Zapotec. Another example of homonymy is *mostaza*. In one case, a speaker, treating an arm irritation, described using the leaves of *mostaza* "the kind with the tubular yellow flower," (*Nicotiana glauca*), not "the kind with the small rounded flowers" (*Brassica nigra*). *Škʷan ghihb* is an additional example of homonymy. The name can denote either *Calea hypoleuca* or *Heimia salicifolia*. The former species can also be labeled *cacahuatón* (Sp.) or *škʷan bižeh* (Zap.), so again, there is a means to resolve any ambiguity about which plant is sought for a particular remedy. In addition, one can describe the plant one means. A final example is the use of the name *škʷan ǰehb las*, which was applied to both *Loeselia caerulea* and to another unidentified yellow flowering mountain herb. By describing plant location and flowers, the two are distinguished. In summary, where speakers have equivalent knowledge of the homonymy contained within the nomenclatural system, they can manipulate names and modifiers to prevent misunderstandings. The use of modifiers to describe the differences between closely related plant classes also creates new potential taxonomic categories at the next lower level in the taxonomy.

An alternative problem for communication built into the nomenclatural system is synonymy. Though usually only one label correctly identifies each botanical species, in Zapotec terminology there is no restriction on the number of names which can be "correctly" applied to one species. This can limit communication, since one may know the plant concept category but not recognize the label and therefore not act on the information presented in an herbal remedy. A Zapotec speaker who knows the plant concept category identified by the label *lengua de vaca* only by the Zapotec label *bala giwi* will fail to respond to the information about the former Spanish name without further consultation with other knowledgeable speakers. Likewise, one may distort a message by designating a different plant than the one intended by the label. Such mistakes can hurt. For example, one uses the plant labeled *yerba de canz* (*Tournefortia hartwegiana*) to wash wounds, and this plant is alternatively labeled *yerba negra*. Another plant labeled *yerba negra* (*Rivina humilis*), is "very strong" and "burns" when applied to the skin. A speaker who does not equate the plant concept category labeled *yerba de canz* with the label *yerba negra* may not only fail to use the plant originally designated by the remedy, but may, in fact, use the wrong plant, which she identifies by the label *yerba negra* and "burn" her patient.

In sum, both synonymy and homonymy potentially distort the accurate information circulated about plants. The mapping between nomenclature and taxonomy is usually consistent, but not entirely so. Mistakes can occur in the transmission of functional information about plants, information which is associated with a particular *name*, rather than with a single plant concept category. Practical and theoretical implications of problems of synonymy/homonymy within the plant classification and identification system can now be discussed.

Pragmatically, the potential inconsistencies in plant use which can result from nonequivalence of mapping between plant names and plant species can be overcome by "conference curing." In practice, herbs are rarely administered or eaten without first discussing them with a more knowledgeable herb gatherer. Women are not allowed to go to the fields or hills alone, and inconsistent identities of particular herbs can be recognized and discussed before herbs are administered.

Alternatively, homonymy and synonymy can be viewed as symptoms of the changing botanical flora and systematic change of such knowledge. Throughout Mexico, where plants are distributed over a wide range, plants with similar qualities of either features or functions tend to be called by the same names. An examination of M. Martínez (1959), *Las Plantas Medicinales de México*, clearly illustrates how one name is applied to several species, often when there is a change of usage. It appears that a use becomes associated with a particular name, and any plant which is said to possess those properties will be assigned the same name. Often it is an outstanding quality of a plant which becomes associated with the remedy and the name, as in the case of *Cuasia*, which is extremely bitter and used as a remedy for *bilis*. According to Martínez, there are two *cuasias*, both of whose roots are extremely bitter and of similar appearance. Both are sold as remedies for *bilis*, but only the "real" *cuasia* seems to be of medicinal value (1959:92-93).

Among the most common species, more than one species is usually associated with a single common name, e.g., *yerba buena, orégano*, since they share functions. Other Spanish names, often denoting function or animals, may also have more than one referent. For example, Martínez cites *yerba del cáncer*, applied to *Cuphea aequipetala* Cav. "and other species" in Mexico, Hidalgo, Puebla, etc. and *Acalypha phleoides* Cav. in Jalisco, Veracruz, Oaxaca, etc. A species of *Salvia* also carries the name in Telolopan, Gro. (Martínez 1959:164-165, 431). Similarly, names may change their referents, as *Bidens pilosa*, named *manzanilla* in Mitla, is *acahuál* in the state of Mexico. Where there is knowledge about synonymy and homonymy there may be no confusion and no growth of information within the system of plant knowledge. However, where the designation of a use (usually a remedy) associated with a plant name becomes extended to include a different species thought to be named by that label, then the knowledge about plant species is changed. In communication terms, the mistakes or "noise" in the system become the source of new information. Though this distortion of the information within the system leads to growth of knowledge, such growth is limited to the extent that there is always recourse to the plant description, rather than just the name, in the actual transfer of knowledge about a remedy. Furthermore, there is often recourse to the specimen itself, so that mistakes will not occur.

PERSISTENCE AND CHANGE IN MITLA ZAPOTEC PLANT KNOWLEDGE

In the foregoing presentation of Zapotec plant knowledge, the kinds of information people use to judge plants similar or different and the ways they act on those principles of classification have been discussed. It has been shown that the native, in contrast to the modern taxonomic botanist, relies on a few salient bits of information rather than a mental key to identify plant conceptual categories. He supplements his systematic knowledge with functional and life stage information in order to classify plants for use. Plant knowledge is systematized, and once he has mastered the several possible modes of classification, he can continually add new specimens into existing categories, expand extant groupings, and add new categories within the structure of the system. The purpose of a folk taxonomy is to organize and communicate information about the botanical world so that information may be quickly retrieved and used, and the Mitla Zapotec method of working between and within classificatory schemes efficiently meets these ends.

Plant knowledge grows in systematic ways. Ecologically, people recognize their flora by zones. They cannot always *name* all of the plant concept categories in a particular environment, such as a milpa, but they have patterned expectations of what plants grow there and can describe the categories, even when each category does not have a specieme label. When new plants appear, they are immediately noted and described as different even though they are usually simply glossed only as *kʷan* with no other name. People wait to observe new plants' habits of growth and patterns of succession, before naming them.

New medicinal plants are constantly being introduced into the local pharmacopoeia. When vendors appear with new useful plants, people observe the morphological, flower, and seed characteristics and learn the name, uses, and origin of the uses. They observe the effects, and all of this information becomes part of the ongoing corpus of plant knowledge. New edible plants are also continually available for experiment. These are largely varieties of well-known cultigens rather than entirely new speciemes, though government programs introducing new grains, such as sorghum and soy, have expanded the number of speciemes known and labeled. As with the older, known varieties, new varieties of maize are coded by color, though their names are prefaced with the general class modifier *"goviern"* (*del gobierno*, "government maize"). Their habits of growth are observed and commented upon much like the established maize varieties. New chile pepper varieties are also common, people either save the seeds of small chiles they like or purchase the plants in the marketplace. Chiles are described and named according to color, size, shape, and potency of the fruit. These contrast with the local *gin skuč* (*chile de palo*), grown in the local gardens and other chiles—*gin miž* ("Mixe"), *gin dzun* "Tlacochahuaya," the names of which code particular type and/or town/region of origin.

Other kinds of plant groupings are also constantly being modified as the locations and particular uses of plants change. Farmers recognize particular compositions of their fields, including the weeds, and can classify plant concept categories according to their place in the orderly succession of plants following the agricultural practices of cultivation, fertilization, and fallow. For example, *Amaranthus* spp. is expected to disappear after a field has been left fallow for two years.

Other speciemes expand their habitats as people remove them from nature to transplant in their gardens. *Lya yodz* (*chapiche*), a common spice eaten with beans, is gathered from the hills or purchased in the marketplace. People recognize that two specimens of it may be "different" if one grows unsown in the dry hillsides and the other is nurtured in the house garden, but they are both still assigned to the same conceptual category. Similarly, medicinal plants, such as *monstranz (monstranza)* and *yag čiǰ (jaras)*, are also sought for transplanting in the household garden. In the ongoing process of "culturalizing nature" Mitla Zapotecs bring wild flora closer to home and expand the ranks of domesticated plants. Though additional plant concept categories might be formed in this manner, in the cases of *monstranz* and *yag čij* the botanical categories did not undergo sufficient observable changes to warrant any change in nomenclature.

Functional groupings also change as people change their assumptions about the useful properties of particular plant concept categories. For example, the medicinal category "plants good for curing cold stomachache" is filled by plants with the chemical characteristic of "sweet" smell/taste. Additional herbs with this quality could be added to this medicinal category without much trouble. Other herbs are tried experimentally for particular ailments and so their use in categories within the medicinal system is expanded. For instance, in the past *lo gid gai* (*ojo de gallo*) was credited with being "good for curing fevers" since this plant was boiled and administered to typhoid victims when all other remedies had failed. A woman with *škʷam bäl* growing outside her door plucked some of the aromatic leaves to place on her son's pimples. If they succeeded in drying the boils, she would add *škʷam bäl* to her list of medicines for skin ailments and simultaneously expand the medicinal qualities attributed to this herb. The medicinal qualities of herbs also expand as the number of categories in the illness classification hierarchy increases. A "bitter" herb like *Artemesia* sp. is now classified as not only "good for curing bilis," a traditional folk illness, but also as "good for curing diabetes," a disease of civilization. *Yahn,* traditionally taken for *pujos* (bleeding dysentery), is now thought to be good for killing amoebas, a disease agent suggested by the doctor to cause dysentery. Conversely, knowledge of the medicinal values of herbs is undermined as pharmaceuticals replace them. Also, the virtues of medicinal plants used to treat "witchcraft" and other folk ailments are reduced as people cease to believe in these illnesses and their remedies.

Hot-cold classifications are also in a process of constant flux. Traditionally, all herbs had their hot-cold designation. If inherited customary knowledge did not supply a hot-cold label, then color, growing location (in the sun = "hot" and in the water = "cold"), seasonality, as well as the "effects" of the herb on the internal body state could be analyzed to achieve a designation (Messer 1975, Chapter 8). People paid attention to the hot-cold dimension of plants and other natural elements in planning their meals, their activities and remedies. Hot-cold thus united the botanical domain with nonbotanical domains of climate, food, illness, and social relations.

Today the hot-cold system continues to be used. Classifications vary between individuals, because people have inherited different knowledge or have different interpretations of the natural signs which point to hot-cold quality. The hot-cold system is open, for new herbs can be added and existing herbs drop out of the hot-cold categories without affecting the classificatory system. It is also flexible in that classifications can vary from person to person without destroying the basic principles of classification, the "principle of opposites."

SUMMARY AND COGNITIVE IMPLICATIONS

Botanical information is highly developed and varied among the Mitla Zapotec. Several kinds of classifications coexist and interact. Plants are known and used according to morphological and other features. Speakers with an adequate knowledge of the local flora and classification systems consciously manipulate the taxonomic and nomenclatural principles to provide selected information to their listeners. The choices of names plus other classificatory modifiers denote the specimens and signify the cultural contexts in and for which the plants are being identified.

In assessing the classifications of plants among Mitla Zapotecs, we can begin from the premise that all people share certain physiological perceptive abilities. Particular stimuli, similarly or universally perceived by individuals in the society, are then grouped into culturally meaningful conceptual categories which are of intellectual and/or practical use for the individuals of the culture. We have discussed three major dimensions in which plants may be grouped (form, function, and hot-cold quality) and these conceptual groupings have been discussed in turn to show how Mitla Zapotec identify, classify, and name plants so that they may be used. These classification principles structure botanical information such that cultural communication and organized social life (with plants) are possible.

Social scientists have continually questioned whether or not natives think differently than modern scientific man. Particularly, they have asked whether traditional cultures think mystically rather than scientifically (Lévy-Bruhl 1926), whether they think purely in concrete instead of abstract terms (Lévi-Strauss 1966), and whether they classify items on the basis of objective, easily communicated criteria (Cole and Scribner 1974).

The foregoing sections have shown that Mitla Zapotec plant science is very highly developed, though it differs from modern Western botanical science in certain regular ways. The logic of classification differs from modern scientific classification in that classificatory activity is for immediate, practical, not philosophical or taxonomic, ends. This means that Zapotecs do not always culturally encode or individually express all of the taxonomic information they see in a plant concept category or specimen. Their classification, which incorporates morphological, economic, and in some cases cosmological information, is a hierarchy of taxa ranked relative to other closely related taxa but not necessarily ranked analogously to the scientific generic-species contrast. Rank appears to be relative rather than absolute.

Furthermore, there does not appear to be a salient difference in the kind of cognitive processing which goes into the recognition of items to a higher or lower level in the taxonomy Berlin et al. have argued:

> ... members of taxa in generic contrast are identified in a psychologically unique fashion, one that is essentially based on instantaneous recognition of the organisms in question. On the other hand, tokens of organisms which are conceptually classified as members of the ethnobiological category we have labelled "specific" are identified by a more formal processing routine that requires rather conscious psychological assessments of contrasting semantic features....
> (1972:238)

On the basis of the Mitla Zapotec data, I would argue that both kinds of identification behavior go on simultaneously, and that the choice of a name from one or another level in the taxonomy is a function of its known existence and the cultural context in which the plant is being used. The choice of a name from a higher level in the taxonomy does not mean that many bits of information which can potentially be used to identify a specimen at a lower level are not being processed simultaneously in the mind of the speaker.

It has been shown that a plant may be classified on the basis of a small number of criteria and identified on the basis of an even smaller number. When closely questioned, a speaker can describe a large number of observations, systematically arranged in contrast sets, which make a particular species unique, but these need not enter into the practical processes of classification and identification. One could argue that discrimination of a large number of features enter into a classificatory decision through a process of "tacit knowing" or "tacit inference" (Polanyi 1967). The speaker would be going through quick mental search procedures without being able to explain, in a step by step systematic fashion, the information processing going on in the mind. Alternatively, one may argue that the cognitive map is "unconsciously" in mind, so the speaker need not express the structure beyond a plant concept category for the cognitive structure to be assumed.

Probably a better explanation is offered by the theory of information processing, where sets of features are conceptually linked and simultaneously judged in a taxonomic and identification decision. Though a speaker may be able to discriminate a plant post facto on the basis of binary attributes, the combination of features which are lumped to reach an instantaneous identification are probably far fewer than the number which he is able to discriminate about the plant. Just as a viewer combines a minimum amount of information from the total amount of information available in a visage to identify a face (Harmon 1973), so the speaker learns to lump a few key blocks of salient information for plant identification and use. Where plant categories are not definitively presented in nature (as in the case of an unflowering specimen which has been goateaten almost to the ground), the speaker may excavate the roots, chew on the stalk, and crush and smell the leaves to identify the plant. Thus there are two routes to knowledge, used together to identify field specimens to concept category: immediate gestalt (pattern) identification and serial analysis of binary information. Speakers use this joint knowledge to assign the concept category its place in systematic and functional taxonomies. The criteria which are used are potentially diverse, to a degree individually variable within a range of possible responses in the cultural repertoire, and are also determined by the context of the communication event in which plant knowledge is solicited.

Third, the Mitla Zapotec classification system, unlike the modern botanical classification system, uses terms polysemously, homonymously, and synonymously. This confuses issues for the modern scientific botanist, but the structure of the system is logical to the native speaker. As Raven et al. have noted:

> A folk taxonomic system is designed not for information retrieval but for communicating about organisms with those who already understand the nature of the organisms being discussed. (1971:1212)

Even though they do not conform to the canons of modern botanical nomenclature, the Mitla Zapotec ethnobotanical system does permit communication about plants on the basis of real properties, using real, objective categories. Their thought is thus logical and comprehensible, even if different from modern botanical thought.

On the issue of whether natives can think abstractly, the collected data shows that Mitla Zapotecs classify items in both abstract and concrete categories. Though one could argue that the plant concept categories existing at different taxonomic levels are not "real" abstract botanical categories, one could not extend this argument to conceptual categories like edible plants, medicinal plants, and hot-cold categories which are clearly abstract. Whether they classify items on the basis of objective, easily communicated criteria, however, varies with the kind of classification being done. Cole and Scribner describe an experiment in which two African natives were placed in adjoining booths. One was asked to describe different botanical specimens set before him so that the other, out of sight of him and the specimens, could match objects from his identical set of plants with the description. The first native proceeded to describe objects along dimensions which could not communicate the salient information to clearly identify the specimens. Expressions like "the long one" or "the curved one" were used in lieu of the salient bits of information necessary to clearly classify the items. From this, the experimenters concluded that natives could not think or classify in terms of objective, easily communicable attributes. As Cole and Scribner note, there is clearly a problem in method in this experiment. It is by no means evident that the subjects understood the task or would be unable to function in normal cultural situations. The Mitla Zapotec, observed in field and home rather than experimental situations, can and do select attributes of plants and communicate effectively about them to perform normal cultural tasks. Salient morphological features are noted and used in classification. Where classificatory attributes are not objective, easily communicated categories, as is the case with the hot-cold quality, this is because they are abstract rather than concrete and inherently malleable to interpretation, both between speakers and over time. There is no "defect" in thought.

CONCLUSIONS

This chapter has presented Mitla Zapotec plant knowledge as a system with highly developed structure. People can add or subtract plants without changing its structure. The system allows for some mistakes, but from such "noise" in the system, the corpus of plant knowledge grows. People can identify and name almost all plants in their environment as a first step towards using them.

In conclusion, the process of plant classification is a multisensory operation. Sight, smell, taste, and touch may all be used. The structure of thinking about plants is hierarchical within taxonomies. The principles for classification are in the human mind, and this organization is used to order nature for cultural thought and cultural uses. Those items which have greater cultural imporatnce and closely resemble other items of cultural importance will be more finely discriminated and named at lower levels in the taxonomy. Usually information supplied in a name below the generic level is lumped so that the name is in the binomial form, with one distinctive feature modifier.

The labeling process can be considered apart from the classificatory procedure. Not all conceivable plant categories have names. Lévi-Strauss (1966) has said that it is not functional criteria which determine classification and naming, but an intellectual criterion, the need to order the world. The Zapotec data have shown that there are two modes of ordering the world: conceptual (through classificatory procedures per se) and linguistic (labeling certain possible conceptual categories and not others).

Native speakers and anthropologists can only learn the meanings of particular labels and the plants to which they are attached by observing all contexts of use. Perhaps not all classificatory schemes are primarily functional in nature and in content; the Zapotec data show that they are not. Nor are all classifications equally useful for conveying all kinds of information. There are problems of level, synonymy, and homonymy, which are problems of the logic of classification and naming, or result from changes in the plant lexicon, the plant domain, or in culturally specific botanical knowledge.

Not all the Zapotec plant information is functional, but a good deal of it is. It is a moot question whether the classificatory schemes were originally "good to think with" and secondarily "good to use." Currently, communication about plants centers around their classification and use for practical concerns. It is to the use of plant names, parts, and stages of growth significant for the proper pursuit of gathering and agriculture, that the discussion now turns.

V

GATHERING AND HORTICULTURE

In anthropological literature there is a definite distinction made between hunting and gathering, horticultural, and agricultural societies. The exploitation of wild food sources is contrasted with the use of domesticated food sources, and similarly, garden production is contrasted with field production.

Data from many areas of the world indicate that agricultural strategies often combine plant production with plant gathering. Even within agricultural field systems, some limited amount of gathering may go on. The purpose of this chapter is to detail the characteristics of gathering and gardening in contemporary Mitla and to show how knowledge of gathered and garden plants articulates with bodies of knowledge about agricultural and medicinal plants. My general thesis is that food production does not involve abrupt changes from one mode of economy to another but instead involves ongoing accumulation of knowledge and technology, derived from using plants for dietary and other purposes. Techniques of observation and classification of plants gathered in the field, hills, or garden are applicable to plants cultivated agriculturally as well. All are part of one body of knowledge, the principles of which extend over all plants. Also, while examining the distribution of plants among ecological and cultural zones, it is possible to see what the population observes about plants and how knowledge is distributed within the population.

GATHERING

Two kinds of gathering can be distinguished in Mitla: (1) exploitation of wild plant resources outside of the agricultural field systems (Sp. *en el campo*, Zap. *lo kamp*); and (2) harvesting of edible herbs which grow within agriculture field systems (Sp. *en la milpa*, Zap. *yähl*). Continuity can be seen by reviewing the archeological, ethnohistoric, and ethnographic evidence.

Plants Exploited outside the
Agricultural Field Systems

The first plants definitely known to be exploited by man in the Valley of Oaxaca were recovered by Flannery et al. (1970) from dry caves near Mitla (Fig. 20). Almost all of these species still grow in the vicinity of the dry caves and are potentially edible. Though maize cultivation may have been carried out on the river floodplain below the caves as early as 4000-5000 B.C., gathering of local wild resources undoubtedly

SCIENTIFIC IDENTIFICATIONS	ZAPOTEC AND SPANISH TERMS
Agave spp.	dohb, maguey
Allium sp.	žiht gihš, cebolla del campo
Arctostaphylos polifolia	žob.nidh, manzanita
Arctostaphylos pungens	manzan.gihš, manzanita
Asclepias sp.	binyah
*Cassia polyantha	Lya gihš, tepeguaje
*Celtis sp.	geč.čehd, rompecapa
Condalia mexicana	žob.binyi
Echinocactus sp.	kehš, biznagre
*Jatropha dioica	susl
Lantana velutina	žob leh, sapotilla
Lemairocereus sp.	bidz lats, pitahaya
*Leucaena esculenta	Lya, guaje
*Lysiloma divaricata	Lya, guaje del campo
*Malpighia sp.	bälwi, nanche
*Opuntia spp.	bia, nopal
Oxalis spp.	guni, camotito
*Prosopis laevigata	beya?, mesquite
*Quercus sp.	žiglanx^w, bellotas

*Denotes plants of which remains were found in the Mitla preceramic period caves (identifications by C. Earle Smith).

Fig. 20. Edible wild plants from nonagricultural zones.

continued alongside incipient agriculture. Plant materials recovered from the dry caves indicate that wild plants, such as maguey, continued to be utilized for food as late as the Postclassic period, Monte Albán V (Flannery et al. 1970). Later, ethnohistoric and historic sources document the ongoing exploitation of the countryside for food. The *Relación de Mitla* (1580) reports no agricultural produce consumed by the Indians, but:

> The provisions with which they sustained themselves were some wild herbs that they did not have a name for except to know them as their food, and some small wild prickly pears and sap of a tree that they call maguey. Some of the upper classes managed to eat rabbits. The peasants seldom ate corn as it did not exist (in sufficient quantity). (del Paso y Troncoso 1905)

The *Relación de Tlacolula* similarly indicates a lack of emphasis on cultivation. The chroniclers report that the inhabitants ate honey, prickly pear, the roots of certain trees, and "from the damp earth they dug up certain nuts which served them as nourishment" (ibid.). From other documentary sources, it is known that there was a highly developed system of maize agriculture in the Valley of Oaxaca (cf. Taylor 1972). The descriptions of the *Relaciones* show that food gathering was being practiced at least through the beginning of the Spanish colonial period. One wonders in what season the scribes observed the Mitla-Tlacolula economies, or whether the accounts were written after a year of poor agricultural yields. Historical sources show how critical the availability of wild resources outside the agricultural zone must have been for the population of Mitla in marginal agricultural years. As recently as 1915, plants in the countryside helped maintain the population of Mitla during a famine year.

With the exception of piñon nuts, all of the major plant resources found in the preceramic occupation levels of the dry caves are still available around Mitla. Among the current population, some people admitted eating some of the plants as part of their seasonal diets. Others remembered having eaten wild plants some time in the past, such as during the famine of 1915. Still others, if pressed, would admit that some members of the population ate wild tubers and berries, with no ill effect, though they, the speakers, did not. The dimensions of the category "edible wild plants" and the relationship between plants which people say are "good to eat" and the plants people actually eat, will be discussed during the presentation of the plants themselves.

Of the edible wild fruits, *tunas* (*Opuntia* sp.) and *nanches* (*Malpighia* sp.) are still favorite sweets, and small boys tending their sheep and goats in the semi-arid foothills strip the area of fruits. Fruit may also be introduced from outside of the immediate vicinity by men and women coming down from the hill towns, where *Opuntia* may be abundant.

In contrast, most people did not remember eating mesquite (*Prosopis laevigata*) or acorns (*Quercus* sp.) and had never heard of piñon nuts (*Pinus* sp.). One woman thought that mesquite pods could be roasted and the seeds eaten, and many people knew that *dulces* ("sweets") of mesquite were made in Tehuantepec. An elderly man remembered that he had eaten mesquite pods boiled into a kind of honey during the famine when he was a child. Some chewed raw pods while "en el campo." Elsewhere in the valley, it is common to eat mesquite. However, most Mitleños agreed that mesquite was "not edible" for human beings and should be eaten by animals, preferably burros. People explained that the mesquite was "strongly sweet" and therefore unpalatable. Even during the famine of 1915, some families did not eat it because it was classified as "inedible" on the criterion of taste.

Acorns were similarly classified as "not edible" by most people. One man had observed men roasting acorns when he was a boy, but not in Mitla. Others had heard that acorns were gathered for food in some of the mountain villages. Within Mitla, acorns, like mesquite, were not considered edible.

Piñon, the pine nut, was unfamiliar to Mitleños, who had never seen nor heard of such food. This is understandable in light of C. Earle Smith's botanical survey. Throughout the Valley of Oaxaca, he failed to discover any of the *Pinus pinyon* species. The presence of piñon refuse in the caves and the absence of current piñon populations can be interpreted in two ways. First, it is possible that collecting parties went great distances to procure it. Collecting parties in search of pine nuts often traveled for several days to their sources in the American Southwest. This was the case among the Papago (Castetter and Underhill 1935). An alternative interpretation is that piñon was lumbered out as a favorite fuel. Since *Pinus* sp. is selectively cut for firewood today, it is quite possible that lumbering eliminated the piñon pine from the Oaxaca environment. This explanation is preferred by Smith and Flannery, who point out (personal communication) that all other plants recovered from the Mitla caves come from close by.

Agave, Celtis, and *Asclepias* are of particular interest, since each genus, still eaten today, is found in the dry caves. Several species of *Agave* are still available in the wild. During the famine of 1915, men collected *maguey del monte,* "from the mountains," and roasted the hearts for food. Today, most maguey is cultivated, either for pulque or mezcal. The hearts of these cultivated species can also be roasted, and are sold as sweets by persons from Matatlán and San Juan del Río. More commonly consumed in Mitla today is *quiote de maguey,* the inflorescence which the maguey plant sends up immediately prior to reproduction. When the inflorescence is cut, the plant concentrates its strength in the heart rather than in the reproductive process. The heart is then consumed or used for the manufacture of mezcal. The tender inflorescence is also roasted and ground into a paste, which is mixed with maize dough to make tortillas. These *tortillas de quiote,* prepared either with sugar or salt, are somewhat of a delicacy today. Though not all young women today know how to make the *quiote* tortillas, the consumption of roasted quiote is probably of great antiquity, since maguey quiotes, as well as quids, were recovered from the dry caves.

Another product of maguey, *aguamiel,* is tapped from certain species of *Agave* to produce pulque. In Precolumbian times, pulque, a mildly alcoholic beverage, was produced by a religious-political elite for ceremonial occasions. Both preparation and consumption were carefully controlled, according to the documentary sources.[1] During colonial times, pulque production became a major industry, particularly in northern Mexico, where maguey was sown in marginal agricultural land, and also in plantations, for the production of aguamiel and the manufacture of pulque. The latter beverage was an important source of calories and nutrients in the lives of most peasants and laborers.[2] Documentary sources for Oaxaca do not elaborate on the production of pulque, and in Mitla today the drink is rarely consumed, except on a few ceremonial occasions such as weddings or mayordomías. The beverage is imported from Matatlán for these occasions. Older people commented that pulque was used as a leavening in earlier times but has been replaced by packaged yeast.

During the famine of 1915, people remembered eating both the roasted hearts and quiotes of maguey. Though the heart is rarely consumed in Mitla, from the months of January through June, men and women search the stands of maguey for tender quiotes. As the price of bread rose during February of 1974, (from 20 centavos to 25 centavos per piece), women organized special outings to search for quiotes. They said that to save money, they would make *tortillas tostadas* ("toasted tortillas"), *tortillas de trigo* ("tortillas of wheat") and *tortillas de quiote* to eat with their morning and evening coffee. Hence, among poorer

[1] According to the documentary sources, the preparation and consumption of pulque was carefully controlled in Precolumbian Mexico, and the plant was of ritual importance. Myths and legends in the codices describe the discovery of maguey and the invention of pulque. From the accounts of Sahagún, quoted by Soustelle (1961), it is also obvious that within the social structure, access to pulque was limited, and often surrounded by ceremony. I thank Judy Nietschmann for bringing this data to my attention.

[2] The Instituto de Nutriologia in 1952 determined that one liter of pulque averaged:

Protein	3.7 grams
Ash	2.4 grams
Calcium	110.0 mg.
Phosphorus	60.0 mg.
Iron	7.0 mg.
Thiamin	2.0 mg.
Niacin	3.5 mg.
Ascorbic acid	51.0 mg.
Folic acid	0.1 mg.
Carbohydrates	8 grams

Source: Loyola Montemayor (1956:82).

households, there may be a movement back to indigenous wild foods as luxury items, to replace the relatively high priced baked goods which have become popular since the Spanish Conquest. An added consequence of the temporarily increasing importance of quiotes was the denial, among some maguey owners that quiotes were a free good, which could be gathered by anyone while "en el campo." On the contrary, they extended their concept of ownership rights to the entire plant, including the inflorescence, as the quiote once again became an important subsidiary item in their diets.

Hackberries (*Celtis* sp.) today are considered to be "inedible" or even toxic by many. Several people believed that the fruit produced drug-like effects or headaches when consumed. Many others, who have eaten the berries on occasion, will ordinarily not eat the fruit because it tastes "too sweet;" they disagree that the fruit is toxic. Whether or not hackberries were said to be edible depended on how people interpreted the question, "Do you eat this?" To the anthropologist asking the question, based on prior knowledge that at least some of the population still eat *rompecapa*, the question seemed straightforward enough, but it was obvious from the verbal (as opposed to the behavioral) responses that this was the wrong question. For example, some people would say with certainty in the home context that *rompecapa* was inedible and only eaten by birds, but in the field, they would pick a few berries off the bush and pop them in their mouths. These people were giving what they considered to be the correct response for their culture. *Rompecapa* is usually not eaten, except when one is "en el campo." People do not go out to the bushes, a short distance from the pueblo and gather the berries the way one goes to the hills to bring back *manzan.gihš*. Hence, the correct cultural response was probably "no, people do not eat *rompecapa*." However, the response is contextualized. If one is "en el campo" and wants to consume fruit, then (assuming that one does not believe *rompecapa* is druglike or poisonous) one may eat the berries. Similarly, most children, when "en el campo" will eat the fruit. In fact, boys tending flocks eat most kinds of the edible wild vegetation, the existence of which the rest of the population is unaware. In the words of one woman:

> You ask whether these fruits (*rompecapa*) are food which people eat. I answer "no," people do not eat them. Sure the little boys can be seen eating *rompecapa* but little boys will eat anything!

Hence, one had to be aware of how people interpreted the questions of edibility for they might apply the question to their culture, to themselves, or to other members of the culture.

Binya (Spanish *gueto*, but always labeled in Zapotec), the edible milkweed pod, was another example of a species found in the dry caves still retained in the memory of the people. Although a majority of the young people did not know to which plant "*binya*" referred, the older generations could recall having eaten the pods in quantity during the Great Hunger of 1915 and eagerly roasted and ate the specimens which I collected in the field. Some families preferred the pure flesh of the roasted pods, other families the flesh with seeds. The remains of desiccated seeds found by Flannery in the dry caves indicate that in the preceramic period the pure flesh was preferred.

Certain species of wild *guajes* are also still consumed. In Corral del Cerro, *guajes del campo* (*Lysiloma divaricata*) are still collected and consumed like the cultivated species *(Leucaena)* with tortillas and beans. The *guajes* of *Cassia polyantha* (*tepeguajes*), which grow near the dry caves, are not classified as edible for humans but edible only for animals. Refuse of both species was recovered in the dry caves.

Certain small tubers are also eaten. In addition to a wild onion, the tuber of a wild bean, *Phaseolus heterophyllus* grows in the vicinity of the dry caves and throughout the general area of Mitla. Small boys tending their animals "en el campo" dig out the sweet tasting tuber. Those who had some familiarity with the countryside mentioned this tuber as one of the "wild" plants which one could eat. This plant was also represented in the dry caves.

The wild squash *Apodanthera aspera*, called "stinking squash" in the local idiom, produces seeds which are, as mentioned in Chapter 4, still eaten roasted. This species was also found in the dry caves.

In summary, with the exception of piñon nuts, all of the species of plants found in the dry caves are currently available in the same vicinity. Furthermore, with the exception of mesquite and *tepeguaje,* most of these plants are still known to be exploited for food.

Other edible plants found outside of the agricultural zones, though not discovered in the cave debris, are also currently gathered and eaten. The cacti near the Mitla caves produce edible fruits and flesh. *Chilillos* (*bidi*) are available at various times during the year but particularly after the rains. More important as a source of food is *biznagre* (*kehš*) which is currently prepared with sugar as a dulce, similar to dulces of *chilacayote* and *calabaza* (squashes). In times of starvation, however, the plant is despined and well cleaned, and the flesh prepared with maize for small tortillas and also for atole. During the hunger of 1915, *biznagre* was very important as a source of food. The plant is mature and of good size after more than one year of growth. Large, "ripe" specimens may be collected throughout the year.

There are also a number of berries, which grow in the Mitla vicintiy: *manzanitas* or *penguicos* (*manzan gihš* [*Arctostaphylos pungens*] and *žob.nihd* [*A. polifolia*]). Also, *Condalia mexicana* has sweet fruits which are considered edible. The tubers of *Oxalis* (*O. galeottii* and *O. latifolia*) are eaten raw, as are the stems and leaves, which are sour and reduce thirst.

In summary, most of the plants known to be consumed prehistorically still form a part, though usually a small one, of the diet and other non-agricultural species are also eaten. During times of crop failure, before the development of a strong, socially concerned central government and modern long distance transportation in Mexico, their importance in the diet was even greater. These uncultivated sources of food in the vicinity of the town of Mitla have been crucial for the preservation of the population during times of famine in the history of this century. Though the historical and archeological record shows an economy dependent on agriculture, during marginal agricultural years there was the subsidiary recourse to the semi-arid hills. During absolute starvation years, there was almost total recourse to the residual vegetation of the region. The old collecting system has persisted alongside the agricultural system. The old does not "drop out," it just is not important in *most* years. During the Classic and Postclassic periods in Mitla, when the environment was not ideal for agriculture, a great civilization flourished. Although one must account for this by the developing agriculture in Mitla and in the eastern arm of the Valley of Oaxaca, one must not discount the contribution of the non-agricultural vegetation to the sustenance of the population during marginal and disaster years.

Information about potential production of edible food from the ecosystem is stored both within the cultural system and outside of the immediate culture. Mitleños observe the practices of other cultures in the hills around Mitla or hear stories about their subsistence practices. In Mesoamerica, there have always been less economically developed cultures still hunting and gathering in the neighborhood of "higher" agriculture cultures. For example, in northern Mexico, the Tarahumara (Bennett and Zingg 1935; Pennington 1963) and Tepehuan (Pennington 1969) continue to use most of the wild resources of their environment without extensive agriculture, in spite of the antiquity of cultivated food sources. Knowledge about the potential resources of the uncultivated plant systems is "stored" through communications about the actual hunting and gathering practices of such groups.

In Oaxaca, the surrounding hill ranchos and the neighboring Mixe territories were poorer than the valley proper. Even today, stories are still related about what these non-Mitleños eat, and travelers to these non-valley regions observe the diets of these other groups. Hence, in times of crop failure, plants located in the Valley of Oaxaca but known to be eaten elsewhere are used for food. There is thus, "a horizontal dimension" to information storage about environment. Though such information is not uniformly useful to the valley cultures due to vegetational differences between zones, it is available to all people through observation or stories. Unlike information stored "vertically" through the experience of the older generation, such information concerning the practices of neighbors is constantly being used, and thus cannot be "forgotten" through lack of use.

Gathering within Agricultural Zones

By 2500 B.C., as agriculture developed, maize production assumed a greater role in food procurement strategies. With its spread, the areas of availability of wild resources would have decreased. However, concomitant with agriculture, with the introduction and manipulation of cultigens, there developed a whole new productive system, which included edible weeds. This meant that though one gathering strategy was curtailed, yet another gathering strategy developed along with agriculture.

C. Earle Smith (this volume) has reconstructed the pristine environment for the Mitla region as exhibiting two principal vegetation zones: an alluvial plain with *Prosopis, Acacia,* and many members of the Burseraceae, Malvaceae, Euphorbiaceae, and Leguminosae, and a thorn-scrub forest, with *Lemaireocereus, Myrtillocactus, Agave, Acacia, Cassia, Opuntia, Dodonaea, Bursera, Jatropha* spp., *Fouquiera,* etc. Into these primary vegetation zones, man introduced new plants and new disturbances, which further affected the composition of the cultural environment.

Probably the most significant change was the development of the agricultural system as a type of ecosystem. This meant not only cleaning out the existing vegetation in the zone but permanently altering the composition of the soils, the availability of seed sources, and the botanical species available for reproduction within the zone. The change in the landscape had wide reaching effects for the region, as the balance of the climax vegetation was upset and the new set of pioneer species introduced. The possibility of the ecosystem returning to its pristine state was reduced, and people had to constantly devise new methods of dealing with their environment for their own actions ensured that the natural context of their survival would constantly change. An adaptation would not only have to meet the immediate requirements for survival, but also be adaptive—to make sure that in the long run the ecosystem would change in a direction within which people would be able to move and adjust.

Botanical changes constructed and restructured particular ecological niches. One might describe the change in terms of ecosystem devolution, the substitution of pioneer vegetation for climax vegetation. In agricultural areas, the principal plants were cultigens and new "weed" species. The latter, described by botanists as "plants growing out of place" (King 1966), were species which preferred the rich, well aerated soils resulting from cultivation of other disturbances. In folk botany they include three functional groups: those which produce leaves edible for humans (*Amaranthus, Chenopodium, Anoda Galinsoga, Crotalaria, Portulaca*); those which produce leaves edible for animals (*Amaranthus, Bidens, Sida, Mollugo, Heliotropium*); and those which are not edible for man or beast but interfere with crop growth (*Rumex, Sonchus*). They are all annuals. If land is left uncultivated, they are replaced within a few years by *Nicotiana glauca, Solanum* spp., *Prosopis laevigata,* and other Leguminosae.

A good study of the vegetation succession in the Valley of Oaxaca would show two sequences: first, the overall pattern of primary succession—an orderly, unidirectional replacement of one set of species by another within a particular zone. This primary succession pattern would be counteracted by a second pattern of sudden destructions, which reduce the vegetation to its pioneer level base, from which the succession would have to commence again. Man, through agriculture, is a principal agent of sudden destructions, causing reversals in the natural maturation process of ecosystems. Man also destroys or alters the composition of the primary environment in which the laws of botanical succession operate. The introduction of new species may eliminate the old by competition, forever altering the successive relationships between species. Other changes to soil and biological community are disruptive enough to permanently set the ecosystem off its trajectory of orderly change. Once the composition of the ecosystem at one stage of progression is sufficiently altered through the introduction of new species or cumulative effects of agricultural practices, the entire ecosystem may be set off in a new direction.

Flannery (1973) discusses the change in ecosystem management in early Mesoamerica in terms of the changing information implied by the signals of the environment. He argues that when maize reaches a critical productive value, it becomes more valuable to plant maize than to continue to gather mesquite, which directly competes with it for land and labor resources. At that point, the presence of a healthy mesquite growth will stimulate cultivation behavior (cut down the mesquite and sow maize) rather than gathering behavior (save the mesquite stand to gather pods in future years). This argument will be discussed further when the question of the evolution of agriculture is treated. For now, the significant results of ecosystem management are 1) the reduction in the absolute area available for non-agricultural gathering; and 2) the creation of a new botanical system, with its own regularity for succession and productive potential. The new botanical system is the field environment, which may have all, or most, of the species listed above. Certain species may be *expected* to appear in the fields, if the fields have been cultivated under certain conditions. This regularity, introduced into the natural environment, means that a new landscape has been added to the environment, and its individual species and their uses, learned.

The gathering of weed species—edible herbs—is the second kind of gathering discussed here (Fig. 21). Weed annuals are only marginally available in the pristine environment. They are differentially available within the cultivated environment, and the ability to exploit these species efficiently is dependent on knowing their habits of growth. Differential exploitation of the species not only provides the human community with added energy from their newly created environment, it also sustains the regularity of that environment, ensuring the continuity and spread of the weed species.

The botanical characteristics and cultural uses of non-cultivated herbs have been noted in other ethnographic areas. *Amaranthus* spp. was an important grain source in Precolumbian times (J. Sauer 1950). The seeds of certain cultivated species are still used, particularly for the manufacture of sweet seed cakes (*alegría*). Among present day farmers in the Valley of Mexico, the tender greens are plucked in the early summer and the seeds harvested in the late fall (Sanders 1957). Young *Amaranthus* leaves are eaten as boiled greens in Yucatán (Standley and Steyermark 1946:155), the Chiapas highlands (Breedlove and Hopkins 1970:283), Guatemala (McBryde 1945:147), and probably other areas as well.

Crotalaria is another genus widely used as a green vegetable in Mesoamerica. Both *Crotalaria longirostrata* and *C. pumila* are commonly consumed. The former, which has a tendency to endure longer than one year in the same location, is planted in Guatemalan gardens (Standley and Steyermark 1946:194; McBryde 1945:147). *Chenopodium ambrosioides* is mentioned both as a spice for beans and as a remedy for intestinal worms in many Mesoamerican ethnographies. *Portulaca oleracea* is similarily eaten as greens.

In Mitla, the weed genera *Amaranthus, Anoda, Chenopodium, Crotalaria, Galinsoga,* and *Portulaca* are the principal edible byproducts of the cultivation system. The tender leaves of *Amaranthus*, preferably those which are mainly "white," are plucked by hand, often with the root which probably aids the men in their weeding activities. When the plant has reached the height of about one meter and has gone to seed it remains useful but only as fodder. The entire plant is uprooted along with associated vegetation when a plot is being cleared.

Anoda cristata and *Galinsoga parviflora* are

SCIENTIFIC NAME	SPANISH	ZAPOTEC
Amaranthus hybridus L.	*quintonil*	gulădz
Anoda cristata (L.) Schlecht.	*violeta*	lakh
Crotalaria pumila Ort.	*chipil*	šiỹ
Galinsoga parviflora Cav.	*beldobes*	bäldohb
Portulaca oleracea L.	*verdolaga*	dzĕdz
Solanum (nigrum group)	*yerba mora*	bityuš bä?k^w

Fig. 21. Most common edible herbs from field systems: Scientific identifications of Spanish and Zapotec common names used in the text.

classified as "edible" during their tender or flowering stages and the leaves gathered for food. Both are used in combination with squash greens and other herbs, or eaten pure as boiled greens. Later, the entire plants may be collected for animal fodder.

Crotalaria pumila, another green used in combination with the herbs above, is considered edible in its tender or flowering stage. It was noted to appear four to six weeks after the onset of the rains and the seeding of the dry farmed milpas in Mitla. It is also eaten, boiled, in combination with maize dough (*tamales de chipil*). Along with the other edible greens enumerated above, it is plucked by enterprising women, who market the herbs in regional markets. In the process of collecting young squashes or picking cash crop vegetables, herbs such as *Crotalaria* and *Galinsoga* form additions to the numbers of marketable vegetables produced in a particular zone. In Mitla, poorer women may gather *Crotalaria* and *Anoda* to sell to other women, who do not have the time to gather them themselves. Thus, an originally "free good" becomes an "economic good" when there is an opportunity cost linked to gathering.

Portulaca oleracea is ordinarily not eaten with the other pot herbs but the tender stems and leaves are either boiled or fried in combination with onions, tomatoes, and garlic. It germinates later than the weeds cited above, but like them, the mature plant may be uprooted and retained as potential fodder when plots are cleared.

Within the genus *Chenopodium*, two main species are recognized in Zapotec. One is divided into two varieties, coded by color; the other is coded by functional role in the preparation of *atole de elotes,* a green maize gruel. Each of the kinds of *bitia?* (*epazote*) grows at the margins of fields. The leaves are collected, branches and all, and may be dried and stored for future use in the spicing of beans (*bitia? nŏl*) or atole (*bitia? zä?*). The locations of these plants are noted by women as they go out to aid in the agricultural process and leaves of the bean spice may be collected on these trips. *Bitia? zä?* has limited seasonal use, usually August through October, when there is green corn to grind into gruel. *Bitia? nŏl,* which is in demand throughout the year, may be uprooted and planted in the home garden or the seeds may be collected and sown. Branches are collected and sold to neighbors or to strangers in the market place.

In contemporary Mitla, not everyone knows what herbs are edible or where they are to be found. People may say that they do not eat the "wild" herbs (*del campo*) for status reasons ("When we have money we won't eat *quintonil* anymore."), but they will recognize that they are edible and that other persons eat them. People may also classify species individuals as edible according to their field location. Those growing in the milpa among the corn plants, are "good to eat" but those growing along the roadsides, or at the borders of the fields, where "the animals go" are "dirty" and preferably not eaten. This pattern of exploitation has two effects. First, it may reduce the spread of certain parasites, whose reproductive cycle includes passage through human excrement. Certainly the ban on eating the greens which spring up in the particularly rich excretory areas of one's houseyard is beneficial for human health. However, there is also a botanical effect of banning the exploitation of plants bordering the fields. Here the vegetation may mature and go to seed and serve as a reproductive source for the entire field, while those plants in among the milpa are cut down. Thus, the attitude of avoiding "unclean" areas, which prevents the harvesting of all the weeds in a field system, is one means of ensuring the continuity of the botanical composition of that field system (Fig. 22).

Edible herbs, unsown and widely available, are a "free good." Anyone may enter a field and pick the greens, provided that he does not touch any of

"CLEAN" *(LIMPIA)*	"DIRTY" *(SUCIA)*
Milpa	Borders of fields where oxen enter
Unsown fields without extensive traffic	Roadways where trash dumped
	House patio
	House corral

Fig. 22. Gathering areas.

the sown crops. Generally gatherers observe this rule. Not everyone knows where the weed species are available in abundance. Familiarity with the layout of fields and the habits of plant growth make the gathering task much simpler for the well informed than for the less informed.

In the early part of the rainy season, *quintonil* is the most widely available green. It grows in prepared fields, which have not yet been cleaned and sown. Since the young, tender leaves are preferred, one must know the cycle of planting and field cultivation to catch the herbs at their choice points.

Quintonil does best under conditions of adequate moisture and fertilization. During 1973, I observed two fields which had been recently fertilized with sheep and goat dung. Their herb growth was outstanding, and each afternoon several families could be seen exploiting the free good. The family of the field owner also exploited their own resource. Other less fortunate people surveyed the milpas in the area for signs of *quintonil* but then had to return to exploit the resource before the field was prepared and sown. During the weeks which followed, I noted that certain women went out daily to gather herbs, either for their families or their animals; they thus were aware of choice locations for *quintonil*. If asked by neighbors or kin, they distributed this information about herb whereabouts. Other women, particularly young girls with little exposure to the fields, would go out gathering and come back almost empty-handed. They had not known in advance where the most likely locations of herb growth would be and had not bothered to ask.

A similar situation prevailed with regard to *chipil*. There are particular locations in the pueblo where the growth is sure, and often abundant. Again, not everyone knew where *chipil* could be found. If a woman wanted to prepare *chipil*, she would start out often after first asking a neighbor or friend where she might encounter the herb. If she was unsuccessful on the basis of her own knowledge, or the communication from her neighbor, she could ask a compadre she encountered along the roadway. She also could ask any of the women traveling along the road or any of her relatives. Any of these individuals could point her to a specific location, sometimes to a specific field. Since *chipil* is a free good, information to aid in the efficiency of extraction is readily accessible, though not necessarily stored permanently by every individual.

In general, women gather herbs for food, but so may men who have been working in the fields. Similarly, though men may be principally responsible for gathering herbs for the animals, it is not unacceptable for women and children to perform this task.

Children differ in their abilities to identify and collect herbs for ingestion by animals and humans. Often it is the young people (around the age of twelve) who collect herbs for the meal, with or without their parents. Very young children may be sent out to gather herbs and grasses to feed the poultry and livestock but may be unable to identify correctly *quintoniles* and *chipiles*. This ability is developed according to the young person's exposure to the fields and willingness to learn the relevant identities. Adults may go to gather herbs as parts of semi-structured parties or as a byproduct of other agricultural pursuits. Children may learn about herbs in some of these contexts. *Chipiles*, eaten in *tamales* (maize dough boiled in maize husks), are a favorite food, and women may form gathering parties on Sundays, the day for rest, relaxation, and often for trips "al campo." Herbs will usually be gathered in the course of observing the fields during the cultivation season. Before the final preparation of the field for sowing, before the cleaning of the young milpa growth, during the *elote* ("green corn") stage, and the final ripe ear stage, herb growth will be noted along with information about the stage of growth of the milpa and herbs gathered for pot herb comidas.

In summary, the exploitation of wild food resources produced within the agricultural system is an important aspect of the diet of Mitla. Knowledge about these plants differs among individuals but is freely communicated through informal discussions and interchange. Individuals who spend more time in the agricultural process are generally inclined to know more about the availability of specific herb species at specific times in specific locations. However, information about availability is also easily stored from year to year since the particular communities are not destroyed, but preserved, through not gathering the herbs at field margins.

Mitla Gathering Compared to Other Zapotec Communities

Combining gathering activities and agriculture is by no means limited to Mitla but applies to other Zapotec and Valley of Oaxaca populations. Kearney reported that the Zapotecs of Ixtepeji gather wild greens and other wild plants in season to supplement their diets (1972:15). Similarly, the Oaxaqueños of Soledad Etla, in the northern arm of the Valley of Oaxaca, gather *chepiches,* a wild green of the hills, and *violeta del campo,* preparing it like the squash blossom. When there are heavy rains, in cultivated lands, there are also "*chepiles,* edible herbs which look like alfalfa" (Iszaevich 1969:38). Iszaevich's description makes it probable that the non-Zapotec residents of Soledad Etla are exploiting some of the same wild plants as the Zapotecs of Mitla.[3] In San Sebastián Abasolo, located between Mitla and Oaxaca City, the Zapotec population ate the same field greens as the Mitla Zapotecs, though they were known by different names.

Not all local populations recognize the same species or all of the same species as "edible." For example, the Zapotec population of Santo Tomás Mazaltepec do not eat *violeta,* which grows in abundance in their area. People said that the green was not eaten by people, though it was gathered for their pigs. Similarly, the leaves of *yerba mora* are not eaten in Mitla, but they may be eaten in other towns. The particular customs of gathering edible wild plants vary from town to town, and people note these differences with reference to their own customs and taste preferences. Persons who do not eat the *yerba mora* leaves say that they are too bitter to consider edible. Those who prefer not to eat the leaves of *violeta* say that they have a slightly thorny texture. Others who do not eat the red leaves of *quintonil* say that they do not look good to eat, since they turn black upon cooking. Thus, the dimensions of preference may refer to the senses of taste, touch, and sight, all of which enter into a traditional and personal system for classifying potential foods as "edible" vs. "inedible," even when people may know that others eat the foods classified as "inedible."

The general principle that supplementary foods may be gathered from the hills and fields is widely shared throughout the Oaxaca area, and probably throughout Mexico. As in the case of the foods gathered outside of the agricultural system, information about the potential edibility of wild herbs is stored in the observable gathering and culinary behavior of other families or other cultures. *Verdolaga* is rarely eaten today in Mitla, but most adults know that it is potentially "edible." The food customs of Tapachula and the Mixe which allow the preparation of *yerba mora* leaves have been observed and noted for future reference by Mitleños. Thus, information about "edible" foods is stored, though the meaning of these plants in Mitla cultural contexts varies.

Eating habits or food classification are one dimension for distinguishing among different cultures. The food customs of the Mixes are one axis on which they are defined as "different" from Mitla Zapotecs. Similarly, each valley town is thought to have its own food customs, a set of cultural practices which establish the identity of the individual pueblo.

Within Mitla, individual families also have their own food customs. Though some wealthy families like the unsown herbs, to others, the consumption of "free goods" in the form of wild herbs is a sign of low status. Hence, manipulation of diet, becomes a sign of economic achievement and advancement. The exploitation of non-sown herbs such as *quintonil* for some households is an index of poor economic status rather than idiosyncratic family tastes. The meaning of wild herb use thus changes from a dietary item, to a self-assessment of inferiority.

Summary

In sum, the wild herbs, gathered within agricultural field systems are nutritious by-

---

[3]*Chepiles* must be *Crotalaria* sp., which resembles alfalfa to a great degree.

products of agricultural activities and botanical community ecology. The herbs have cultural meaning, through their interpretation as members of the field system and their classification as "edible." That not all of the herbs potentially edible within the field system are recognized as edible has implications for three dimensions of plant knowledge. First, Mitleños do not know about all of the matter potentially edible within their field systems. We cannot judge whether this knowledge has been lost in recent history or whether it simply never existed. In other parts of Mexico, or of the world, species of *Sonchus, Rumex,* and *Tridens pilosa,* all represented in the Mitla field systems, supply "edible" leaves,[4] though Mitleños do not know they are edible. Second, local cultures establish their homogeneity in contrast to other cultural units by many dimensions, one of which is diet. Mitla customs vary in contrast to other towns. Third, individual food customs vary within a local population. Given a set of categories of "edible" foods, individuals will select preferred foods according to individual sensory preferences, availability, and value judgments about preferred foods.

HORTICULTURE

We have discussed unsown resources in two contexts: non-agricultural and agricultural. Another dimension of plant production is horticulture, which takes place in residential houseyards. These gardens fit very well Edgar Anderson's and Carl Sauer's descriptions of back yard gardens. Partially dump heap and partly clever potpourri of condiments and vegetables and fruits, these gardens give the family spices, food variety, and remedies.

Horticultural practices indicate types of marginal agricultural activities and feedback between agricultural strategies and garden production. By horticultural, we mean the home garden, usually on the house lot, as opposed to the milpa (maize field system), which is usually removed from the residence area and may be three to four miles (or more) from the home. A rich variety of botanical species (and folk species) may be seen in the typical garden. These plants are grown for both ornamentation and consumption. Since one major use of plants is ceremonial adornment of altars, growing one's own flowers gives one a ready supply, a beautiful yard, and an economic saving. Gardens also contain a variety of herbs for medicine and condiments. *Epazote, cilantro, yerba buena* are fairly standard, while up to fifty different herbs may be contained within one garden. The precise composition of a garden may vary, depending on the season and the success of the horticulturalist. Most gardens are hand-watered and cultivated.

The continuum between gardens and milpa may be just conceptual or physical. A garden will usually contain at least one maize plant, carefully or casually sown. Maize plants are allowed to grow where they germinate. They are not classed as undesirable and are not removed. If the yard is large, it may be cultivated as a small milpa, making its distinction from the larger milpa negligible. Kitchen gardens usually include some squash and beans which are well watered. *Chayote,* green vegetables, and green condiments are also favored to produce a supply of culinary ingredients close to the home.

In addition to cultivation of "garden crops" on a small scale, botanical experimentation can also be observed in horticultural activities. Women may go out to the fields, gather mature *chipil,* carefully save the seeds, and then sow them. This way they have a supply on hand for future use. Standley and Steyermark may be indicating this is the practice with *Crotalaria longirostrata,* another species of *chipil* which is found in the wild but also in the house gardens in Guatemala (Standley and Steyermark 1946). *Epazote* is sown in kitchen gardens; the entire plant is uprooted from its wild location, and then it is replanted. The leaves are frequently plucked, removing whole stems, but the plant soon regenerates with new shoots and leaves. *Yerba buena,* though it does not grow wild, is treated in exactly the same manner.

---

[4] African maize field systems, including the edible weeds within them, are extensively reviewed by Miracle (1966, 1967). Bennett and Zingg (1935) and Pennington (1963, 1969) list the edible plants consumed among the Tarahumara and Tepehuán in northern Mexico. It can be noted that there is much more potentially edible matter in the Zapotec field systems than is currently recognized as "edible" and eaten.

Young shrubs may be carried from their foothill habitats and replanted in gardens. *Dodonaea (jaras)* did not fare well under these attempts, but there were successful examples of *Menthus* sp. *(pitiona)* growing in the pueblo. Seeds of husk tomatoes, *Physalis* sp. *(miltomates)*, were saved and planted. In several cases, I observed young plants being uprooted from their field or border locations and carried home to be transplanted in gardens. Fruits and avocado trees also were planted from saved seeds and carefully nurtured. Other vegetables, fruits, and herbs (*manzanilla*, etc.) were planted from purchased seed sources, carefully watched, and the seeds saved for future generations of plants.

In summary, horticulture involves small-scale cultivation activities, and the kinds of keen observation, nurturing, and manipulation which help develop new seed sources for cultivated crops. There is conscious selection; seeds of particularly good tomatoes and the pits of sweet freestone peaches may be saved and sown. There is an attempt to expand the seasonality of green plants ("We save the *chipil* seeds to plant *for the time when there are none in the fields* so we will have greens to eat.") This could be how other agricultural species originally began to be used. People probably saved seeds to sow during times and in areas where the desired plants were not naturally available. There is experimentation—a few maize seeds of a non-local variety will be planted to see how they grow. Above all, the system is open—accepting vegetable seeds from a government teacher, maize seeds from a neighbor. Hence, one sees in the kitchen garden a keen awareness of how plants grow—where, when, and under what conditions—and an appreciation for their integration into the life of the home.[5] By examining the range of natural and domestic plant production, one can see how these cumulatively form one conceptual system of thinking about plant growth and availability. The total range of contexts in which plants are viewed and used illustrates the range of empirical knowledge available to individuals within the culture. The step to full agriculture, as indicated by the ethnographic and historical data, need not have been a large one.

---

[5] Though my interviews included the topic, "What is appropriate for a garden?", the general response on the home garden tour was "What is pleasing" or "What is useful and brings in money."

VI

AGRICULTURE

Cultivation, the deliberate propagation of plant species from seeds, has probably been practiced in the Mitla area since at least 6000–8000 B.C. Beginning with occupation of the dry caves (Flannery et al. 1970), there developed an agricultural tradition which substantially altered the environment. Agriculture was practiced in a continually changing social and biological environment. In each period, a particular system of land exploitation advanced the general goal of human survival.

PRECOLUMBIAN AGRICULTURAL PRACTICES

Mitla agriculture can be divided into three major periods: Precolumbian, colonial, and modern. Precolumbian agriculture can be reconstructed through archeological evidence and ethnohistorical documents written at the time of and shortly after the Conquest. The archeological evidence provides two sources of data: paleoethnobotanical specimens and general settlement pattern information. Botanical specimens, both micro-fossils (pollen) and macro-fossils (charred seeds, desiccated plant remains, charred wood) are good indicators of the kinds of plants that were available during particular prehistoric periods. Such data are useful for the reconstruction of the diet of the population, the local environment, and particularly, the local field systems. Analysis of settlement pattern data sets the empirical botanical data in the context of social life.

Archeological evidence for agriculture is available from several sites in the Valley of Oaxaca. There is evidence for agriculture during the Formative period (1500 B.C.-A.D. 100) at Huitzo (Flannery et al. 1970), San José Mogote (ibid.), and Fábrica San José (Drennan 1976) in the northern arm of the valley, and also from San Sebastián Abasolo (Flannery et al. 1970) and Santo Domingo Tomaltepec (Whalen n.d.) in the southeastern arm. On the basis of pollen samples taken from Guilá Naquitz Cave and from the site of Gheo-Shih, Schoenwetter believes that maize agriculture may have been practiced near Mitla as early as 4000-5000 B.C. (Schoenwetter 1974).

Crops

In the previous chapter, it was noted that agriculture not only introduced new cultigens but also new plant communities. In searching for the origins of agriculture, one can look for not only evidence of maize pollen and macro-fossils in early contexts but also examine pollen data for evidence of changing plant communities. Pollen collected in Formative village deposits showed higher percentages of Chenopod/Amaranth pollen than in earlier periods. Flannery and Schoenwetter (1970) originally wondered if the 40% Chenopod/Amaranth pollen figure indicated some change in climatic conditions to a cooler, moister environment. Through later experiments, Schoenwetter (personal communication) has discovered that Chenopod/Amaranth pollen shows higher frequencies on house floors in villages (both Formative and modern) than out in the countryside. Pollen evidence can also be supplemented by recovery of weed seeds from Formative archeological contexts.[1]

From site excavation reports, there is evidence that agriculture included maize, beans, squash, tree crops, and fibers. From the later periods, Classic and Postclassic in caves near Mitla (Monte

[1] Archeologists can recover weed seeds by screening with a .5 mm micromesh. Experiments with such mesh in the Mitla caves yielded grass seeds but no Cheno-Ams comparable to the Formative sites.

Albán IV-V), a form of Chapalote maize, large black twining beans, short bush beans, pumpkins, yellow chile peppers, white zapotes, avocados and cotton (Flannery et al. 1970) are all indicated. During Monte Albán V, there is also evidence for maguey roasting pits. All of these finds were recovered from Guilá Naquitz Cave and are from the period when Mitla was at its height as a ceremonial center for the valley.

Precolumbian Technology

The technology of Precolumbian agriculture was quite simple and caused a minimum of environmental disturbance. Plots were cleared of mesquite and other growth and then seeds were placed in holes excavated by a digging stick. To complete the maize field system and supply a full diet, beans and squash were probably sown along with maize. When not permanently fertile, plots were probably rested until the soil regenerated and supported a healthy growth of mesquite. No domestic animal fertilizer was available, though nightsoil or bat guano may have been used. There is no documentary evidence for the use of composting, ash, or other village debris for fertilizer. However, prior to the introduction of domestic animals, there would have been no economic value attached to maize stalks, which might have been mulched and put back into the soil.

In summary, the technology of early agriculture would have been simple and supplementary to gathering and early horticulture. It was probably similar to the milpa cultivation using a digging stick (coa), which will be described below. Environmentally, agriculture disrupted the natural succession of plants and introduced a complement of weed species where mesquite had dominated before. Agriculture would have created a multi-crop environment, exploited at different seasons for herbs and for grain. Agri-

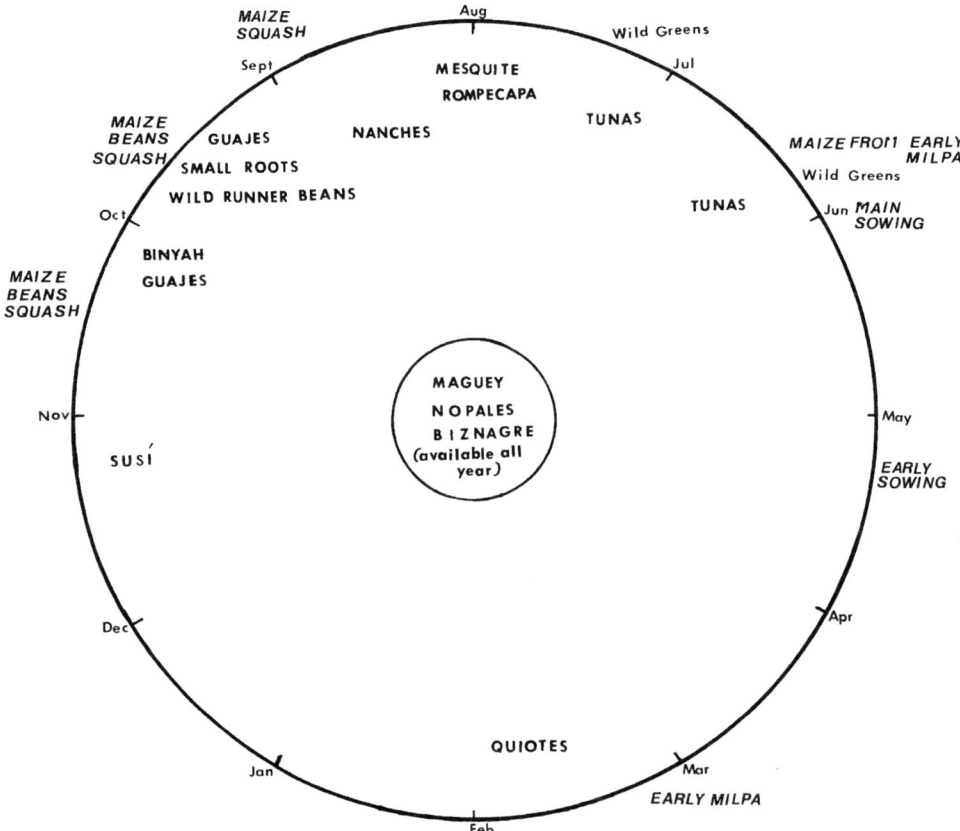

Fig. 23. Plant availability in combined agriculture and gathering.

culture would not have provided absolute security from famine. As shown by the ongoing archeological evidence of maguey exploitation and the reports of the Spanish chronicles, wild foods were still exploited.

AGRICULTURE DURING COLONIAL TIMES

With the introduction of the colonial system, the Indian population was forced to produce crops not only to sustain their own nobility but also to feed the growing urban population and monastic estates. In Oaxaca, in contrast to northern Mexico, Indian holdings remained relatively intact (see Chevalier 1963; Taylor 1972). Taylor suggests that this was because the Spanish were dependent on the Indians' food production and the Indians knew the law. The post-Conquest conditions of production suggest that a highly effective pre-Conquest productive organization was transferred directly to the new ruling elite.[2]

Indian holdings discouraged the development of large estates. Records show that estate holdings were economically unstable as was ownership. The Indians who were forced to work on projects such as the mines would sooner flee than serve, and the Spanish estates were constantly plagued by a shortage of labor. There was no economic security to be gained through farming, and in general, landholding produced downward economic mobility. The only large estates which were profitable were devoted to stock raising. Despite the difficulties of landholding, the creoles and mestizos conspired within the political structure to try to force land and labor abuses on the Indians. Much of the unprofitable private land eventually passed into the hands of the church. The monastery of Santo Domingo became the largest landholder in the valley, with seven estates, including Xaagá, totaling over 20,000 acres (Taylor 1972, passim).

Mitla's community boundaries did not go untouched in the early colonial period. Estates owned and managed by non-Indians were an alternative economic form which accompanied but did not replace Indian community agriculture. Between Mitla and Tlacolula, the tracts which are today called Don Pedrillo and Hacienda Tanivé were acquired in the sixteenth century. The former was originally a grazing site; the latter agricultural as well. Xaagá was at first primarily used for cattle and later for goats and horses. Mitla also lost land between the sixteenth and eighteenth centuries when Santa Catarina and San Miguel split away and became separate towns with their own lands. As a result of these changes in territory, Mitla was in frequent conflict with Spanish estates over borders and water rights (Taylor 1972:106-107).[3]

Within the remaining community lands, individual and town land holdings in the Mitla-Tlacolula arm of the valley were relatively large, due to infertility and aridity. Taylor estimates that each farmer commonly owned at least two plots of land, or 11-17 acres (5.6-8.5 acres per plot) (Taylor 1972:77).

---

[2]Immediately prior to the Conquest, the valley was under Aztec control. The production organization of the Aztec and Zapotec elites was probably utilized by the Spanish. Taylor estimates that the numbers of Nahua soldiers and laborers in Oaxaca during the sixteenth century may have increased to as many as 4000, but that the Aztec influence was considerably greater than their numbers (Taylor 1972:22-23).

[3]Taylor describes the territorial relations of Mitla: "Although owning sufficient lands, Mitla was the one large community of the eastern section of the Valley frequently in conflict with Spanish estates. In the eighteenth century the town was bordered on the east by the Hacienda Xaagá, on the north by the rancho el Fuerte, on the northwest by the sitio de Don Pedrillo, and on the southwest by the Hacienda Tanibé. The extremely bitter land disputes between Mitla and the Hacienda Xaagá started in the mid-sixteenth century over water rights; a ranching tract that later became part of the hacienda contained one of Mitla's two principal sources of water. A 1791 land map indicates that the dividing line drawn by Mitla and Tlacolula in 1553 [1549, according to the map] was still intact, although Don Pedrillo and del Fuerte had since been established on Mitla's side of the line. The map does not show Mitla's two sheep ranches, obtained by merced in 1565 and 1594, but it does show arable land and pastureland south and west of the town. By 1791 Mitla had lost the extensive community lands to the north described in the *Relación Geográfica* of 1581, owing not to Spanish encroachment but to the splitting away of Santa Catarina and San Miguel, which became separate towns with their own lands" (1972:106-107). In more recent times, claims to wooded lands are also a major source of contention between Mitla and surrounding political units.

Effects of Domestic Animals

Animals greatly changed the patterns of land use. First, the introduction of draft animals and the iron-tipped plough greatly changed the relationship of labor to land. Extensive tracts could be cleared and planted. Hand cultivation was probably relegated to marginal importance, as it is now. Plow agriculture, with quick, thorough cleaning and seeding of land, brought less productive lands under cultivation. Though the Indians continued the system of maize agriculture for their own consumption and tribute payments, the agricultural technology, the relationship of labor to land, and the total output were greatly changed. The new productive system had two additional byproducts. First, the increased use of land, combined with grazing, gradually degraded agricultural land. Second, the vegetative parts of maize and other plants assumed economic importance as fodder.

Domestic animals also affected Precolumbian patterns of land use. Marginal agricultural land became important for livestock grazing. Animal husbandry interfered with cultivation and water distribution rights in agriculture. Conflicts between communities and estates, as well as land erosion, were byproducts of stock raising.

In Mitla, animals as beasts of burden affected the economy. By 1580, The *Relaciones* report that members of the population engaged in trade, using pack-horses to take goods such as salt, chile, and other small items to other towns. Several 1576 documents mention that Teotitlán del Valle, Macuilxóchitl, Mitla, Tlacolula, and San José Teitipac had "many traders and merchants" (Taylor 1972:103-104). Thus, salt production and trade—supplementary or alternative incomes to agriculture—were affected by the introduction of pack animals. Mitla, given its location, was probably a center of tumpline trade in Precolumbian times. However, the quantities of goods and distances that they moved greatly increased after the introduction of domestic animals.

Introduced Crops

Spanish introductions also affected crop mix. By 1580, the *Relaciones* list quinces, oranges, wheat, garlic, onions, cabbage, turnips, radishes, lettuce, and grapes grown along with native zapotes and avocados. Maguey, distilled into mezcal, also received new prominence, superceding its original importance for pulque and for carbohydrates in the diet. Also, cochineal dye production became a major industry for the Valley of Oaxaca.[4]

Production by Indians was also affected by the schedules of church tithes. When it was decided in 1543 or 1544 that Indians would pay tithes on the three Spanish-introduced cash crops (wheat, silk, and livestock) the Indians stopped raising them.[5] Later, under the Dominicans, these distinctions were erased, as all crops introduced from Spain, as well as indigenous tribute crops, were tithed (Borah 1941).

Summary

The Spanish introduced new technology, new dietary items, and a new religion. In spite of the Indians maintaining their land intact, the quality of life changed. The new agricultural technology affected the fertility of the soil, patterns of crop rotation, and land fallowing. Grazing animals and husbandry reduced the amount of land available for cultivation.

Spanish fruits and vegetables, development of trade, and religion were probably less disruptive. They embellished patterns of horticulture, alternative incomes to agriculture, and belief systems which had existed previously. The plant classification systems easily accommodated new elements. European herbs were sown along with indigenous herbs in gardens and fields. At the crossroads of the mountains, the coast, and the

---

[4] Cochineal dye is relevant to agriculture in that the larvae producing the dark red dye are grown on *Opuntia* sp., and the industry provides another alternative income to agriculture.

[5] Originally, Indians were not subject to the tithes, since the Fathers thought this might interfere with the conversion process. In 1530, tributes to the Crown were raised to increase revenues without the introduction of tithes. The tithes of 1543 and 1544 were a compromise measure. Indians were also subject to tithes on crops raised on land leased or bought from Spaniards, and caciques were required to turn over one tenth of all tributes paid to them in the fashion of Spanish encomenderos (Borah 1941).

valley, Mitla had probably always been a center for trade. The volume and the variety of that trade was altered, as well as the facility with which goods could move between regions. However, Mitla was probably maintaining rather than beginning an economic role as a trade center.

Analyses of recent Indian agricultural beliefs and customs in Mitla show that there is still much that is "Indian" in Zapotec Catholicism. Some agricultural beliefs and customs probably began in Precolumbian times. Today the saints are still addressed at predictable times that correspond to sowing and harvest. Thus, the position of maize did not change with the introduction of new technology and crops. Rather, the form in which maize fertility was sought and thankfully received was translated into the idiom of the Catholic church and sacred calendar of saints' days. San Isidro became the saint responsible for agriculture, propitiated along with the local patron, San Pablo. In addition to blessing fields and first fruits, the priest might bless draft animals or, more recently, farm machinery.[6] In the event of a drought, the image of the Virgin might be taken out of the church and paraded through the town to see the crops suffering. In summary, Spanish introductions did not change the chief agricultural concerns of the people. Maize remained the crop par excellence for cultivation, diet, and cultural concern. However, new agricultural technology, along with husbandry, changed the composition of land. New crops and religious symbols could be accommodated within old patterns of sowing and worship, but the environment was inexorably altered.

CONTEMPORARY AGRICULTURE

Plants are a major topic of discussion and concern for people in Mitla, many of whom still wrest their living from the soil. During the month of June, when most milpas are planted, casual conversations are about the rains, the readiness of land, and individual household planting strategies. The diet in Mitla is mainly vegetarian. Maize, in the form of tortillas, is still the staple food, eaten with beans and other vegetable complements. Meat, fish or poultry are infrequent dietary elements in poorer households. Much of the maize still is grown locally. Beans and squash, the other two basic dietary items, are also cultivated on local lands.

The following sections will deal first with agricultural ecology. Agricultural plant classifications will be discussed in terms of both production and consumption. The conceptions of these plants, the understanding of their habits of growth, developmental stages, and distinctive varieties will be considered in the descriptions of the staple species: maize, beans and squash. Finally, agriculture will be briefly considered in relation to the total economy and the total culture. Distribution of knowledge about agricultural plants and opinions about their role in the lives of the people will form an integral part of the discussion.

As we will see in the following sections, the natural factors in agricultural production are land, climate, and plant populations; these are manipulated by human energy and technology to produce food. Since most farming in Mitla is rainfall dry farming, Zapotec farmers have the least control over water resources and the most control over their seed resources.

Land

Land is classified according to general and specific geographical locations, soil depth, color, and consistency. The most general contrast is between *tierra caliente* ("hot land") and *tierra fría* ("cold land"). "Hot lands" refer to Tehuantepec coast, and "cold lands" indicate the land in the Valley of Oaxaca. Mitla is called *tierra fría* to denote vegetation associated with temperate land, rather than tropical land. The terrain may also be contrasted with the land of the high mountains *(el cerro grande),* which has vegetation distinctive from the valley vegetation. Within the valley, *tierra de humedad* ("humid earth") or *tierra de jugo* ("juicy earth") may be

---

[6] In May, on the "day of the bulls" when plow teams are adorned with streamers and flowers and blessed by priests, the tractors in some communities are blessed also.

contrasted with *tierra seca* ("dry earth"), the dominant land type of Mitla.

Within Mitla, one can speak of several contrasting types of land. The land along the river, which is permanently humid, is glossed *tierra de humedad* in Spanish and *yuh kohp* in Zapotec; it contrasts with dry land, *tierra seca (yuh bidz)*. There is also description of land in terms of soil depth: *tierra gruesa* ("thick land," *yuh naL*) or *tierra delgada* ("thin land," *yuh lǎs*). These distinctions reflect soil quality. Thick land is referred to as *de primera,* "first class," land. Thin land, is *de segunda,* "second class," while the land in the low hills, not consistently farmed, is labeled *tercera,* "third class," land.[7] These designations of first, second, and third class lands are also nationally recognized. Other national designations are climate (hot, temperate, or cold) and quality (the assessment of which includes the availability of seasonal or irrigated water). If thick land is sufficiently moistened, its yields will be higher per hectare than thin land or mountain land. Land may also be described in terms of its soil color, e.g., "black" soil of first class thick land, or in terms of consistency e.g., "stony" hill land (Fig. 24).

The yield of first class land depends mainly on the availability of moisture during the growing season. Most water is supplied through natural rainfall, from the end of April through the beginning of November. The quantity of rainfall, as well as the timing, determine to a great extent the success of the agricultural cycle; ability to predict small fluctuations in rainfall and to act on these signs during the agricultural season help farmers to intensify the benefits and mitigate the hazards of rainfall patterns during the agricultural season.

[7]The Agrarian Law, drawn up by Zapata and his colleagues to accompany the Ayala Plan of 1911, was original, forceful, and specific. It was designed to ensure holdings for the common man and also to assure him access to water for irrigation by declaring water to be national property (Articles 32, 33, 34).

Also of interest for the present study are the limitations on the amounts of each of the different classes of land that may be held by an individual. Considered in the land evaluations were classifications based on climate (hot, temperate, and cold), quality (prime, secondary, and poor), and water (irrigated and seasonal) (Womack 1970:Appendix).

Water

The farmer takes into consideration the annual cycle of rainfall as well as differential ranifall on his various fields. For example, fields at the western extreme of Mitla, near the Matatlán crossroads, generally receive less rain and are ready to be planted later in the season than fields near the cemetery on the outskirts of the town proper. Thus, there is order to the timing and distribution of rainfall, which is noted by the farmer, who is experienced with evaluating annual rainfall and creating a successful agricultural strategy.

The farmer also takes into account the particular incidence of rainfall within any given year. The precise quantity and timing of the rainfall in a given area will, to a large degree, determine the time of planting in that particular terrain for a given year. Kirkby, who interviewed farmers about their rainfall perceptions and related planting strategies, found that most people in her sample group relied on the current year's rainfall up through June for their planting dates. People tended to plant earlier (with greater risk) in mountain and piedmont zones (Kirkby 1973:85-88). My data largely concur. The farmer, in setting out his fields, considers both the overall picture of the usual cycle of rains and also the micro-picture of the immediate moisture availability of his plots.

Rainfall is largely unpredictable. Experienced farmers sometimes talk about "signs" of rain, both as omens for the coming rainy season or as portents of immediate precipitation, but most of these are casual observations rather than firm beliefs. For example, one elderly farmer commented that cold weather extending into February boded ill for the coming rainy season. In contrast, "out of season" rain on January 29, the day of San Pablo, patron saint of Mitla, is supposed to be a good sign, presaging a season of abundant rain. Though it is related that one year, following torrential rains on San Pablo's Day, farmers immediately planted their fields and suffered complete crop failure as a result, such general seasonal observations usually have no direct bearing on subsequent cultivation strategies.

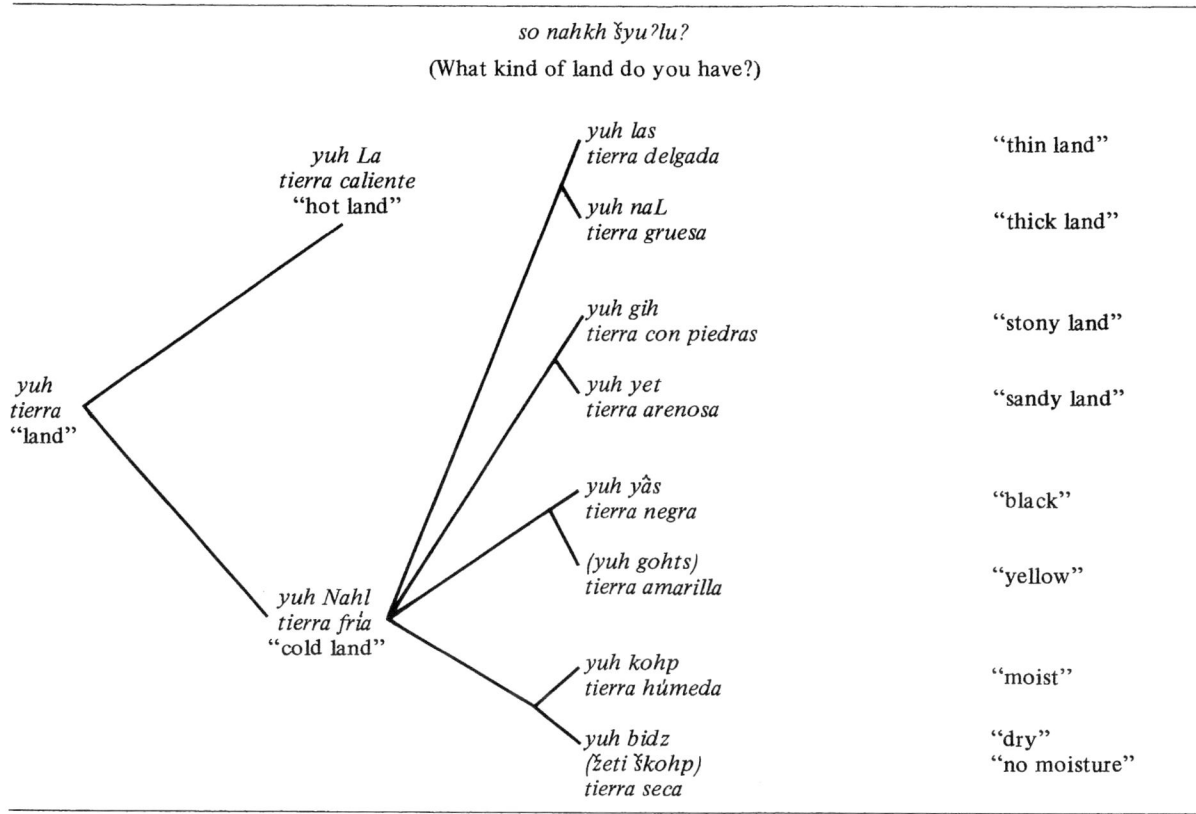

Fig. 24. Land types. Land may be generally categorized as "hot country" or "cold country." All Mitla terrains are "cold." They may be described according to dimensions of consistency, texture/composition, color, moisture. Moisture may be the criterion to describe humid land near the river versus other types of land or the humid (versus nonhumid) state of another kind of land, e.g. "thick land" with "humidity."

During the rainy season, remarks about signs of rain are made less casually and have much more meaning for agricultural behaviors. For example, rains beginning early in April are thought to denote a good rainy season, and planting may be carried out early. Early planting on land moistened by the first rains is a gamble that the rains will continue, ensuring that the seeds and young plants will not be eaten by birds and lizards. In June, when the majority of fields are planted, the skies are watched anxiously for signs of rain. An experienced farmer commented that a cock crowing in the morning was a sure sign that rain would fall, while the cock crowing in the evening was a sign that a week of rains had ceased.

The lunar cycle was also considered to be a good guide to the pattern of rains. If the moon was in the first quarter (or for some, within the first half), this was supposed to be the "time" of the rains. One woman thought that if the rains started during this critical first period of the month, they would continue for the duration of the month. Winds are also associated with rain but are a negative sign. If the skies are overcast in the morning but accompanied by winds, then there will probably not be rains later in the day. Thus, the pattern of rains is associated with idiosyncratic indicators such as the timing of the cock's crow, meteorological indicators such as the wind, and the time cycle indicator, the moon.

In addition to these environmental indicators, the religious calendar is also supposed to be a guide to the incidence of rains (Fig. 25). The weeks of San Antonio (ca. June 13) and San

---
CHRISTIAN REFERENCE FOR MAIN PLANTING SEASON

May 15 San Isidro Labrador, patron de los campesinos (early planting; blessing of animals and farm equipment)
June 13 San Antonio (week for planting)
June 18 El sagrado corazón de Jesús (farmers give thanks; ordinarily do not work)
June 24 San Juan (good week for planting)
June 28-30 San Pablo y San Pedro (Mitla pueblo fiestas; good week for planting)

Fig. 25. Agricultural calendar (source: Maino Galván Rivera, *Calendario para 1971*).

Juan (ca. June 24) are supposed to be rainy weeks. The influence of the saints is invoked during these weeks, and conversations about rain often make reference to the religious calendar. On Sunday, June 10, 1973, the *vísperos* of San Antonio, light rains were taken as a sign that the saint was already present in Mitla. Farmers predicted that there would be adequate rainfall on the coming Wednesday, the precise day of the saint's celebration. Planting dates are also expressed in terms of the timing according to the Catholic cycle of saints' days. Thus, one plants one's beanfield during "Carmen" (July 15).

In addition to natural rainfall, there are other means by which moisture may be introduced into fields. Natural means include floodwater farming along rivers. In both the ejido land of Tanivé and along the Río Mitla within the pueblo proper, farmers rely on the natural moisture of the river to irrigate the fields during the rainy season. When it is raining in the mountains above either area, the water may come down and flood the lands adjoining the river. Cultivation procedures may influence the effectiveness of this water in two ways. First, the sides of the fields must be kept clear of extensive vegetation, so that the water can enter. In Tanivé, farmers must clear out the *chamizo* and associated riverside vegetation every two or three years, or the river will not flood the adjacent field. Farmers may also have to construct some kind of drainage area, so that the water will not stand for long periods of time in the milpa, damaging the plants.

Farmers may also irrigate artificially. This requires access to either river water or to a well. Pumping is an expensive procedure (70 pesos per day), and use of someone else's well may cost even more (75 pesos).[8] Most farming on land away from the river floodplains is still dry farming, though some farmers, having lost crops due to drought, have in recent years invested in pumps and constructed wells.

Finally, the farmer may also affect the moisture in his field by careful cultivation of the soil. Through a preparation including two plowings, the soil may be better able to absorb and hold moisture. This is an indirect means by which a farmer may improve the quality of his land and potential yield.

Soil Fertility

In addition to classification of different kinds of land according to thickness, color, consistency, and location, there is limited consideration of soil fertility. Floodwaters entering a milpa along the river deposit both water and silt. With careful cultivation, this fertile floodplain may be double cropped.

In lands not in the floodplain, the problem of keeping nutrients on the land is difficult. Though most farmers mix leguminous plants with maize in their milpas, there is still danger of yields decreasing over time. One farmer dumps his manure and trash on his fields, each of which he cultivates once every two or three years. Since he owns cows and bulls, he deposits their manure. Animal manure is the most frequently-used nutrient material, and the most favored is that of goats. Farmers say that they do not favor chemical fertilizers since they are expensive, must be applied every year, and also "burn" the land or the crops if there is inadequate rainfall following application. Since rainfall is unpredictable in Mitla, chemical fertilizers are a risk. Plant manure is infrequently used since corn stalks and even larger dried herbs are of value as animal fodder. They are cut, tied, and removed from the land,

---
[8] All costs are in pesos ($.08 U.S. in 1975). The maize produced at these operating rates yielded a return of 1.60 to 1.80 pesos per kilo.

but their nutrients may be reintroduced eventually through animal wastes.

Since fertilizers are expensive, some farmers do not want to use them. Diminishing yields are often blamed on decreasing rainfall over the years, without reference to soil fertility. One farmer, owner of a plot for eleven years, commented on his poor returns from maize. The milpa is set out between rows of *maguey espadín,* which are also doing poorly. While he attributes the poor growth of the maguey to the numbers of weeds competing for the moisture and nutrients of the soil, he attributes the poor growth of the maize to inadequate soil moisture resulting from inadequate rainfall. In his eleven years of ownership, he has never applied chemical or animal fertilizer to his plot, but he never mentions soil exhaustion as a cause of poor yields. He does not consider letting the land lie fallow. It is difficult to say how widespread this lack of perception of soil exhaustion is.

Along with the physical soil-sunlight-water system in which the maize and other cultigens develop, the associated botanical and zoological populations must also be considered. In well cultivated, well watered terrain, "weed annuals," including *Amaranthus, Tithonia,* and *Sida* flourish. They compete for sunlight, nutrients, and moisture with the sown crops. In the cultivation strategy, weed control must also be considered to maximize yields of seed cultigens. The association of luxuriant weed growth with newly fertilized terrains is noted,[9] and additional clearings of such lands are necessary. Weeds are a product of the agricultural system which man produces and annually renews, and farmers are familiar from years of observation with the growing habits of weeds. The agricultural behavior associated with weeds will be discussed below.

In addition, there are plagues associated with individual cultivated species, which appear during particular kinds of agricultural seasons. For example, a maize worm strikes during extremely dry years. It is believed to come from the mountains, dropping like a fog or mist to the hills on the horizon. If the soil is cultivated and hilled when too moist, the borer enters the maize plants. Thus, agricultural behavior is integrally related to both the flora and fauna within a given field system.

Agricultural Strategies

In any given year, a farmer's agricultural strategy is a result of his perception of the general constraints provided by the annual seasonal cycle, the quality of his lands and seed mix, the particular constraints caused by moisture availability, his economic position, and the availability of resources in cash to perform necessary cultivation operations. Since maize farming is the most important activity, it will be discussed first and will be followed by a consideration of cropping apart from the maize field system.

CULTIVATION STRATEGY FOR MAIZE

As noted above, most plots of maize are sown in June, when the land is sufficiently moist. This is calculated so the plants can resist the effects of the *canicula.* If one planted earlier, maize would dry up in the green corn stage, and the ears would never fill out properly. In contrast, the June or early July planting means that the plants are small but will be resistant if drought occurs in mid-July. The plants will continue to grow with available water during the drought, and when the rain begins again, as it usually does the last week in August, the milpa will be in spikelet, and the elotes will begin to grow. This maize will be ready to harvest after Todos Santos.

People begin to check their land after the first heavy rains of the season. Thin land is wet after one or two heavy rainfalls. Thin land will yield well in a season of low rainfall, but the crop may be endangered by too much water. In contrast, thick land may take longer than thin land to get wet enough for planting, but it will hold the moisture longer and produce a greater yield in most years, given adequate rainfall.

---

[9] At the onset of the agricultural season, 1973, one milpa of land in the section called *yeo wih* had an abundant growth of *Amaranthus* spp. The abundance of the herb there, in contrast to the surrounding milpas, was attributed to the soil preparation, which included the application of goat manure.

Most farmers own at least two plots of land, generally with opposite characteristics.[10] One may be near the river, the other away from the river. One may be thick land, which will yield well in a season of sufficient rainfall, the other may be thin land, which will provide a crop in a season of marginal rainfall when first class land suffers. In the past, when most citizens were dependent to a great degree upon agricultural yields for a living, the diversity of holdings kept an individual household from losing all of its crops, except in extremely dry years.

With his eye on the calendar and on weather conditions in which it is favorable to plant maize (mainly June), the farmer examines the soil for signs of readiness. The soil is usually prepared at least once and cleaned of weeds (see Fig. 26). The soil must be wet, but not too wet. If the farmer sows land that is too dry, the birds and the lizards will eat the seed. If the soil is too wet, it is difficult to work the land, the plow sticks in the mud, the draft animals flounder, and the soil dries to a kind of crust through which the young maize plants find it difficult to penetrate. An additional problem of sowing when the land is too wet is weed growth. Existing weed growth is removed either immediately prior to or during the sowing. If the soil is wet, then the weeds get a head start on the maize.

In the old days, the people had the custom of planting and harvesting with the full moon. This custom no longer exists, and people plant on the basis of land/soil readiness and plowteam availability. A white, dry layer on top of the earth, with moisture a few centimeters beneath means the soil is ready. If there is a heavy soaking prior to planting, soil (depending on its thickness and consistency) may take another three days to dry to this point again. Thus, there is some anxiety about getting the services of a plow team and seedsman *(sembrador)* at the right moment of soil preparation. The *patrón* hiring a plow team is at the mercy of the schedule of the team's owner, who often has a number of requests for its services during the last weeks of June, when most people want to seed. Thus, in recent times, the decision of when to plant is determined not only by the signs of the soil but also by the schedules of the plowteams.

VARIETIES OF MAIZE

Seed selection is based principally on availability. Farmers try to save seed from their previous harvest to maintain the same seed stock in the same fields. Maize is classified by type and color. Type usually denotes origin, the most common distinction being *maíz criollo* (the local Valley of Oaxaca maize, grown in Mitla) and *maíz delgado,* the "thin," *híbrido* maize which comes from outside of the Valley of Oaxaca and is used in surrounding towns. The latter does not yield in Mitla. Though people show an eagerness to experiment by growing foreign seeds in gardens, including the seeds of government maize, "foreign" maize never forms ears.

Maize is further classified by color. Most of the maize grown and sold in Mitla is white or yellow. Though black and purple varieties of maize grow well in Mitla, the dark maize is said to be attacked more quickly by insects than white or yellow. Also, since people in Mitla do not have the custom of making and eating blue tortillas, there is no market value for blue maize. Red maize, though rare within Mitla, is highly valued. It is grown by a few farmers in Corral del Cerro. The large kernels of red maize may be saved for seed by those who grow or purchase the ears.

Maize is also distinguished by habits of growth. Four to five month varieties are planted most often. They yield full-sized stalks, six feet or taller in tassel with large ears. Alternatively,

---

[10]The median total holdings, usually distributed between two plots of land, was 10 almudes, or 2.5 hectares. This coincides nicely with Kirkby's median analytical figure, also 2.5 hectares. However, the figure is deceptive for two reasons. First, the amount of seed which a plot of land could take was not a fixed figure, but a judgment on the quality of the land, including its preparation. A lower alluvium field with thick soil and good drainage could be worked to increase its capacity from 8 to 10 almudes of maize seed. Second, according to the current landholding and agricultural working arrangements, the owners of plow teams often get half of the crop instead of cash payment. Though they are not the titular holders of the land, they still receive half its produce. Hence, not just the amount of land held, but also the state of the land and the economic arrangements for agricultural production must be considered.

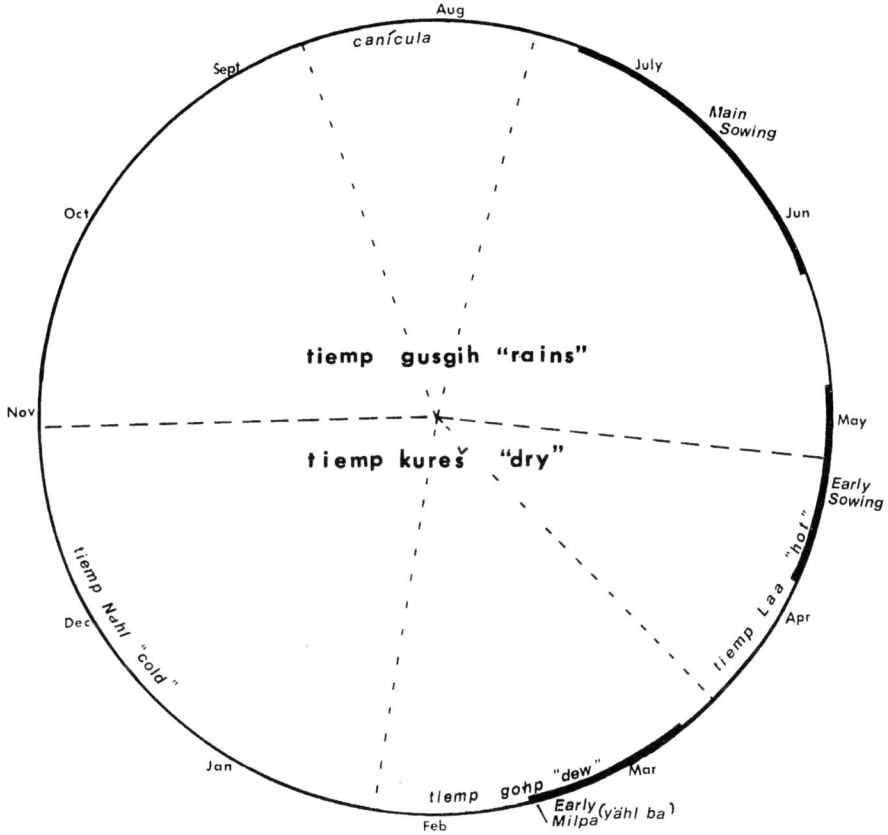

Fig. 26. Seasonal cycle of agriculture: sowings.

three to four month varieties of maize produce smaller ears and stalks. Their demand for moisture is smaller, and their growing time is shorter, so they may be preferred in marginal land. If one has good terrain, the greater economic advantage of the maize stalks for fodder make the larger, four to five month maize more desirable.

Stocks on hand are the chief source of seed maize. Since most maize grown in Mitla is white, white maize is perpetuated within the field systems. If the farmer owns all valley land, he may use the same seed stock (usually white maize) to plant all of his fields. In contrast, farmers with hillside plots may sow yellow maize, or a mixture of white and yellow maize there. Some farmers believe that yellow maize is hardier than white maize and also that certain varieties grow faster than white. One farmer working a second class field was planting both white and yellow maize in each furrow; he rationalized that if one variety did not grow, the other would. Another farmer purchased some yellow seed to sow his hillside plot, while the rest of his lands he sowed with white maize that he had stored from the previous year. Another who had planted four month white maize knew of three month yellow and three month black varieties, which he thought would give faster and perhaps greater yields, but he planted white because he did not have the other kinds of seed on hand. Thus, the convenience and cash savings of home seed stores are chief determinants of maintaining local seed stocks.

If one does not possess a stock of seeds, maize kernels from the centers of large kerneled ears will be sought first within Mitla, and then probably at the Sunday Tlacolula market. Seed maize is relatively expensive (8 pesos per almud in contrast with 5.25-5.50 pesos for ordinary maize) and often it is not readily available. Certain owners of stocks of seedcorn will sell only selectively within the pueblo, apparently hoarding their own stocks. People are generally reluctant to buy maize from outside Mitla, since it may not yield well in local terrains.[11]

SOWING MAIZE

In addition to his choice of seed, the farmer also has a choice of techniques for preparing and sowing his land. Though most land is still worked by a plow team pulling a steel tipped wooden plow, there are two tractors in Mitla, as well as additional tractors in surrounding towns. In the long run, tractors are not more costly than plow teams and may be economically more efficient. The total cost of team plowing, with a maximum of four preparations, may be as high as 180 pesos, compared to 150 or 160 pesos charged by the tractor owner. The latter, in one morning, can plow an entire hectare, overturning the soil to a greater depth which gives the soil better aeration. Thus, many farmers are turning to tractors for the initial preparation, if not for seeding. In the one instance of tractor sown land that I observed in 1973, the tractor covered four hectares in one morning, with eleven sembradores running behind him. This contrasts greatly with the plow man, who with one or two sembradores, covers only half a hectare per working day. Since land cultivation often requires the time of the landowner, the savings may be significant for all concerned. One drawback to the tractor is that it cannot enter all terrains, and therefore, cannot be considered for lands with no road access or with sharply sloping terrain.

There is no automatic sowing machine, so all seed is still sown by hand. On the average, each hectare takes four almudes of maize, along with some proportion of beans and squash. Thick, fertile, well watered land may take slightly more seed, while thin, hilly land may take slightly less, but four almudes per hectare is the figure by which terrains are measured.[12]

Young men or women, working as sembradores, follow behind the plow team or the tractor, dropping four to five seeds (3 maize, 1 bean, 1 squash; 4 maize, 1 squash, etc.) into each furrow, about two-thirds of a meter apart in thick land; two to four seeds slightly farther apart in thin land. Sembradores describe the work as very hard, since they have to kick the hill of the furrow back over the seed. Mainly men and boys do this work within Mitla, though women are often seen to be working in the mountain ranchos, such as Corral del Cerro and Xaagá, surrounding Mitla.

Two almudes or one half hectare are sown per day by the traditional plow method. All of the seed is supplied by the landowner, even in cases where the land is being sown *en medio* (for half shares) by someone else. In addition, the landowner supplies the major meal each day for the field laborers.

SUMMARY

Agriculture has an ancient history which has had certain effects on the environment and on the social network of Mitla. The farmer traditionally takes stock of land, moisture, seed, and technology, and works with them within one agricultural system. Though rainfall, floodwater, and soil seem to be ecological "givens," through judicious working of land, management of riverside terrains, irrigation, and introduction of fertilizers, the Mitla farmer is able to create a productive niche which produces not only sown crops, but also a variety of weed annuals and animals. Though ultimately, the farmer is still dependent on the seasonal rains, he can manipulate what water there is to produce results far different than those which would be produced at random in a natural system.

Looking for signs in the social and natural environment, the farmer takes account of the

---

[11] During 1973, many farmers found themselves without stocks of seed maize due to the crop failure of the year before. Several who had purchased seed in Tlacolula watched their milpas grow tall and green but fail to fertilize. They attributed their low crop yields to bad seed.

[12] Land is usually not measured in areal units but in terms of seed capacity.

AGRICULTURE

timing of rains, often expressed in terms of the ceremonial calendar and ritual, and the seasonal cycles of plants to produce a greater yield of food. Though some of the perceptions of factors affecting yields may be imperfect, such as the failure to add fertilizer to exhausted fields, there is still an intimate knowledge of the nature of agricultural systems, the relationships among the plant populations, and the relationships between plant populations and animal populations, which helps guide his agricultural strategies in particular ways.

IMPORTANT CULTIGENS: MAIZE, BEANS, SQUASH

Maize

STAGES OF GROWTH

Culturally, maize is the most important plant in Mitla. The attention devoted to milpa cultivation, the vocabulary used to describe the maize plants and fields in contrast to other cultivated and noncultivated plants, and the care with which maize and the natural factors affecting its growth are watched, set maize off from other classes of flora (see Fig. 27).

Maize begins to break through the soil eight to fifteen days after sowing. In Zapotec, the young milpa is called *yähl bäz*, "baby" or "small" milpa. If the milpa is sown at the optimal point of soil readiness, the young maize has a good head start on the weeds. For example, one milpa, early in the season, was sown on moist ground, followed by a dry spell, and the milpa was outstripping the herbs. Another was sown on moderately dry ground, but immediately after, the river flooded the land. This inundation was followed by a dry spell, and the weeds had a lag period behind the growth of the maize. Toward the end of the planting season, one farmer planted his terrain dry. Shortly afterwards, there were heavy rains, with the result that the weeds got the same good start as the maize. The farmer did not regret his decision, since the time to sow maize was quickly passing. In cases where heavy rainfall has followed immediately on the planting, the wet soil may cake and smother the nascent seedlings. In such cases, goats and sheep are sometimes introduced to soften the earth with their trodding, to facilitate germination.

Three to four weeks into the cultivation season, the milpa is cleaned and hilled. By this time, maize is about a meter in height, and the weed growth between the rows is substantial. The plow creates furrows, eliminating weed competitors and opening up the soil so that water can enter. The young plants are then firmly braced into small mounds of soil (*levantando*, "raising" or "hilling" milpa). The appearance of the fields at this stage depends to a great extent on the cleanness of the terrain when the seeds were planted and on the timing of the rains during

ZAPOTEC	SPANISH	STAGE	WEEKS AFTER PLANTING
yähl	*milpa*	"maize plant"	1-2
yähl bäz	*milpa chiquita*	"small maize plant"	3-4
a gohl huh yuh yähl	*diyerbar la milpa*	"weed the maize field"	6
žadz lahg	*en hoja ancha (señorita)*	"broad leaves" (ready to form spikelets)	
yuʔ doh	*espigando*	in "spikelet" stage	
akabeh yäični	*empieza hacer elotes*	"beginning to form green corn"	
yuʔ zäʔ	*elotes*	"green corn"	12
a gohl dzub yahl nu agudeh yuʔ zäʔni	*tiempo para quemar copal*	"season to burn the *copal*"	
yähl rats	*está amarillando*	"yellowing or ripening maize"	
anakni niz kayak niz	*mazorcas*	"ripe ears"	16

Fig. 27. Milpa stages (Zapotec, Spanish, English) with associated agricultural behavior.

planting. Once the maize has been in the soil a month, the farmer is usually anxious to remove the weed competition and set the plants upright so that they are more resistant to entering water.

In the beginning of July, farmers with plow teams divide their time between planting the last milpas and weeding the milpas sown near the end of May or the beginning of June. Since rainfall and soil conditions are the critical factors for both cleaning and planting, there is often some conflict in scheduling. Generally, the plow team owner, who is an experienced farmer, evaluates the conditions of the fields and either plants or weeds according to which land he believes is ready and which activity can less dangerously be postponed. If there is a shortage of fodder for his animals and the farmer needs cash, he may opt to work for hire in preference to giving immediate attention to his own fields.

Fields may be weeded once or twice, depending on the weed growth and the availability of plow teams. A farmer may simply plow between the rows and hire a workman to remove noxious weeds by hand uprooting or with a digging stick. On the other hand a farmer may carefully plow back and forth between the rows, weeding them well. If there is to be a second weeding, this must be done before the maize flowers. Once the maize is in spikelet, it must be left undisturbed for fifteen days since such activity would disturb the development of the green corn.

In Mitla Zapotec nomenclature, the month-old milpa is called *yähl lagz*. At this stage in the cultivation cycle, one says, *a gohl huh yuh yähl*, "It is time to clean the herbs from the milpa." By the time of the second cleaning, the maize plants have grown into the "broad leaf" stage (in Spanish, *ya mero en hoja ancho*), and are ready to spikelet. In Tehuantepec, farmers may say that their maize is "in maidenhood" *(en señorita)* when it is still in the broadleaf stage prior to flowering. Mitla farmers occasionally refer to their maize by this figure of speech.

Approximately fifteen days after the milpa has been cleaned, the plants may begin to flower. Zapotecs describe the spikelet stage as *yu? doh (espiga)*. On thin land, the spikelets are removed after the fertilization process, because the green corn will not fill out otherwise. This extra measure does not have to be taken on thick land, which supplies better nutritive and moisture support to the green corn.

While the green corn is growing, it may be necessary to weed again. Since the corn is high, this weeding is done by hand, with a digging stick or spade. Removing the weeds at this point has two functions. First, it removes competitors for the moisture and nutrients of the soil. Second, cleaning within the fields and around the edges removes nesting ground for rodents, which pillage the green corn.

During the stage of the forming and filling out of the *elote* ("green corn") there are certain dangers to avoid. The fields, if dry, must be irrigated or the harvest will be lost. If there is too much water on the fields, it must be pumped out, or the harvest will be lost. Thus, the rainfall should be adequate but not overly abundant.

As the elote forms, people watch the process with great concern and admiration. After the first signs of elote (in Zapotec *a yu? zä?*, "there are elotes"), one carefully observes that when the elote is fresh, the beard of the elote is wet, and the ear sticks to the leaf of the central plant. As the kernels of green corn fill out, the elote unsticks itself from the leaf, the beard appears dry, and the elote is formed. Each of these observations is carefully noted in the Zapotec discussion of the growth of maize. The duration of the process from elote inception to the beard drying out is approximately eight days.

Within a month after the fertilization of the milpa, the green corn should be in full kernel. The ripeness of the elotes is judged by feeling the green corn ears and ripping open a few of the elotes in the field. If the elotes are full, a party—sometimes the whole nuclear and extended family—goes out to the fields to pick some of the green corn. Many elotes are stripped and degrained. The kernels are ground and form the basis for either *atole de elotes* ("green corn gruel") or *tamales de elotes* ("green corn tamales"). Both delicacies are eaten only during the green corn season. With the boiling tamales are placed the remainder of the elotes, which are eaten as corn on the cob.

A household invites most of its relatives and neighbors to its green corn celebration. Stalks of the green corn flank the altar, and copal is burnt. Before eating the green corn, the head of the household may bless the gathering. In one celebration, the grandmother, feminine head of the household, blessed an assembly which included the three nuclear families that normally ate together in their kitchen, plus all of the other relatives who had been invited in passing.

In Zapotec, the time when the elotes are full, *yuʔ zäʔ*, is also called "time to burn the copal," *a gohl dzub yahl nu*. Thus, the religious behavior associated with this stage in the maize cycle becomes an alternative linguistic reference used to describe the state of one's milpa. The green corn celebration is of great traditional value and brings families together, both men and women, to pick the green corn, prepare the delicacies in a common kitchen, and eat until bursting of the first fruits of the milpa.[13]

Following the elote stage, the maize begins to ripen and dry, in Zapotec *kayak niz*. The ripening maize (in Spanish, *mazorca*) is also described as "yellowing." The kernels within the ears (in Zapotec, *niz*) dry out, as the vegetative parts of the plant also begin to dry. Depending on the timing of the rains, and the subsequent timing within the agricultural season, milpas will be ready to harvest anywhere from the end of August (April-to-May-sown milpas) to the first two weeks of November (June-to-early-July-sown milpas).

Harvesting is a significant expense for the household. One must pay workmen, provide the cart or truck to bring the maize back to the house, and furnish food for the workmen during the day. Many families are forced to sell livestock at this time, to pay cash for the harvesting.

Maize is picked in a traditional manner, with each workman running through one furrow at a time, with a basket on his back. He cuts or pulls the ears off of each plant as he passes and tosses them over his shoulder into the basket. If there has been a good harvest, this is backbreaking work, as the basket is weighted down with maize at the end of each furrow.

A woman, usually the field owner's wife, is in charge of preparing refreshments for the work crew. Before going out, she has supplied the workers with their *almuerzo*. In the field, around 10 or 11, she supplies a beverage, usually *pozole* or *tejate*, which has a maize base, and at midday or early afternoon, she supplies a major meal, usually with meat, sometimes with eggs. In addition to supplying the food for the group, she also repicks behind the workmen. The custom of repicking, gleaning the leavings of the field, exists in Oaxaca as in many other parts of the world. Usually, the women who are repicking are invited by the patron of the field; others must ask permission to glean. Women may also help to pick the squash and green beans during the harvest day. Once the harvest day is over, the woman returns home to serve the men coffee and bread, with additional food if they are hungry. In the afternoon, the men are given mezcal, to relieve the physical strain of the work, and bring about rejoicing which accompanies the harvest.

During the harvest, it is possible to see the botanical results of various cultivation strategies. If the milpa has not been carefully weeded in the later stages of maize growth, there will be dense weed growth. *Bidens pilosa, Tithonia repens,* and *Amaranthus hybridus* will all be 1.5-2.0 meters in height, in flower or seed stages, in direct competition with the maize. If the farmer is interested in maximizing fodder, rather than maize yields, and if he has worked an extensive number of fields during the season, this may have affected his decision to be less than conscientious about removing the herbal growth from around the maize plants. People without plow teams, who have someone else sow *en medio* on their terrain, sometimes complain that the plow team owner is more interested in fodder for his animals than cleaning the fields to favor the maize.

---

[13]One man explained that the old custom was to go out on the first Sunday in October (Sunday of *Rosarios*) with a cart and a group of people to pick elotes. The whole company returned home, and a pot of atole was made, which was sent to neighbors and served to relatives and friends. Then all those present helped to make *tamales de elotes*. One placed *atole* and *tamales* on the altar, flanked the altar with all of the *zacate* and *elotes* from some of the maize plants, and then one burned *copal*.

Thus, maize yields may be slightly reduced by the priorities of the cultivator.

A NOTE ON FIELD MIXES

It is possible to see great variations in the incidence and variety of particular botanical species other than maize within the field systems. Some farmers plant mainly maize, while others liberally mix their seed with beans and squash. Again, part of the rationale for the particular mix is the seed on hand.

Weed species also show great local variations. For example, very little *Anoda* and *Galinsoga* are found in Mitla, while these species are plentiful in the ejido lands of Tanivé and Don Pedrillo. Similarly, *Crotalaria pumila* is found frequently in the milpas sown alongside rows of maguey on the northeast side of the pueblo, but less frequently in other locations. Since these three genera, and particularly *Crotalaria pumila,* are occasionally sought after as food, their location in particular fields is noted. An efficient woman keeps herself well informed of the whereabouts of particular classes of herbs.

Farmers attribute the general incidence of weeds to cultivation strategy—how well the land has been worked—but they attribute the particular incidence of weed species to the presence or absence of seed stocks. For example, one field in Tanivé was almost devoid of *Amaranthus hybridus,* a common weed species throughout the local milpas of Mitla. The farmer explained that there was no *quintonil* here because there were no seeds. Similarly, the absence of *Crotalaria pilosa* in fields on the west side of the pueblo is attributed to lack of seeds. In addition, people associate the successful *Crotalaria* community with the maguey sown on the northeastern side of the pueblo. Not only are there seeds there, but the *chipiles* can develop because the spines of the maguey keep the animals from eating all of the plants. Thus, *chipil* is protected within this particular field system.

FACTORS AFFECTING MAIZE YIELDS

As they survey the harvest, farmers have the opportunity to evaluate factors which have produced or limited the yields, and reassess the interrelationships of the factors for the future. Though the farmer has no control over rainfall, he can isolate those points in his strategy which may have increased the dangers wrought by the natural cycle. For example, one milpa suffered drought when it should have been forming green corn. The field's owner resolved never again to lose the harvest for lack of water at the critical time and invested time, labor, and a certain amount of cash in the construction of a well for the following season.

Another woman, noting that many of the milpa plants had been bitten by worms, attributed the attack to the timing of the field weeding. The plow team had entered when the soil was very wet, and as a result, the soil had dried to a consistency favoring the insect plague. If there had been rains following the drying of the soil, this would have removed most of the effects of the plowing/plague relationship, but instead, there was dry weather.

Farmers may also assess the quality of their seed and plan changes for the following year. For example, one field, sown with seed purchased in Tlacolula, had grown, but had not flowered during August, (*encañando y engañando,*" "growing [tall] into cane and deceiving" according to the local Spanish expression). Only one milpa in three was fertile. Part of the blame was attributed to the timing of the rains. However, the poor outcome was ascribed to the combination of the varieties of seed planted in this particular soil/ moisture matrix.

At the time of the harvest, the farmer may also decide to fertilize his fields in the coming year to increase yields. Since the initial preparation of terrains can also take place in the fall, he can begin to plan for the following year. Also, he arranges for the distribution of the non-food part of the maize plant. Zacate or fodder, as mentioned above, is a commodity of great economic value, particularly in seasons of low vegetative maize yields. One farmer, reckoning his profits, estimated the returns on his zacate to be in excess of 2000 pesos and considered the returns on the *totomostle* (Hispanicized Nahuatl for "green maize sheaths") and food grain as profits above and beyond the major source of revenue, the zacate.

In summary, the milpa has a central place in the agricultural life of Mitla. Through the agricultural cycle, one recognizes certain signs in the growth of maize and performs particular acts of a technical or religious nature in accordance with those signs. Through agricultural practice and observation, one learns to recognize certain key associations between the natural elements and the biological populations existing within the milpa field system.

Beans

Most beans (Sp. *frijoles,* Zap. *bisya*) sown in Mitla are black (Sp. *negro,* Zap. *yǎs*). They are divided into categories of "thin" (Sp. *delgado,* Zap. *lǎs*) or "large" (Sp. *grueso,* Zap. *roʔ*). In addition, certain varietal names are applied to particular types of seed, e.g., *bisya gu, bisya pelón.* These are "thin" also. Few people sow white beans, but a variety of other colors, ranging from yellow to speckled or bright red may be sown.[14]

Beans, like maize, have their predicted season. Large beans (from the milpa) will never flower until July, no matter when planted. They are not sown in the early milpas of February since they only produce vegetative parts. Even if sown in May, they will not flower until July, and the beans will not ripen until November. These "large beans" may be planted along with maize and squash seeds when one sows the milpa. *Bisya gu* may be planted when weeding the milpa. If beans are sown in milpa fields without maize, these are also called *bisya gu.* One wise farmer commented that if one saw beans growing in June or July, they were surely *bisya gu.*

Bisya lǎs, "thin beans," are sown separately from the maize also. In contrast to the other beans and maize, which are sown in furrows, thin beans are sown throughout a plot. The farmer

[14]The genetics of these varieties may not be well understood, since more than once I was shown a number of different shapes and colors of beans which had resulted from sowing just black and *bayo* ("buff") seeds. The farmers were mildly inquisitive but mainly amused by the unexpected variety.

then works back and forth across the field in crisscross fashion covering the bean seeds. Thin beans may be sown during July and the first part of August. They do not need much care and sometimes are not weeded. Mountain land is considered excellent bean land, as are stony soils. However, yields are inconsistent. Bean land is reported to yield well one or two years in succession, after which the crop usually fails. One local explanation for the delicacy of beans and bean land are species-specific insect plagues.[15]

Beans are described by a particular set of stage name descriptions (Fig. 28). When "small," the plants are called *bäz,* as are other herbs and maize. The next noted stages are "flowering," "small beans" and finally, "good to pull up." Though some beans are picked while tender to be sold as green beans, most are left to ripen and dry in the fields. During the ripening, they must be carefully watched. If they are very ripe, they should be harvested in the morning to prevent them from splitting open.

Squash

Squash (Sp. *calabaza;* Zap. *giht*) are rarely sown apart from the milpa except in home gardens. Economically, they are important for both the green squashes, which they produce throughout the summer, and for the flesh and seeds of the mature specimen. There are several varieties of squash. Only *giht gec* has "edible"

ZAPOTEC	SPANISH	ENGLISH
bisya	*frijoles*	"beans"
bisya bäz	*frijoles chiquitos*	"small"
akabeh gi	*todos floriando*	"all in flower"
akaˆkah bisya bǎz	*ejotes chiquitos*	"small beans"
a gol giliayač bisya	*bueno para arrancar*	"good to pick"
teh žahn yak bisya	*una mata de frijol*	"a bean bush"
bisya yaʔ	*ejote*	"young bean"
		"green bean"
bisya bihdz	*frijol seco*	"dry bean"

Fig. 28. Beans: descriptive stage names.

[15]*Bisya lǎs* suffer from an insect called *mahn škäʔ*, described as "round like a ball, with yellow and reddish colorings, and having lots of legs."

guías ("tendrils"). Of the others, the tender squashes or the mature squashes may be eaten (but not the tips, flowers, and leaves.)

When describing squash (Fig. 29), one may refer to the stage of growth of the leaves. *A yuʔ lo kʷan yaʔ* means that the plant has leaves that are ready to cut and eat. Cutting of guías and tips of the squash plant is believed to result in the appearance of *calabacitas* in the very near future and to be good for the growth of the plant. The flowers of the squash *(gi kʷan yaʔ)* and the green squash (*giht bäz* or *giht řen*, "tender") are also cut and stewed with the leaves. Since squash leaves are a very important dish in the local diet, one can often see women in their milpas, cutting the fresh greens for dinner. From late July through the harvest, squash leaves are usually available in field systems, while the plants sown in gardens yield squash during most of the year.

When choosing green squash, one distinguishes between "tender" or "baby" squash and "riper" squash *(aguyahlni)*. The distinction between baby, tender fruits or plants and older, riper fruits or plants, is the same as that used to distinguish the growth stages of noncultivated plants. Finally, the very mature squash are harvested along with the ears of maize in the milpa. The first fruits for cooking *(giht rseʔ)* are usually cut into pieces and boiled in an *olla* ("pot") with *panela* ("brown sugar"). During the rest of the year, the squashes will be cut open and the seeds *(bedz giht)* removed, washed, and sun-dried for consumption. If the flesh has not dried within the thick skin of the squash, it may be prepared with panela and eaten as a sweet.

From the local viewpoint, the most valuable part of the squash plant is the seeds. There is a story about Mitla farmers who had a bumper crop of squash in their milpa in Tanivé. Since they could not transport all of those squashes to Mitla without hiring more workmen and carts, they offered them as a gift to the local people. The local people, who did not want to cart the heavy squashes back to their homes either, simply smashed open the fruits and scraped out the seeds, which they carried home for consumption. As the story goes, the Mitla farmers followed the

ZAPOTEC	SPANISH	ENGLISH
kʷan yaʔ (*a yuʔ lo kʷan yaʔ?*)	*guías* (*hay guías*)	"squash leaves"
giht bäz (=*giht řen*)	*calabacita*	"small squash," "tender"
aguyahlni	*maduro*	"mature," "ripe"
giht řsyeʔ	*calabaza*	(first fruits to cook as ripe mature squash)
PARTS OF THE SQUASH PLANT		
yahg kʷan yaʔ	(*la planta*)	"squash plant"
kʷan yaʔ	*guías*	"squash leaves" (edible)
gi kʷan yaʔ	*flor de calabaza*	"squash flowers" (edible)
giht	*calabaza*	"squash fruit" (edible)
bedz giht	*semillas*	"squash seeds" (edible)

Fig. 29. Squash: descriptive stage names.

local villagers' example in subsequent years! In addition, the green parts of the plant are still an important source of pot herbs, though most women only gather the leaves of plants within walking distance from their homes. Before the introduction of European greens, squash leaves may have been even more important in the diet. Older people still refer to guías as a staple of "the Indians'" diet.

OTHER CROPS

Garbanzos

In addition to the beans and squash ordinarily planted along with the maize in the milpa, garbanzos may also be introduced into the field system. Some farmers sow garbanzos when the milpa is hilled and cleaned, a month into its growth season. Others sow a garbanzo crop after the maize season. October is considered the best month to plant, so that the plant can withstand the occasional hailstorms and frosts of the cold season, November through February *(tiemp*

Nahl). These garbanzos are then ready to harvest in March, and the field can be prepared for the next milpa planting.

Wheat

Wheat is only occasionally planted, and then in the mountain plots. The timing of the crop overlaps with that of maize, so that one must forego maize land to plant wheat. Though Mitleños eat large quantities of bread, bakers purchase the flour from outside of Mitla. One only rarely hears of tortillas or atole of wheat; these staple foods are produced from maize. Thus, there is little wheat farming in the immediate vicinity.

Sunflowers

Sunflowers (Sp. *girasol,* Zap. *yäb*) are occasionally sown along with the milpa. They produce abundantly, and seeds can be saved from season to season. Unfortunately, there is little market for the seeds. Though women said that they began raising sunflowers in home gardens because they had heard that the seeds were valuable for their oil, they could find no place to market them. So far, people do not toast and eat sunflower seeds like squash seeds.

Maguey

In addition to the maize, beans, and squash planted within field systems, maguey may be sown as a long term investment. The major importance of maguey currently is as a cash crop. Two kinds of maguey are sown in Mitla: *dohb gih (maguey espadín)* and *dohb neph* (pulque maguey). Both are sown in surcos in the maize fields, and maize is usually planted between the rows. Both are long term crops, espadín maturing over eight years, pulque maguey over twelve. The former variety is purchased by the manufacturers of mezcal, a distilled liquor made from the juice of the roasted heart. Pulque maguey is used principally in the manufacture of pulque, though the heart may also serve for the manufacture of mezcal. Other uncultivated classes of maguey are exploited in the Mitla hills: the pencas (leaves) for fiber; the quiotes (inflorescence) for food. In addition, during marginal years such as 1915, the hearts were roasted as food. Maguey is carefully cared for. Seedlings are tended in seed beds, and then the baby plants are transplanted into furrows. The delicate care given the seedlings is comparable to the care given vegetables in seedbeds in most garden crop systems.

After transplanting in fields, maguey is carefully weeded during the rainy season since weed competitors sap the moisture and nutrients from the soil and can adversely affect the growth of the maguey. When the maguey is mature, it sends up an inflorescence as do the wild varieties. As with the wild varieties, the quiote is cut off to concentrate the energy of the mature plant in the underground heart, which is now the valuable part.

Though we do not know when maguey began to be cultivated, it is of interest to analyze current practices. The relationships between weed competitors and the growth of maguey are carefully noted and the effects of competition seen. People know that it is necessary to clean out the weeds between the maguey rows to avoid a diminished crop. People also notice the interrelationships between milpa and maguey. One man pointed to two adjacent fields, neither of which had been fertilized. The maize in one was small and yellow, the maize in the other larger and greener. He said that both fields had been sown with the same seed, but that the rows of maguey, interspersed with the milpa rows, sucked nutrients from the soil and harmed the milpa. Another man attributed the poor performance of his milpa to the fact that the field had not been fertilized since the removal of the mature maguey the previous year. Thus, in cultivating maguey, the interrelationships of the field system and the energy relationships of the different plants are noted and interpreted. Strategies to assure maximum yield, such as weeding the maguey each rainy season and resting or refortifying land on which maguey has grown, are considered.

Maguey is of interest because it is a plant that

began to be exploited extensively when wild and that has been cultivated with new interest in post-Hispanic times. The parts of the plant—quiote, pencas, and heart—are still labeled the same and may be treated the same, but the plant has achieved new importance. The heart is now a commercial crop rather than a starvation food, but the plant life cycle remains unchanged. People still pursue quiotes for food as in pre-Hispanic times.

The use of pulque maguey has also changed since the Conquest. It is also used for mezcal. The blue pencas, which give this variety the alternate name, *maguey azul,* are also used to shelter roasting meat in sheep and goat barbecues.

The economic botany of maguey, then, has changed since the Conquest, and the genus *Agave* has become a cultigen of extreme importance as a cash crop and as a long term investment. Though in pre-Hispanic times maguey was undoubtedly very important, particularly in marginal agricultural zones as a source of pulque, today there is a premium on mezcal manufacture.

In its relationship to maize and to the total economy, maguey plays a role similar to that of domestic animals. In Mitla, pigs, for example, are kept as investments which can be sold for cash at some critical time in the future. Piglets are purchased, fattened on maize, *salvado* (a prepared, powdered feed mixed with water), and slops. If one has mazorcas on hand, the only real expense is prepared feed, since the slops and labor are available in the household. In this manner, maize is converted into animal protein, which is sold for cash.

Maguey, too, is a long-term investment, and at the end of the growth cycle, one can get a lump sum return for the product of the field. Though the returns are less striking and strung out over a longer period of years than the returns from animal husbandry, investment in maguey can be "like a pig." Both consume potential food for humans: the pigs directly by eating maize which people could eat, the maguey indirectly by reducing yields on land which could produce food for humans.

In summary, the place of maguey in the agricultural system has shown two major changes since the Spanish Conquest. First, it has become a minor source of income because the juice of the roasted heart can be distilled into mezcal, a liquor not known in pre-Hispanic times. Concomitant with this change in function, maguey has come to be regarded as an investment which will be a future source of cash income. In spite of these changes, maguey is still classified traditionally according to its varieties, each of which has its function, parts, and life stages that are still recognized by the same signs and labels. Traditional use of the parts of maguey, such as the eating of the quiote, go on alongside the changed major function of the plant for mezcal manufacture. Thus, classification system, labels, and recognition of life stages go on unchanged for the uncultivated and cultivated varieties of maguey. The plant genus continues to persist within the botanical system, though its role in the economy has changed. Since its place in particular field systems may have long-run effects (in that it removes nutrients from the ground and hence causes permanent soil exhaustion) it may have direct implications for change in the field system.

Castor Beans

Castor beans (Sp. *grilla,* Zap. *baláp*) are also a garden or field crop of some commercial value. They are raised primarily for their seeds, which vary greatly in value.[16] Though castor beans in the past have been sown in fields and are still occasionally seen in milpas, most castor bean plants today are grown in home gardens. There are two recognized types: Sp. *colorado* (Zap. *šnyâ,* "red") and Sp. *blanco* (Zap. *nŏl,* "white") (For their classification, see Chapter 4).

Economically, the chief product of castor beans is their oil-producing seeds, used commercially in the preparation of certain medicinal and lamp oils. Locally, the plant's leaves are also exploited in several different remedies, for which

---

[16]Over a one week period, the price of castor beans at the Tlacolula Sunday market fluctuated from 3.5 to 6.0 pesos.

the coding of the varieties and the stage of leaf growth are extremely important. The growth characteristics of the castor bean plant are well noted by those who cultivate the seeds for sale and occasionally exploit the leaves for medicine. In addition, people know the growth habits of castor beans, which rob the soil of nutrients and which also make castor bean plants almost impossible to eliminate from land on which it has once been sown.

In addition to the major cultigens which enter into the maize field systems in Mitla, Mitleños exploit the noncultivated, harvested part of the field system—the milpa herbs and the cultivated and noncultivated plants harvested from gardens outside of the major agricultural areas.

DISTRIBUTION OF KNOWLEDGE ABOUT AGRICULTURE

In considering what people know about the agricultural systems within Mitla and how this knowledge is distributed throughout the population, one begins with the assumption that knowledge is patterned. A child begins with no knowledge of agriculture or the natural world. Gradually, through social channels, he or she develops a working knowledge of the agricultural technology, seasonal cycle, and products. Then, he or she is able to integrate the role of agriculture into that larger pattern which becomes loosely, the cultural world view.

Agricultural Knowledge Among Children

To investigate how knowledge about agriculture is developed in the minds and behavior of children, I interviewed a number of young people, under the age of 13 in their homes. In addition, I talked to children who were with their parents, in the course of my daily rounds to the fields. Knowledge about the relationshps between land and seed depended both on the exposure of the child to information on this agricultural topic and the interest of the child in the information. For example, the questions: "What are the different kinds of land?" and "What particular crops do you sow on each kind of land?" received a number of responses indicating total ignorance: "I do not know anything about land. We have never sown a milpa" (Girl, age 12). "There is thick land and thin land, and my father has both, but I do not know which plot is which. My father sows white maize on one class of land, and yellow maize on another, but I do not know where. I think he plants beans in a separate field, but I do not remember which kind" (Girl, age 12). "I do not know anything about land, but my mother does. We planted white maize in our mountain land; I do not know how to tell different kinds of land apart" (Boy, age 12). In the first instance, the girl has had no field experience and knows nothing about her plant environment except what she observes in her yard. In the second two cases, the children have been taught but have not cared to learn the informational signs of the environment or the mapping between soil types and seed types. The boy had actually aided his (single) mother in the fields. The girls had only participated in repicking activities, where they had accompanied adult women in providing meals and gleaning activities.

In Mitla, most agricultural activity is performed by males. Though women of the ranchos seed, clean and raise milpa, and generally work along with the men, Mitla women are less often seen in the fields doing the physical labor. As one young girl remarked, "Better we should hire a *mozo* ["workman"]." This may affect the kind of exposure young women currently have to knowledge about agriculture, though sexual division of labor and knowledge may have been less divided in older generations. Among my agricultural guides, I found at least two women as well informed as the most knowledgeable men. They stated quite simply that they loved the work of the fields more than other work and had indulgent husbands. The superior knowledge of these women probably is also a result of their general shrewdness.

For the young man, field experiences usually start at the age of 13 to 14. He begins as a sembrador, a seeder who follows the plow team with a bag of mixed maize, squash, and bean seeds. The work is hard and low paying, which is why many young men prefer other pursuits. The sembrador in 1973 earned 15 pesos, in contrast to 20 pesos which he would get in most other activities, at much less physical cost to himself. In addition, boys may work weeding and hilling milpa. Usually, they are recruited by a plow team owner, an experienced farmer who needs a helper and teaches the young men facts of agriculture while helping their fathers in the field. Now, the rarity of plow teams eliminates this traditional family source of information and instruction.

Before the age of 13, most boys are considered too young to help in the fields. One father, bringing his 11 and 8 year-olds, commented that they were too young to work, and besides, they had to attend school. The older boy helped his father weed and helped with the animals while the younger boy cut the sharp tips off the maguey with a scythe, but both were present for the agricultural field exposure rather than as great increments to agricultural labor.

At the age of 16, a boy may begin to learn how to control the plow and ox team. I never saw women performing this agricultural activity, though women did pasture bulls in the open fields and hills when they were not plowing. Women may occasionally help out in the weeding and raising milpa activities, particularly if there is a reluctance to hire an additional workman or a shortage of men willing to work. In one field, which had healthier *acahual* than maize given the wet soil of planting time, a woman spent two days with a machete chopping away at the weeds. Her neighbor's children accompanied her but did little work. The cost of such activity was high, since she worked ordinarily as an accomplished seamstress.

Women enter the fields at sowing and harvest times to deliver the meals for the workmen. Part of the wages of mozos is in their comidas. Giving the working men a hot meal rather than cold tacos in the middle of the day also gives the women a chance to get out to the countryside and fields. The women may use this opportunity to gather edible herbs such as *chipil* and *quintonil*, which only some men will bring home from their field cleaning activities, or they may gather medicinal herbs such as *billushit*. The only other opportunity women have to go to the field is to leave a meal, and they may combine the trip with gathering firewood.

As agricultural days involve some opportunity costs for men, the trip to bring a meal to the field usually involves some opportunity cost for women. In addition to the daily routine of cooking, cleaning, and washing, most women also have an income activity, such as tying the points of *rebozos*. To leave this activity for a day usually involves some financial hardship for the woman. The trip to leave the meal at the site of work does have real benefits, however. It brings the family together and reinforces the positive value of milpa. It gives order to the seasonal cycle of agricultural activities and relieves the drudgery of the daily routine of the woman in the home. In addition, it creates an ideal family learning situation for young people of both sexes. It is in these trips to the campo, often in the context of helping mothers, aunts, or grandmothers leave meals, that young girls are shown some of the facts of the fields and a great many other natural plants of which they had no prior knowledge. Thus, the milpa has a very important place in the socialization and learning processes for young people. They participate in a common work experience with the rest of their family. In the context of sharing food, they are shown the custom of hospitality. In brief, they learn through a combination of observation, verbal instruction, and participation in agricultural or gathering activities.

Differences in Adult Agricultural Practices

While participation in milpa activities at two or three times during the year helps teach the young people about the milpa and also helps gives them an appreciation of nature and agriculture in their society, there do exist definite differences of knowledge among adults. First, not all know equally well how to work their land. Men in their middle to late fifties, who had been working their plots all of their adult years, were not equally familiar with the effects of physical factors on the soil and milpa. For instance, one farmer tried to raise up his maize plants after they had been knocked down by a flood entering the field. Alarmed, he then consulted with the farmer whom he employed as his plowman. The latter told him to leave the plants alone; he would do more harm than good by tampering with them. If the plants were strong, they would raise themselves up. If they were not strong, tampering with them would be of no use.

Obviously, here was a recognized difference in knowledge between two farmers about the growth habits of maize, and the less knowledgeable consulted the "expert" farmer. At planting time, farmers with less developed senses of the signs of soil readiness for planting may ask more knowledgeable plowmen to evaluate the best time to plant.

Second, there are probably differences in farmers' awareness of the needs of milpa at particular times during its growth. This leads to differences in cultivation strategies and differences in yields beyond those caused by natural differences in soil/moisture/seed combinations.

For example, one experienced farmer cuts in an extra row between the maize plants shortly before the plants flower, to take maximum advantage of what water there is in a marginal season. This gives his field an extra advantage in a marginal year. Another farmer knows that to protect his crop from a drought during the elote stage, he must pump in water. Another farmer realizes that to protect his milpa during heavy rains, he must pump out water at a critical point, or the plants will yellow and die.

These are bits of practical knowledge—knowing how to recognize the environmental signs of the milpa system and being able to coordinate agricultural behavior to meet the demands set by those signs. Different agricultural abilities also affect planting strategies and yields. White maize is preferred among the population of Mitla. Though yellow maize may fare better in the hillside milpas and may fare equally well on the valley land, there is little effort among most farmers to sow yellow maize. Some do not know of the strategy of planting yellow maize, or yellow maize mixed with white, to ensure a better harvest in most years. For others, the preference for white maize as well as the possession of white seedcorn overrides practical reasons for planting an alternative variety.

In the effort directed toward weeding milpas, one can also notice variations. Some farmers invest the minimum of time and labor to weeding their fields. Milpas are weeded and hilled one month into the growing season, and afterwards, the weeds are left alone, to compete with the milpa. There may be several reasons for this. First, there may be a limited awareness of just how damaging the weeds are in terms of competition. Second, there may be no knowledge that luxurious weed growth encourages the nesting of rodents, which eat the elotes. On the other hand, there may be some knowledge that these factors interfere with the growth of the ears, but the knowledge does not produce a disturbance great enough to stimulate action. For example, one farmer sowing *en medio,* was quite content to let the weeds compete with the milpa, since he was getting only half of the maize grain anyway and could lump the weed growth with the zacate for his animals. Since he was farming a large number of plots, he felt that the effort required to perform an extra weeding was not worth a small increase in the number of ears to be harvested.

Similarly, farmers who divide their time between agriculture and domestic labor may decide that an extra day in the field would be better spent earning the secure returns of his other occupation. Thus, the field may go unworked for the extra day of domestic labor. Finally, there are those who in any case feel that an extra day of back-breaking labor will not yield added returns sufficient to warrant their straining themselves in the field. This last factor has affected the labor pool available for agricultural work in recent seasons. Since agricultural work is difficult and relatively low paying, the option to weave or sew is often taken. In sum, there is both differential knowledge and differential interest in the maize cycle and the yields of the agricultural system.

Given real differences in technical knowledge about agricultural processes and in conceptions of the importance of agricultural behaviors for providing one's income, it remains to be demonstrated how these differences in knowledge and attitudes arise within the population. It has been noted that learning about agriculture usually takes place in the field. Traditionally, boys have learned to plow and girls have learned to help out with auxiliary activities "en el campo." This is the traditional route to knowledge. Given their more central role in the procedures, the boys might be expected to have a more thorough working knowledge of the relationships between land and plants.

The Role of Women in Field Agriculture

Among adult agriculturalists some of the women knew as much and often more than the men. They could examine the conditions of their fields and determine the right moments for planting, cleaning, and harvesting. They could evaluate what factors were affecting the harvest adversely. If the maize plants were attacked by maize worms, for example, they could talk about the life cycle of the plague, its incidence in the particular year, and the timing of plowing on wet land, which had set up conditions favorable to the worm's attack.

These women were very familiar with the growth habits of squash and could explain how cutting the tendrils seemed to force the production of the small squashes. Examining their fields, they could identify *by name* all of the herbs named by the most knowledgeable of the men and would comment upon which herbs appeared to be recent introductions. One woman, going through her maize and beans, plucked an herb and commented that it seemed to have invaded only within the past three years; prior to that time she had never noticed it.

Women were also shrewdly aware of the economic hazards of maize farming in Mitla. They could recite the costs of sowing, weeding, and harvesting, as well as add into their accounts the costs of supplying food and mezcal for the laborers. In sum, some women were the equals of men in their command of technical information about agriculture and agricultural systems, in their comprehension of the life cycle and growing habits of maize and other cultigens, and in their knowledge of the qualities of seed and the advantages and costs of different agricultural strategies.

The attitudes of these women toward agriculture were more like those of men than of most women. They took pleasure in participating in agricultural production. One woman admitted that she could have spent her time in Mitla keeping a shop or a home, but she preferred the life "en el campo." Since her father had had extensive land holdings, she was familiar with the agricultural operations and enjoyed working out of doors. When she inherited a large portion of land at her father's death, she continued to farm, with the help of her husband. Holding lands along the river, they cleaned away the vegetation at the land's edge, so that the water could enter the fields, allowing them to harvest two crops a year. She could explain in great detail the life cycle of the milpa, as well as the system of double cropping. In brief, she was a most valuable teacher.

Another woman, old and partially lame, had inherited a large portion of land on the death of her husband, and continued to work on her own lands and his with the aid of *medieros*. Though she herself could not plow and only with difficulty could oversee the operations of her fields, she had a thorough command of the mechanics of agriculture, as well as an appreciation of differences in knowledge and commitment among those who now farmed. Commenting on the agricultural performances of her various medieros, she noted that one did not seem to have the agricultural acumen to wrest an optimal return from land in marginal years. Though she was too tactful to comment on the intellectual performance necessary in agriculture, she did attribute some of the problem of poor performance by one mediero to his lack of dedication to agriculture as opposed to other occupational pursuits. Describing the more successful of her medieros, she said that they were "pure *campesinos*." From the time they got up in the morning (6 a.m. or earlier), they had nothing but agriculture on their minds.

In a third case, the woman of the household always accompanied her husband into the fields, which were irrigated ejido land, due to his insistence and her enjoyment of the milpa. She was highly knowledgeable about the local relationships between sown plants and plants which invaded the agricultural soils. Though she considered herself not very knowledgeable about other herbs, she was familiar with the agricultural procedures after years of exposure. She not only brought meals to the fields, but also very efficiently helped in the harvest of beans and squash.

What is common to each of these three cases is a great enjoyment of the milpa and of agriculture and extensive exposure to the fields. An added factor affecting their exposure to the land might be childlessness. In each case, the woman was married but had no natural children. As seen in the discussion of gathering, young women may accompany their husbands to the fields and hills in search of herbs or in conjunction with agricultural tasks, but these activities may be curtailed once the woman is "tied down" with children. Though women continue to come to the fields with their children to bring comida, if their aid in cleaning the fields and other agricultural pursuits is not absolutely necessary, their energies will be expended mainly in the home. Though women may become more active in agriculture once their youngest children are mobile, they will have lost the continuity of exposure to particular lands, and this might affect their perceptions of particular agricultural strategies.

In addition, there are certain social attitudes conspiring against the women's full exposure to and participation in agricultural activities. One is the tacit or expressed idea of sexual division of labor in agriculture which currently exists in Mitla. The woman brings the food to the field and gleans but generally does not participate in the central agricultural work. This is both a social attitude and a reflection of real economic priorities. Currently, in addition to the chores of cleaning and keeping the household, the women also work, either sewing, tying the points of rebozos or retailing commercial textiles to tourists. The opportunity costs for women's presence in the fields can be high. Unless they enjoy agricultural work, they may appear in the fields only when they deliver food.

Moreover, there are emotional factors keeping women from working in the field. A man should be able to pay a mozo and maintain the existing division of labor in agriculture. Relationships between the sexes are also so structured that certain males may be *muy celoso* ("very jealous"), which further works to confine the young woman to the home, under the care of the other female relatives of the man. If he is economically well off, so as not to need her help, and in addition, jealous, but possesses a kin network which will oversee his wife, the young woman may find herself sheltered from field experience.

On the other hand, young women of any age, who have a part in making up the household budget, may be very much aware of the costs of agriculture in relation to current and projected income. Their economic activities and assessment of expenditures may play a part in determining whether to plant or not to plant in years when the household budget is barely meeting expenditures. They keep account of many of the hidden costs of agriculture, such as the numbers of fowl or pesos of meat bought in the preparation of meals for agricultural workers. Throughout the agricultural season, women take notice of the factors affecting agriculture, principally rainfall, even if they rarely enter the fields, since the unpredictable returns to agriculture will greatly affect the household budget and composition of the diet for the coming year.

In addition, women find it economically advantageous to be aware of the stages of growth of various milpas within walking distance. This is because the herbs which are stewed as greens or fed to animals are produced within the field systems at particular times. Following May and early June rains, there may be extensive growths of *quintoniles* in fields where the land has been well prepared but not yet sown. It is beneficial for the woman to know where the herbs are available, as well as the conditions of the soil, so that she may gather the green vegetables before the field is sown and they are removed. Once the agricultural season is in full operation, she will still find it profitable to be aware of lands sufficiently fertile and moist to produce herbs and of the stage of growth of the milpa, which will let her exploit the herbs before they are weeded out.

Through using the products of the field systems, women become more aware of the natural cycle of development of the fields and the probable areas of availability of economic products, both cultivated and noncultivated. They take a great interest in agriculture, both for its direct products, the maize, beans and squash, and its indirect products, such as herbs. The agricultural cycle also affects the organization of women's lives, as it is a certain series of interruptions scheduled throughout the year. Finally, agricultural yields are of concern to women as much as to men, since the women have the task of buying the goods which are not produced through subsistence agriculture. It is through women's auxiliary field activities and gathering that the agricultural cycle as a whole is integrated into the fabric of their social life and into their conception of the organization of the natural world.

Summary

The distribution of agricultural knowledge is ordered by age, sex, and occupation. Differences in knowledge between individuals are due to their exposure to and interest in agriculture. Curiosity and occupational commitment to agriculture usually result in a greater mastery of the agricultural factors.

CHANGING AGRICULTURAL CUSTOMS

Agricultural knowledge and behavior are changing. The changes involve both the use of technology and the allocation of time and interest to agriculture. Observations gathered over a period of four years in Mitla will be discussed first, followed by predictions of long-term change and explanations of change.

Technology

Though most farmers in Mitla today still employ the plow team, two alternatives exist. Either the farmer can sow his milpa with a coa, a human labor intensive process, or he can rent a tractor. Early milpas, sown in February and March along the riverside, are still cultivated by the digging stick method. Several workmen punch holes into which four or five maize seeds are dropped. The seeds are sown at sufficient depth to take advantage of the moisture available in the soil, due to its proximity to river's edge. The February sowing is usually harvested in June, after which the land is immediately cultivated by plow team, and another crop sown by early July. Only those without resources to hire a plow team still use the coa for the second, main crop. Since plow teams usually cannot approach the high milpas, because of the roughness of the terrain, these third class mountain lands are also sown with coa. The lands belong to the pueblo until they are cleared and worked. Then, by usufruct, the worker of the field can become its legal owner.

Working of third class land is a good example of how the old planting customs now include certain modern elements, while some of the basic agricultural strategies and organizational ideas have persisted unchanged. An area with natural thorn forest mountain vegetation is one type of third class land that is worked. Considerations in choosing it may be its accessibility to the main pueblo, estimates of its fertility, and the proximity of water to it. The land is prepared in the manner described below.

A group goes out to clear the land of vegetation. In the case I witnessed, a father, son, and a hired worker formed the work party. They brought along matches, a crow bar, a pick, one long handled hoe, and one short handled hoe. The female members of the household, the mother and her 11 year old daughter, accompanied the men and would prepare food. During the initial clearing and sowing, the family lived for three days in a temporary shelter on the milpa site, but subsequent journeys were for full days only. In each case, sufficient food was brought along, fires set at the field's edge, local fuel collected, and water carried from a nearby pool.

Land was first cleared by setting fire to the dense *espinas* ("thorny vegetation") and brush. Then the larger and smaller rocks were removed with hoes and crowbars. Low vegetation was chopped out with the hoes, loosening up the soil considerably. The work was extremely taxing, even with the aid of the metal tools. In the process of clearing the vegetation, several different tubers were unearthed. These were examined, tasted, and identified by the father, who taught the boys (and the anthropologist) to identify a few new plants. The women did not choose to participate in clearing but prepared meals, gathered flowers, and brought water.

Work had begun in the morning, and by late afternoon, the men were sowing maize and beans. In June, one almud of white maize was sown, together with some seeds of *bisya gu*. In mid-July, some yellow maize and 40 centavos of *bisya lǎs* were sown. The latter was broadcast, not placed in holes. While clearing and seeding, the father explained to the boys about the rainy season, about which they had little knowledge. By sowing first in June, and then in July, he calculated that the maize and beans would be able to last through the *canícula*, which would occur around July 22 and last until August 23, with the effects of the drought probably lingering another week. He also explained to the boys about the classes of maize and also about the growth habits of the two kinds of beans. Thus, the agricultural procedure itself was an important learning situation.

The two principal situations in which there is still coa agriculture, (sowing the early milpa [*yähl bah*] along the river floodplain and clearing and sowing third class mountain land) are both good examples of the combination of modern tools with traditional agricultural methods. The farmer must consider the cycle of seasonal rainfall and the life cycles of maize and beans, no matter what method of cultivation he uses.

Sowing an early milpa along the river is slightly different. Here, iron tools are employed, making the work easier. In the harvest season, the reaping is aided by either a truck or oxcart, further reducing the human labor required. Some farmers sowing early milpas also use pumps to irrigate. In this case, they are removing themselves from the direct exigencies of the natural system and temporarily creating an agricultural system freed to some degree from the limitations of natural rainfall, river flooding, and soil humidity retention. Even so, they must continue to recognize the signs of soil moisture and act correctly. Once one has irrigated the early field, it must be sown while the top of the soil still retains some humidity; otherwise, one can lose this crop.

There is no question that modern technology has relieved some of the natural constraints on agriculture, but the system of knowledge, by which the factors of agricultural signs are organized, persists no matter what the level of technology.

Water continues to be a major factor in dry farming. In very recent years, Mitleños have purchased pumps and constructed wells to remove some of the uncertainties of the agricultural cycle. If one has the money and a well, there is no longer any reason to plant one's field dry, since it can be irrigated to give the seeds the optimal start. Yet, one must still recognize the signs of soil readiness to reach that optimum point. Similarly, one must continue to recognize the critical points in the maize life cycle when water must be introduced in dry years or reduced in wet years, or no amount of technical imput will save a harvest.

Vehicles

Tractors are beginning to have a major influence on land preparation, labor and capital outlays. One tractor can plow a hectare of land and thoroughly aerate the soil in a morning, while a plow team may labor six days on the same amount of land. Given the estimated costs of agriculture for 1973 to 1974, it may be cheaper to hire a tractor than to hire a plow team. Moreover, the two operations are not strictly comparable since the tractor does a more thorough job.

Tractors may also revolutionize traditional methods of sowing. In one six-hour day, a three-disc tractor with 11 seedsmen can do the work that one plow team with one seedsman would have taken four days to complete (i.e., sow 8 almudes of maize).

In the harvest, though men still pick the maize, trucks usually carry it. Though this procedure has little direct bearing on field strategy, it does reduce the use of bull teams. In combination, tractors and trucks could reduce the work loads of draft animals in the future. This would not only change agricultural practices but also have great repercussions on the use of the products of the field systems. Removing animals from working the land is just one aspect of the change. Animals consume the products of the land, and if the number of animals owned were reduced, this might affect the use of zacate and herbs for fodder. Though beef and milk animals might consume the products of the fields, these animals are mainly pastured in the campo, and there might be some far-reaching change in the total maize cycle.

Planting

Planting customs are changing. Few people sow with the coa, since there is little time and reason to expend energy in labor intensive agriculture when other income is available. Few campesinos without an alternative source of income remain in Mitla, and those who do remain are not encouraging their sons to enter into a struggle with the soil.

In spite of the trend away from agriculture, land is continually sown, usually without lying fallow. This is due to the economic costs of maintaining plow teams. If one has animals and is forced to feed them, one will sow as much as possible, to use animal energy to produce more energy in the form of maize ears and zacate. Though at one time there may have been a natural cycle of fallowing land, not all farmers practice this now. If the fertility of the land is not constantly maintained through fertilizing with animal manure, yields will decrease as the land becomes exhausted.

The allocation of land to agriculture also continues to change. As the population of Mitla increases, land which once was planted is converted into house sites. This may have already reduced available land to such an extent that fallow periods have been reduced.

CHANGE IN ATTITUDES TOWARD AGRICULTURE

Most persons said that the trend toward abandoning agriculture as an occupation began approximately ten years ago. Some mentioned an illness of draft animals that killed them before they could be slaughtered for meat. When the animals died, for the most part, they were not replaced. Previously, almost every landowner possessed his own plow team; after the plague, most relied on hired plow teams. Others, also pinpointing a change about ten years ago, said that there had been an extremely marginal agricultural year. Though everyone had invested time, labor, and seed in planting, the rains did not come, and the crop was lost. After the poor returns of this harvest, many persons decided to invest their time in less risky endeavors, such as weaving and sewing. Thus, because of the diminishing returns, people began to remove investments from agriculture.

With the change in the agricultural system, people have come to have a different attitude toward the milpa and toward the rains. Some people see the changing occupational preferences and the new social attitudes of the young (who are said to have no respect for elders and no respect for the traditional religious values, including the milpa) combining to create a situation in which rain will continue to decrease in Mitla as a kind of divine decree. Elders, observing the changing times, both environmental and social, think the deterioration in both areas is related.

Explanations for change in the Mitla rainfall cycle show a curious mixture of folk, religious, practical, and modern thought. The low incidence of rain in Mitla, in contrast to the surrounding towns in the valley and in the mountains, is attributed to Mitla's "high" location.

According to folklore, Mitla is the center of the world, where the dead souls gather, and higher than surrounding pueblos. Because it is the highest spot, rains do not fall in Mitla.[17] Some juxtapose the traditional belief and explanation with the scientific observation that the mountains around Mitla block the rain. Folklore and the recognition of rainfall shadow effects meet in topographic explanations.

Some say that abandonment of traditional agriculture, family structure, respect for elders, etc. has led to "bad times." Experienced agriculturalists, who insist that the rainfall pattern has changed for the worse, are inclined to link their explanations to an avenging God. The times are bad because people are bad; they have no respect. The weaver who is trying to dry his shawls and the woman who wants to attract tourists to her retail business want sun. The different ideas about what constitutes "favorable" weather are said to have almost led to violence between farmers and retailers during the drought of 1972.[18] In sum, the religious argument linking behavior and God's rainfall takes into account social factors (respect of the young for the old), religious factors (respect for traditional views of world organization), and economic factors (changing occupations and desires for rain).

Other persons offer further scientific and apocalyptic explanations of diminishing rainfall. Some mention that extensive tree cutting in the hills around Mitla has reduced rainfall, for trees are believed to hold the clouds which bring rainwater. Since the demise of the hacienda system, there has been unlimited cutting of firewood, denuding the hills. Certainly, the recognition of linkages between deforestation and diminishing returns to agriculture is correct, though the precise cause and effect sequence may not be. Some also mention that cutting down trees has resulted in deterioration of land and soil in the hills.

Another man said that he believed atomic explosions had reduced rainfall. He had heard on the radio how atomic fallout "dirtied" the atmosphere, reducing the rain. He recalled that as a child, he had observed sufficient rainfall and planting by San Isidro (April 29),[19] but currently, rains were both later and scarcer. Memories of the past and scientific explanations of atomic fallout blend into an apocalyptic explanation: the end of the world must be coming as a result of both social evils and atomic explosions.

The variety of explanations about decreased rainfall and decreasing returns from agriculture illustrates the diversity of routes to knowledge. Folk beliefs are passed down from old to young within generations of family members. These traditional channels are still open, and children hear the traditional stories, even if they do not actively "believe" that Mitla is the center of the world and the highest spot of the surrounding countryside.[20] Mass media, particularly the radio, have continual effects on people's conceptions of the world. The national culture and the mass media create desires which cannot be met from the proceeds of subsistence agriculture. Thus, in addition to adding new "scientific" explanations to the thought of Mitleños, they also indirectly influence cultural attitudes toward agriculture.

A good gauge of the changing place of agriculture in the Mitla economy and world view are parents' plans for their children. Among those interviewed who could be considered full-time campesinos, not one thought the returns from

---

[17]Though some rain does not reach Mitla due to its height, neither do plagues, so it is said that height is an advantage as well as a disadvantage. However, this favorable aspect is rarely mentioned in discussing Mitla's place in the universe.

[18]During the height of the drought, the farmers wanted rain, but the retailers enjoyed the benefits of many tourists visiting the ruins on sunny days. One day in July, a woman selling at the ruins was heard to remark that she hoped it would not rain, since that would hurt her business. A farmer watching his mi'pas suffer was outraged at the remark, and an altercation ensued. Local informants reported that all of the people present joined the argument on one side or the other, and there was almost civil war in the pueblo. Though the report is probably exaggerated, there are basic conflicts over the weather.

[19]Elsie Clews Parsons (1936) also noted that most farmers planted in April, so observations about changing rainfall patterns may have some basis in fact.

[20]Elderly persons may know the folklore explanations but not believe them either. An 80 year old man, corrected me by saying that Mitla was *not* the center of the world, but someplace in Venezuela was. He had heard the fact on the radio.

agriculture were sufficient to encourage his son(s) to enter that occupation as a sole source of income. Agriculture may still be one means of livelihood, but it is no longer the only one. One plow team owner said that he was going to encourage one of his sons to be a mason, the other to be a baker, and his daughter to be a seamstress. He still cultivated land, but his immediate agricultural goal was to harvest enough maize and zacate to buy two pigs, which he would then fatten and sell, to buy his daughter a sewing machine. Thus, subsistence agriculture has changed along with the rest of the economy.

Though in traditional Mesoamerican economies the milpa is a place where a man finds his manhood (Kirkby 1973:53), in Mitla agriculture no longer is it a necessary religious and social value in the life of every individual. The milpa is still of value for its products; locally grown maize is still preferred to other maize, and it may still be economically feasible in most years to grow one's own subsistence crops.[21] The milpa is still the system which activates certain formal and informal channels of communication carrying ecological and social information. The agricultural cycle is still surrounded by religious ritual and is still one means of bringing together the family unit and learning about the natural world. In sum, in spite of the technical and environmental changes which have occurred in the agricultural and social systems, the agricultural pursuits continue to have importance for the world view and life of Mitleños.

[21] In 1974, landowners said they would sow their milpas in spite of the chance of low yields and the high costs of labor and technical energy, because one still had a chance of coming out ahead by growing one's own maize, due to the high price of purchasing this staple food.

VII

CONCLUSIONS AND PRACTICAL IMPLICATIONS

The preceding chapters have presented several different aspects of Mitla Zapotec plant knowledge, some of which can now be integrated with general ethnobotanical theory. Plants can be viewed as parts of ecosystems and parts of cultural systems. Plant taxa have multiple sets of attributes, which place them in systematic and functional categories.

Both systematic taxonomy and functional (e.g., medicinal plant) taxonomies are hierarchically structured. Mitla Zapotecs know plants by sight and by name. Not all nodes in the systematic taxonomy are labeled. These unlabeled nodes include both covert categories (Berlin, Breedlove, and Raven 1968) and unlabeled, lower level taxa. The latter can be discovered in the course of field trips and interviews with men and women. People can point to a plant without naming it, but assign it a place, along with other named generics and specifics, in functional taxonomies.

Many of the functional criteria used by Mitla Zapotecs to classify plants are somewhat foreign to the Western taxonomist. Rather than using a visual key to identify taxa, the Mitleño groups salient features in the identification procedure, i.e., he "chunks" information (Miller 1956). In addition, he uses chemical information processed through the senses of taste and smell as important parts of the identification procedure. Unfortunately, the bits of information used to assign plants places in functional taxonomies are difficult for the uninitiated to assimilate. For instance, terms like "hot" as opposed to "cold," "white dysentery reduction" versus "*empacho* reduction" are salient features of today's Mitleño medicinal plant taxonomy. When these symbolic categories that link plants to people cease to be understood, knowledge of the value of the plants will disappear. Likewise, if the functional taxonomies based on the folk illness category attributes dissolve, the meaning of medicinal plants will vanish. On the other hand, as new sets of symptoms are labeled and treated successfully by particular taxa, new meaning is added to a taxon, and new functional schemes (though not necessarily functional taxonomies) are created.

The Zapotec systematic taxonomy is inherently more stable than the functional taxonomy. Although items may be added or substracted from the content or juggled between different levels, the structure is sound. New garden herbs and flowers as well as new field grains and weeds can be added at the generic level without affecting the classification structure. Even if people learn fewer plants beyond the life form or generic levels, the conceptual categories should remain the same. As long as the plants as conceptual categories are part of the environment, they should persist as visual conceptual entities, even if their meaning—their roles in the ecosystem and cultural system—and their depth in the taxonomic nomenclature are reduced. In contrast, the deeper levels of the taxonomic nomenclature should easily provide slots for introduced plants, such as new maize varieties, since Zapotecs already distinguish maize on the basis of size and shape of grain and on the basis of color. Other characteristics of new maize, such as texture for tortillas, may add a new dimension to the systematic taxonomy of maize or merely may be added to descriptions.

Adjustment to sweeping changes in the ecosystem may be more disruptive to plant knowledge. In the chapters on gathering, horticulture, and agriculture, we saw that knowledge of the ecosystem is somewhat specialized according to sex, age, and occupation. Many wild plants are known only by older persons who have experienced famines or by younger persons who are marginal in the social structure, since now wild plants' edibility is experienced only by socio-economically marginal people or in marginal times. People who occasionally eat wild plants but do not admit eating them do so only under special circumstances—when they are "en el campo" and either hungry or thirsty. As food preferences turn away from wild foods, information about edible wild plants will be lost.

In addition, the relationship of the local population to the local ecosystem is changing. In lieu of great dependence on both cultivated and uncultivated zones in times of crop failure, Mitleños now are linked to the state economy. From 1972 to 1973 when Mitla suffered a great crop failure, people did not revert to gathering in the countryside as before but relied on the government, which sent in maize. Though the maize was not *criollo,* it did enable people to manufacture maize tortillas. In the past, the local population relied to some extent on purchasing maize grown nearby to supplment low stores of grain in bad years, and they supplemented their subsistence purchases with gathering outside of the field systems. Today, when few households rely entirely on agriculture for income or subsistence, people are dependent on the market mechanism and government redistribution. Some of the flexibility provided by relying on the total ecosystem has been lost, as people lose knowledge of the edible potential of the total environment. However, in the long run, they may be better off, since despite exploitation of a broad spectrum of resources, many people died in 1915, the "time of hunger," when there was not yet a concerned central state.

Modern technology and political, social, and economic programs affect people's knowledge of the local environment. In the chapter on agriculture, we saw that even with piecemeal additions of modern agricultural technology, farmers still have to have knowledge of the traditional agricultural factors. Tractors can plow the soil deeper and pump irrigation can extend or insure the agricultural season, but farmers still have to master the signs of soil fertility, soil/moisture readiness, and weed growth interference for a successful cultivation strategy. Fields are communities of plants, both cultigens and noncultigens, many of which have their place as both human and animal food.

New agricultural packages could alter this. Though the "Green Revolution" has not had an extensive impact on Mitla agriculture, it could transform existing field systems. The International Maize and Wheat Improvement Center (CIMMYT) has introduced not only new seeds but new cultivation strategies as well. The results of the Puebla Project implemented in 1967 to develop, field test, and refine a strategy for rapidly increasing maize yields under natural rainfall conditions, have implications for dry farming communities such as Mitla. The agricultural package given to Puebla farmers included maize seed, fertilizers, herbicides, and cultivation instructions. They followed the directions and increased their gross income in maize production by almost fifty percent (Díaz-Cisneros 1974:457). People used their additional income in maize to fatten farm animals and fowl, to improve their houses, and to add protein to their diet. Attitudes toward farming became more favorable, and people invested in fertilizer, grew garden crops, and dug wells for irrigating gardens and fields. Traditional agriculture and horticulture were transformed by the new agricultural technology. People wanted to return to the land not for the traditional reasons of "each man in his milpa" but for the potential financial gain which could be experienced.

The implications of such agricultural programs are great. First, the project created a monocrop maize system, since herbicides eliminated beans as well as all weeds. With new technology, the botanical populations and interactions of the local agricultural systems are transformed; the ecosystem is changed, and traditional knowledge about the environment no longer applies. In addition to the botanical changes, the traditional signs of soil fertility are also rendered irrelevant with chemical fertilizers. Second, the increased maize yield was used by the Puebla farmers mainly to fatten pigs and chickens. They expanded the trophic level of primary (nonhuman) energy consumer within their local energy system while expanding the role of animals as capital investments for their crops. People used the

CONCLUSIONS AND PRACTICAL APPLICATIONS

traditional energy recycling system to convert their increased crops into income. Third, people applied what they had learned in the new agricultural package to their garden crops with success.

As a total package, new seeds plus chemicals could transform Mitla agriculture. The soil and plant composition of the field system as well as the cycles of energy exchange could be altered. Maize now supplies both people and animals with food. The grain is fed to humans and pigs, the herbage to oxen. The oxen then supply the mechanical energy as well as manure for agriculture. With new technology, the roles of oxen and maize in the ecosystem would be permanently altered. With the introduction of plow agriculture and domestic animals, the Spanish changed the cycling of nutrients through the Precolumbian milpa system. New agricultural technology could again change these relationships among plants, people, animals, and land. So far, people have experimented with tractors, fertilizers, new seeds, and foods, but as a whole, they have maintained their traditional field systems and traditional diet. Both ecological and nutritional knowledge about plants would be affected by new agricultural practices which create a new monocrop ecosystem.

To the extent that traditional agriculture continues to be practiced, traditional plant knowledge will continue. Information about plants will be altered as dietary and medicinal preferences change, but the structure of the systematic taxonomy as well as many of the functional classifications will accommodate new information while some of the old is discarded. Only a radical change such as a complete agricultural package offers a clear alternative to the traditional Mitla Zapotec system of plant knowledge. Otherwise, the traditional system can continue to accommodate new information from botanical, animal, and mineral domains.

APPENDIX I

SYSTEMATICS

All plants listed below, with their collection identification numbers, were identified by Professor Rogers McVaugh of the University of Michigan Herbarium, with the aid of additional authorities where noted. Specimens are deposited at the University of Michigan Herbarium. Duplicate specimens were sent to the Herbario Nacional de Mexico, Mexico City.

The prefix 71 denotes collection date during the 1971 field season; 72 denotes the 1972 field season. All specimens are from San Pablo Mitla, except where otherwise noted.

PTERIDOPHYTA
  Selaginellaceae
    Selaginella pallescens (Presl) Spring 72/25.

SPERMATOPHYTA
  GYMNOSPERMAE
    Cupressaceae
      Juniperus sp. 71/205. (San Antonino Ocotlán).
    Pinaceae
      Pinus teocote Schlecht & Cham. 71/228.

ANGIOSPERMAE

DICOTYLEDONEAE

Acanthaceae
  Anisacanthus quadrifidus (Vahl) Standl. 72/112, 139.
  A. sp. 71/94, 218.
  Ruellia nudiflora (Engelm. & Gray) Urb. 71/116.
Aizoaceae
  Mollugo verticillata L. 71/181; 72/89.
  Trianthema portulacastrum L. 71/111. (Abasolo).
Amaranthaceae
  Alternanthera repens (L.) Kuntze 71/194; 72/50, 180.
  Amaranthus dubius Mart. 72/152a.
  A. hybridus L. 71/194, 201, 209b; 72/114, 147, 183, 208.
  A. powellii S. Wats. (?) 71/24 Possibly hybrid *A. hybridus* x *A. powellii;* 72/117a (Identifications E. L. McWilliams).
  Guilleminia densa (Willd.) Moq. 72/69.
Anacardiaceae
  Schinus molle L. 71/51.
Apiaceae
  Coriandrum sativum L. 71/18 (Abasolo).
  Foeniculum vulgare Mill. 71/186.
  Hydrocotyle ranunculoides L.f. 71/166.
Apocynaceae
  Plumeria rubra L. 71/129; 72/169.
  Thevetia thevetioides (H.B.K.) K. Schum. 71/191.

Asclepiadaceae
  Asclepias elata Benth. (?) 71/76.
  A. glaucescens H.B.K. 71/82.
  A. linaria Cav. 71/64, 69.
  A. oenotheroides Cham. & Schlecht. 71/161; 72/46.
  Marsdenia mexicana Decne. 71/105, 214; 72/39.
Asteraceae
  Artemisia sp. 72/79, 191.
  Baccharis pyramidata (Rob. & Greenm.) Rzedowski = *Haplopappus pyramidatus* (Rob. & Greenm.) Blake 71/220. (Rzedowski identification).
  Baccharis salicifolia (R. & P.) Pers. 71/84; 72/78, 135.
  Bidens pilosa L. 72/129, 204.
  Brickellia veronicaefolia (H.B.K.) A. Gray. 71/54; 72/35, 165a, 198.
  Calea hypoleuca Rob. & Greenm. 72/110, 123, 144.
  cf. *Calendula arvensis* L. 72/187.
  Chrysanthemum parthenium (L.) Bernh. 71/58; 72/192.
  Coreopsis pinnatisecta Blake 72/145. (det. D. J. Crawford, 1974).
  Dyssodia decipiens (Bartl.) M. C. Johnst. 72/167.
  D. cf. *sanguinea* (Klatt.) Strother 72/148a.
  Eupatorium espinosarum A. Gray 71/68, 96, 118; 72/143, 155.
  E. sp. 72/80.
  Flaveria trinervia (Spreng.) C. Mohr 72/4, 177.
  Florestina platyphylla (Rob. & Greenm.) Rob. & Greenm. 72/148d.
  Galinsoga parviflora Cav. 71/5; 72/1.
  Gnaphalium spp. 71/147, 170; 72/133.
  Grindelia sp. 72/17.
  Gymnolaena serratifolia (DC.) Rydb. 71/217; 72/100, 132, 172
  Gymnosperma glutinosum (Spreng.) Less. 72/121.
  Haplopappus pyramidatus (Rob. & Greenm.) Blake 72/74 = same species as *Baccharis pyramidata*.
  Heterosperma pinnatum Cav. 72/105; 122.
  Hymenostephium guatemalense (Rob. & Grennm.) Blake 72/111.
  Malvastrum coromandelianum (L.) Garcke 72/2.
  M. spicatum (L.) A. Gray 72/107.
  Melampodium divaricatum (Rich.) DC. 72/119.
  Montanoa cf. *microcephala* Sch. Bip. 72/150.
  M. tomentosa Cerv. 71/95, 215.
  Parthenium hysterophorus L. 72/59.
  P. tomentosum DC. 72/26.
  Pinaropappus roseus (Less.) Less. 71/12, 148, 260.

Pluchea odorata (L.) Cass. 72/68, 81.
Porophyllum tagetoides (H.B.K.) DC. 71/14, 168a.
Rumfordia floribunda DC. 71/256.
Sanvitalia procumbens Lam. 72, 29a.
Senecio praecox (Cav.) DC. 71/174.
Simsia lagascaeformis DC. 72/90, 151a-b, 162.
Sonchus oleraceus L. 71/30; 72/19.
Stevia lucida Cav. 72/115.
S. sp. 72/128.
Tagetes lucida Cav. 72/115.
T. remotiflora Kunze 72/158.
T. sp. 71/75; 72/94.
Tithonia rotundifolia (Mill.) Blake 71/42.
T. tubaeformis (Jacq.) Cass. 72/160.
Tridax coronopifolia (H.B.K.) Hemsl. 71/3.
Verbesina abscondita Klatt 72/51, 120.
V. sericea Kunth & Bouche 72/126.
Vernonia monosis Sch. Bip. 71/244; 72/75, 124, 156.
Viguiera dentata (Cav.) Spreng. 72/174a-b.
Xanthium strumarium L. 71/45, 237.
Zinnia peruviana (L.) L. 72/12a-b, 27, 29b.

Bignoniaeceae
Parmentiera edulis DC. 71/190.
Tecoma stans (L.) H.B.K. 72/205.

Boraginaceae
Cordia curassavica (Jacq.) R. & S. 71/113, 162, 254a, 270.
Heliotropium procumbens Mill. 72/10, 102a, 201.
Tournefortia hartwegiana Steud. 71/59; 72/93, 131.
T. volubilis L. 71/101; 72/67, 86.

Brassicaceae
Brassica campestris L. 71/198, 199 (Nochixtlán Valley).
B. nigra (L.) Koch 71/39, 230.
Eruca sativa Mill. 71/111, 183.
Lepidium virginicum L. 71/13, 154; 72/144.

Burseraceae
Bursera glabrifolia (H.B.K.) Engl. 71/172.
B. sp. 71/66.

Cactaceae
Mammillaria sp. 72/30.
Opuntia spp. 71/36, 37 (Abasolo).

Caprifoliaceae
Sambucus mexicana Presl 71/222.

Celastraceae
Wimmeria persifolia Radlk. 71/254b.

Chenopodiaceae
Chenopodium ambrosioides L. 71/1, 2, 99(?).
C. berlandieri Moq. 72/161b.
C. murale L. 71/83; 72/62, 134.
C. sp. 71/46.

Cistaceae
Helianthemum glomeratum (Lag.) DC. 72/142, 170.

Compositae: see Asteraceae

Convolvulaceae
Dichondra argentea Willd. 72/70.
Evolvulus sericeus Sw. 71/243.
Ipomoea muricata Cav. 71/146.
I. pauciflora Mart. & Gal. 71/56, 92, 255.
I. purpurea (L.) Roth 71/34 (Abasolo).
I. sp. 72/181.

Crassulaceae
Crassula? 72/81.

Cucurbitaceae
Apodanthera aspera Cogn. 72/21. (Det. J.V.A. Dieterle).
Echinopepon floribundus (Cogn.) Rose 72/71, 130.
Microsechium? 72/56.

Ericaceae
Arctostaphylos polifolia H.B.K. 71/223; 72/141.
A. pungens H.B.K. 71/225; 72/137.

Euphorbiaceae
Acalypha monostachya Cav. 71/137, 241.
Croton ciliato-glanduliferus Ort. 71/77, 126a, 140; 72/31.
Euphorbia dentata Michx. 72/11. (San Antonino Ocotlán).
E. graminea Jacq. 72/175.
E. heterophylla L. 72/176.
E. hyssopifolia L. 72/5.
E. indivisa (Engelm.) Tidestr. 72/113.
E. maculata L. 71/31, 188, 234.
E. stictospora Engelm. 71/180.
Jatropha dioica Sessé 71/63, 121, 175; 72/43.
Pedilanthus tomentellus Rob. & Greenm. 72/99.
Ricinus communis L. 71/213a-b.

Fabaceae
Acacia farnesiana (L.) Willd. 71/164, 259.
A. aff. *macracantha* Willd. 71/107.
A. sp. 71/253.
Calliandra malacophylla Benth. 71/247.
Canavalia villosa Benth. 71/247.
Cassia holwayana Rose 72/127, 157, 186.
C. polyantha Colladon 71/71; 72/65.
Cracca mollis (H.B.K.) Benth. & Oerst. 71/239.
Crotalaria incana L. 72/118.
C. pumila Ort. 71/9.
Dalea capitulata (Rydb.) Harms 72/154.
D. citriodora (Cav.) Willd. 71/10.
D. sericea Lag. 72/164.
D. sp. 71/211; 72/166 (Abasolo).
Desmanthus virgatus (L.) Willd. 71/189.
Indigofera suffruticosa Mill. 72/108.
Leucaena esculenta (DC.) Benth. 72/96.
Lysiloma divaricata (Jacq.) Macbr. 72/168.
Melilotus indica (L.) All. 72/9 San Antonino Ocotlán).
Mimosa biuncifera Benth. 71/168.
M. deamii Rob. 71/238, 258.
M. polyantha Benth. 72/20.
Nissolia fruticosa Jacq. 72/14 (Abasolo).
Pachyrrhizus erosus (L.) Urb. 71/206.
Phaseolus atropurpureus DC. 71/112, 179.
P. heterophyllus Willd. 71/117, 138.
Prosopis laevigata (Willd.) M. C. Johnst. 72/34.
Stylosanthes spp. 71/141; 72/102.
Zornia diphylla (L.) Pers. 72/103.

Fagaceae
Quercus glaucoides Mart. & Gal. 71/127, 251; 72/140.
Q. near *obtusata* Humb. & Bonpl. 71/229.

Q. urbanii Trel. 71/226; 72/138.
Q. sp. 71/250.
Fouquieriaceae
   Fouquieria formosa H.B.K. 71/130.
Hydrophyllaceae
   Nama undulatum H.B.K. 71/184.
   Wigandia sp. 71/177.
Labiatae
   Marrubium vulgare L. 71/49, 93.
   Mentha rotundifolia Huds. 72/92, 188.
   Ocimum micranthum Willd. 71/150; 72/16.
   Origanum vulgare L. (probably) 71/19 (Abasolo).
   Rosmarinus officinalis L. 72/194a.
   Salvia amarissima Ort. 71/98, 106.
   S. fruticulosa Benth. 71/132; 72/165b.
   S. misella H.B.K. 72/195.
   S. sp. 71/62; 72/195.
   Satureia mexicana (Benth.) Briq. 71/80, 195; 72/207.
Lauraceae
   Persea americana L.
Leguminosae, see Fabaceae
Loasaceae
   Mentzelia hispida Willd. 71/160, 212c; 72/47, 85.
Lobeliaceae
   Lobelia laxiflora H.B.K. 71/25, 86, 87 (Abasolo).
Loganiaceae
   Buddleia sessiliflora H.B.K. 72/40, 87 (Rzedowski identification).
   Polypremum procumbens L. 71/16 (Abasolo).
Loranthaceae
   Phoradendron carneum Urb. 72/185.
   Psittacanthus schiedeanus (Schlecht. & Cham.) Blume ex Schult. 71/248.
Lythraceae
   Heimia salicifolia Link 71/81, 139, 232; 72/38, 125.
Malpighiaceae
   Bunchosia montana Juss. 71/65, 120.
   Malpighia punicifolia L. 72/22.
   Mascagnia seleriana Loes. 71/122.
Malvaceae
   Abutilon sp. 72/153.
   Anoda cristata (L.) Schlecht. 71/8, 40, 194b, 197, 233.
   Malva parviflora L. 71/17, 41.
   Malvaviscus sp. 72/146.
   Sida procumbens Sw. 72/102b.
   S. rhombifolia L. 72/58, 88, 136, 203.
   S. sp. 72/77.
Martyniaceae
   Proboscidea triloba (Cham. & Schlecht.) Decne. 71/178.
Menthaceae: see Labiatae
Mimosaceae: see Fabaceae
Myrtaceae
   Psidium guajava L. 71/110; 72/76.
Nyctaginaceae
   Boerhaavia coccinea Mill. 72/33.
   Commicarpus scandens (L.) Standl. 72/57.
   Mirabilis jalapa L. 72/54.

Salpianthus purpurascens (Cav.) Hook. & Arn. 72/52, 63, 109.
Onagraceae
   Gaura drummondii (Spach.) T. & G. 72/42, 60, 152b-c.
   Ludwigia repens Forst. 71/167a.
Oxalidaceae (Melinda Denton identifications)
   Oxalis galeottii Turcz. 71/201.
   O. latifolia H.B.K. 71/7, 67, 128.
   O. magnifica (Rose) Knuth 71/246 (Nochixtlán).
Papaveraceae
   Argemone mexicana L. 71/15.
   Polanisia uniglandulosa (Cav.) DC. 72/66.
Papilionaceae: see Fabaceae
Passifloraceae
   Passiflora foetida L. 71/249.
Phytolaccaceae
   Rivina humilis L. 72/41.
Piperaceae
   Peperomia cf. *campylotropa* A. W. Hill 72/73.
   Piper sp.
Plumbaginaceae
   cf. *Plumbago* 71/100, 221.
Polemoniaceae
   Loeselia caerulea (Cav.) G. Don 71/182; 72/182, 197, 199.
   L. mexicana (Lam.) Brand 71/224; 72/206.
Polygonaceae
   Rumex mexicanus Meissn. 72/18.
   R. obtusifolius L. 71/38.
Portulacaceae
   Portulaca oleracea L. 71/4, 48, 202.
   Talinum sp. 72/72.
Primulaceae
   Anagallis arvensis L. 71/231.
Rhamnaceae
   Condalia mexicana Schlecht. 71/73.
Rubiaceae
   Bouvardia xylosteoides Hook. & Arn., ex. descr. 71/136.
Rutaceae
   Casimiroa edulis Ll. & Lex. 71/35.
   Ruta graveolens L. 71/20.
Sapindaceae
   Dodonaea viscosa (L.) Jacq. 71/70, 123, 144, 176.
   Sapindus saponaria L. 71/104.
Scrophulariaceae
   Bacopa monnieri (L.) Pennell 71/167b.
   Castilleja arvensis Cham. & Schlecht. 72/106.
   Penstemon campanulatus (Cav.) Willd. 71/168b.
   P. sp. 71/134.
Solanaceae
   Capsicum sp.
   Cestrum dumetorum Schlecht. 72/200.
   Datura meteloides L. 71/219, 240.
   Lycopersicon sp.
   Nicotiana glauca Grah. 71/89.
   Physalis nicandroides Schlecht. 72/179.
   P. viscosa L. 72/171.
   Saracha procumbens (Cav.) R. & P. 72/55.

Solanum laurifolium Mill. 71/64; 72/36.
S. mitlense Dunal 71/90, 133, 242, 236.
S. (*nigrum* group) 71/49, 212a; 72/61.
S. rostratum Dunal 71/57.
S. sp. 72/83.

Tropaeolaceae
Tropaeolum majus L. 72/190.
Turneraceae
Turnera diffusa Willd. 71/135, 145, 171.
Ulmaceae
Celtis sp.
Umbelliferae: see Apiaceae

Verbenaceae
Aloysia triphylla (L.'Her.) Britton 72/193 (Rzedowski identification).
Lantana camara L. 71/53, 61.
L. velutina Mart. & Gal. 71/114, 192, 210a, 212b.
Lippia alba (Mill.) N. E. Brown 71/21.
L. graveolens H.B.K. 71/142, 165, 193.
Vitaceae
Cissus sp. 72/49.
Zygophyllaceae
Tribulus sp. 72/264.

MONOCOTYLEDONEAE

Agavaceae
Agave spp.
Amaryllidaceae
Zephyranthes sp. 71/74, 108, 208.
Cyperaceae
Cyperus? 71/29 (Abasolo).
Liliaceae
Echeandia sp. 71/125.
Nothoscordum bivalve (L.) Britton 71/128.
Orchidaceae
71/72.
72/202b.
Poaceae
Cenchrus echinatus L. 72/101b.
Cynodon dactylon (L.) Pers. 71/26 (Abasolo).
Eragostris tephrosanthos Schult. 72/103.
Paspalum notatum Flügge 72/103.
Rhynchelytrum roseum (Nees) Stapf & Hubb. 72/101a.
Setaria verticillata (L.) Beauv. 71/28, 44.
Sorghum vulgare Pers. 71/245.
Zea mays L.

APPENDIX II

SPANISH, ZAPOTEC, AND BOTANICAL NAMES OF PLANTS

In this appendix, plants recognized by Mitleño informants are listed alphabetically, both in Spanish and in Zapotec. The format is as follows. First come plants whose Spanish name begins with an A, then plants whose Zapotec name begins with an A; next, plants whose Spanish name begins with a B, then plants whose Zapotec name begins with a B; and so on to the end of the alphabet.

SPANISH NAMES	ZAPOTEC NAMES	SCIENTIFIC IDENTIFICATIONS
abrojo	geč bióp	*Tribulus* sp.
acahual	yäb	*Melampodium divaricatum* (Rich.) DC.
		Simsia lagascaeformis DC.
		Tithonia rotundifolia (Mill.) Blake
		T. tubaeformis (Jacq.) Cass.
		Viguiera dentata (Cav.) Spreng.
agrios	guni	*Oxalis galeottii* Turcz.
		O. latifolia H.B.K.
		O. magnifica (Rose) Knuth.
aguacate	yehš	*Persea americana* Mill.
ajo	až	*Allium sativum* L.
alfalfa	kʷan	*Medicago* sp.
anís del campo	anís gihš	*Tagetes* sp.
anís estrella		*Illisium anisatum* L. (Martínez 1959:38)
beldobes	škʷam bäldohb	*Galinsoga parviflora* Cav.
biznagre	kehš	*Echinocactus* sp.
	bala giwi⁷	*Buddleia sessiliflora* H.B.K.
	bala šoh	*Piper* sp.
	bala šoh gihš	*Marsdenia mexicana* Decne.
	bala wäh	*Wigandia* sp.
	baláp	*Ricinus communis* L.
	bälwi	*Malpighia* sp.
	bälwi bäz	*Bunchosia montana* Juss.
	bäwi	*Psidium guajava* L.
	bedz viv	*Sapindus saponaria* L.
	bia sa⁷	*Opuntia* spp.
	bia bäz	
	bia de castiy	
	bia kʷiot	
	bidu geč	*Parmentiera edulis* DC.
	bidz lats	*Lemairocereus* sp.
	bidz žob	*Myrtillocactus* sp.
	bini	*Pedilanthus tomentellus* (Rob. & Greenm.)
	biniỹ bido	*Datura meteloides*
	binya kačä	*Asclepias oenotheroides* Cham. & Schlecht.

SPANISH NAMES	ZAPOTEC NAMES	SCIENTIFIC IDENTIFICATIONS
	binya xŏl	*Asclepias* spp.
	binya bä?kʷ	*Asclepias elata* Benth.
	bisya	*Phaseolus vulgaris* L.
	bitia?	*Chenopodium ambrosioides* L.
	bitia zä?	*Chenopodium* sp.
	bityuš bä?kʷ	*Solanum* (*nigrum* group)
	bityuš gŏn	*Physalis nicandroides* Schlecht.
	bityuš gihš	*Physalis* sp.
	bityuš lahn	*Passiflora foetida* L.
	bityuš su	*Lycopersicon* sp.
	bityuš zah	*Physalis viscosa* L.
cacahuatón	škʷam bižeh, škʷam ghihb	*Calea hypoleuca* Rob. & Greenm.
cacalosuchet	gi golti	*Plumeria rubra* L.
calabaza	giht	*Cucurbita* spp.
calabaza amarga	giht lahn	*Apodanthera aspera* Cogn.
camote blanco	gu nŏl	*Ipomoea muricata* Cav.
camote morado	gu morad	
camotito	guni, gužehl	*Oxalis galeottii* Turcz.
camotito (jicamita)	gužehl	*Phaseolus heterophyllus* Willd.
carrizo	ya biki	*Arundo donax*
cebolla	žiht	*Allium cepa* L.
cebolla del campo	žiht gihš	*Allium* sp.
cedrón		*Aloysia triphylla* (L'Her.) Britton
copal	yahl	*Bursera galeottiana* Engl. *B. glabrifolia* H.B.K.
cuajilote	bidu geč	*Parmentiera edulis* DC.
chamizo blanco	yak šeh	*Baccharis salicifolia* (R. & P.) Pers.
chapiche (chepiche)	lya yodz	*Porophyllum tagetoides* (H.B.K.) DC.
chayote	gihtia?p	*Sechium edule* L.
chayotillo	geč gitia?p	*Xanthium strumarium* L.
chicalote	geč.niz	*Argemone mexicana* L.
chilillo	ya bidi	*Mammillaria* sp.
chipil	šiǰ	*Crotalaria pumila* Ort.
chipil del campo	šiǰ gihš	*Crotalaria incana* L.
cholla	geč gol	*Opuntia* sp.
dimoriale		*Salvia misella* H.B.K.
doradilla (siempre viva, yerba de piedra)	kʷan gih	*Selaginella pallescens* (Presl) Spring
	dohb	*Agave* spp.
	dut gih	*Grindelia* sp.
	dzědz	*Portulaca oleracea* L.
	dzedz nihs	*Ludwigia repens* Forst.
epazote	bitia?	*Chenopodium* spp.
espinosilla (yerba de espanto)	škʷan ǰehb	*Loeselia mexicana* (Lam.) Brand.
espule (espulga)		*Pinaropappus roseus* (Less.) Less.
eucalipto		*Eucalyptus globulus* Labill.
fresno		*Fraxinus* sp.

APPENDIX II

SPANISH NAMES	ZAPOTEC NAMES	SCIENTIFIC IDENTIFICATIONS
frijolón		*Canavalia villosa* Benth.
flor de gallo	kʷan gid gai	*Zinnea violacea* Cav.
		Z. elegans Jacq.
		Z. peruviana (L.) L.
flor de novio	gitia?p geč	*Echinopepon floribundus* (Cogn.) Rose
flor de perrita		*Gaura drummondii* (Spach.) T. & G.
flor de sau (sauco)		*Sambucus mexicana* DC.
flor de zopilote		*Asclepias linaria* Cav.
girasol	yăb	*Helianthus annuus* L.
golandrina		*Euphorbia indivisa* (Engelm.) Tidestr.
		E. stictospora Engelm.
gordolobo		*Gnaphalium* sp.
granada	žob.štil	*Punica granatum* L.
guaje	Lyá	*Leucaena esculenta* (DC.) Benth.
guaje del campo	Lyá gihš	*Lysiloma divaricata* (Jacq.) Macbr.
guajillo	Lyá lăs	*Desmanthus virgatus* (L.) Willd.
	geč.beh	*Prosopis laevigata* (Willd.) M. C. Johnst.
	geč.bigin	*Solanum rostratum* Dunal.
	geč.bióp	*Tribulus* sp.
	geč.buɬ	*Fouquieria formosa* H.B.K.
	geč.čahd	*Acacia farnesiana* (L.) Willd.
	geč.čehd	*Celtis pallida*
	geč.šihd	*Mimosa polyantha* Benth.
		M. biuncifera Benth.
		M. deamii Rob.
	geč.gitia?p	*Xanthium strumarium* L.
	geč.giža?	*Rhynchelytrum roseum* (Nees) Stapf & Hubb.
	geč.gol	*Opuntia* sp.
	geč.gusohp	*Solanum laurifolium* Mill.
		S. mitlense Dunal.
	geč.niz	*Argemone mexicana* L.
	gi.bakan	*Thevetia thevetioides* (H.B.K.) K. Schum.
	gi.bigu.štil	*Tagetes erecta* L.
	gi.lahk	*Stevia* sp.
		S. rhombifolia H.B.K.
	gi.lahk	*Stevia lucida* Lag.
	gi.no?č	*Zephyranthes* sp.
	gi.reh	*Ipomoea purpurea* (L.) Roth
	gi.ɬtsun	*Verbesina abscondita* Klatt.
	gi.stehn ya.luǰ.dahn	*Psittacanthus schiedeanus* (Schlecht. & Cham.) Schult.
	gišlobeh	*Malva parvifolia* L.
	gi.ste.bakeč	*Parthenium hysterophorus* L.
	gi.togol	*Tagetes remotiflora* Kunze
	gi.togol kʷa?č	*Dyssodia decipiens* (Bartl.) M. C. Johnst.
		D. sanguinea (Klatt.) Strother
	gi.tohb	Unidentified
	gi.tohts	*Cassia holwayana* Rose
	gi.tsl	Unidentified

SPANISH NAMES	ZAPOTEC NAMES	SCIENTIFIC IDENTIFICATIONS
	giht	*Cucurbita* spp.
	giht lahn	*Apodanthera aspera* Cogn.
	gihtia'p	*Sechium edule* L.
	gihtia'p geč	*Echinopepon floribundus* (Cogn.) Rose
	gol.bets	*Polanisia uniglandulosa* (Cav.) DC.
	gubetunth	*Anisacanthus quadrifidus* (Vahl) Standl.
	gubenig^w	*Cordia curassavica* (Jacq.) R & S.
	gubezehd (gubezihd)	*Brickellia veronicaefolia* (H.B.K.) A. Gray
	gu gihš	*Gymnolaena serratifolia* (DC.) Rydb.
	guladz	*Amaranthus* spp.
	gu malvarisk	*Sida rhombifolia* L.
	gu morad	*Ipomoea muricata* Cav.
	guni	*Oxalis* spp.
	gu nŏl	*Ipomoea muricata* Cav.
	gurak^w	*Commicarpus scandens* (L.) Standl.
	gu.zehd	*Mentzelia hispida* Willd.
	gužehl	*Phaseolus heterophyllus* Willd.
higo		*Ficus* sp.
hoja blanca		*Vernonia monosis* Sch. Bip.
hoja sén		*Flourensia cernua* DC. (Martínez 1959:186)
jaras	yak.čiǰ	*Dodonaea viscosa* Jacq.
	k^{w}an ɨgid	*Mentzelia hispida* Willd.
	k^{w}an šnaš	*Croton ciliato-glanduliferus* Ort.
	k^{w}an zahn	*Pluchea odorata* (L.) Cass.
lanté		*Plantago* sp.
laurel (flor)	gi.baláš	*Plumeria rubra* L.
lechuga del campo	lečug gihš	*Sonchus oleraceus* L.
lengua de vaca	bala giwi'	*Buddleia sessiliflora* H.B.K.
limón		*Citrus aurantifolia*
	lakh	*Anoda cristata* (L.) Schlecht.
	lakh gon	*Salpianthus purpurascens* (Cav.) Hook. & Arn.
	lo bidzun	*Saracha procumbens* (Cav.) R. & P.
	lo.gid.gai	*Sanvitalia procumbens* Lam.
	luhč.bä'k^w	*Rumex mexicanus* Meissn.
	Lya	*Leucaena* sp.
	Lya kunef	*Cracca mollis* (H.B.K.) Benth. & Oerst.
	Lya gihš	*Cassia polyantha* Colladon
maguey	dohb	*Agave* spp.
mala mujer	geč.bahd	*Jatropha urens*
malva	gišlobeh	*Malva parvifolia* L.
malvarisco	gu malvarisk	*Sida rhombifolia* L.
mandarina		*Citrus reticulata*
manzanita	manzan.gihš	*Arctostaphylos pungens* H.B.K.
manzanilla amarga (Santa María)	manzaniy La	*Chrysanthemum parthenium* (L.) Bernh.

APPENDIX II

SPANISH NAMES	ZAPOTEC NAMES	SCIENTIFIC IDENTIFICATIONS
manzanilla dulce	manzaniy štil, neš	*Matricaria chamomilla* L.
marijuana		*Cannabis sativa* L.
marrubia	pition. gihš	*Marrubium vulgare* L.
mesquite	geč.béh	*Prosopis laevigata* (Willd.) M. C. Johnst.
miltomate	bityuš.gihš	*Physalis* sp.
mirhto		*Salvia* sp.
monstranza		*Mentha rotundifolia* Huds.
montwerz		*Tropaeolum majus* L.
monzi		*Malvaviscus* sp.
mostaza	mostas gihš	*Nicotiana glauca* Grah.
	mostas štil	*Brassica nigra* (L.) Koch
	madokh	*Casimiroa edulis* Ll. & Lex.
nanche	bälwi	*Malpighia* sp.
naranja		*Citrus sinensis*
orégano		*Origanum vulgare* L.
oreja (orejita) de ratón	gubezehd	*Brickellia veronicaefolia* (H.B.K.) A. Gray
pájaro bobo	ya.banuh	*Ipomoea pauciflora* Mart. & Gal.
palo santo	ya.gitič	*Senecio praecox* (Cav.) DC.
pata de cabrón	geč.bigin	*Solanum rostratum* Dunal.
pegajoso	kʷan ĭgid	*Mentzelia hispida* Willd.
perejil		*Petroselinum* sp.
pericón		*Tagetes lucida* Cav.
pierna vieja	siǎk	*Lepidium virginicum* L.
pinocote	ya.gehd	*Pinus teocote* Schlecht. & Cham.
pirú	ya.luǰ	*Schinus molle* L.
pitiona		*Lippia alba* (Mill.) N. E. Brown
poleo	wǎs	*Satureja mexicana* (Benth.) Briq.
pulgo	pez.nis	*Peperomia* cf. *campylotropa* A. W. Hill
	pition.gihš	*Marrubium vulgare* L.
quintonil	guladz	*Amaranthus* spp.
rábano del campo	rab gihš	*Eruca sativa* Mill.
rejalgar	gi.bakan	*Thevetia thevetioides* (H.B.K.) K. Schum.
romero		*Rosmarinus officinalis* L.
romero del campo	romer gihš	*Haplopappus pyramidatus* Rob. & Greenm.) Blake = *Baccharis pyramidata* (Rob. & Greenm.) Rzed.
rompecapa	geč.čehd	*Celtis pallida*
rosa de castilla		*Rosa centifolia* L.
ruda		*Ruta graveolens* L.
salvia amarilla	salb gohts	*Lippia graveolens* H.B.K.
salvia blanca	salb nŏl	*Turnera diffusa* Willd.
San Cayetano	geč.gusohp	*Solanum laurifolium* Mill. / *S. mitlense* Dunal.
San Pablo		*Solanum* sp.
Santa María (Manzanilla amarga)	manzaniy La	*Chrysanthemum parthenium* (L.) Bernh.

SPANISH NAMES	ZAPOTEC NAMES	SCIENTIFIC IDENTIFICATIONS
sauco		*Sambucus mexicana* D.C.
sauce	yahg.yehs	*Salix* sp.
siempre viva	kʷan gih	*Selaginella pallescens* (Presl) Spring
sia	siǎk	*Lepidium virginicum* L.
sinasle	kʷan šnaš	*Croton ciliato-glanduliferus* Ort.
sinsontle	gi.šte.bakeč	*Parthenium hysterophorus* L.
susenneh	gi.noʔč	*Zephyranthes* sp.
	škʷam.bäl	*Eupatorium espinosarum* A. Gray
	škʷam.behd	*Chenopodium murale* L.
	škʷam.bižeʔ	*Calea hypoleuca* Rob. & Greenm.
	škʷam.bižeʔ yäl	*Tournefortia* sp.
	škʷam.bizin	*Microsechium* sp.?
	škʷam.butz.šnyâ	*Rivina humilis* L.
	škʷan.ghihb	*Heimia salicifolia* Link.
	škʷan.gurakʷ	*Euphorbia maculata* L.
	škʷan.gušat	Unidentified
	škʷan.ǰehb	*Loeselia mexicana* (Lam.) Brand.
	škʷan.ǰehb lǎs	*Loeselia caerulea* (Cav.) G. Don
	škʷan.kunef	*Tridax coronopifolia* (H.B.K.) Hemsl.
	škʷan.tst	*Stylosanthes* sp.
	susi	*Jatropha dioica* Sessé
tepeguaje	Lya gihš	*Cassia polyantha* Colladon
togoles	gi.togol	*Dyssodia* spp.
toloache blanco	biniǰ bido	*Datura meteloides*
tomates	bityuš	*Physalis* spp.
tormache		*Proboscidea triloba* (Cham. & Schlecht.) Decne
toronjil		*Dalea capitulata* (Rydb.) Harms. *D. citriodora* (Cav.) Willd. *D.* sp.
trobadora	gibakan gihš	*Tecoma stans* (L.) H.B.K.
uña de gato	ya.geč	*Acacia* spp.
verbena	zeh.La (zeh.La.gič)	*Salvia amarissima* Ort.
verdolaga	dzědz	*Portulaca oleracea* L.
violeta	lakh	*Anoda cristata* (L.) Schlecht.
yerba de aigre	škʷam.bäl	*Eupatorium espinosarum* A. Gray
yerba de aretes		*Boerhaavia coccinea* Mill.
yerba buena	bäč.štil	*Menthus* spp.
yerba de canela	kʷan zahn	*Pluchea odorata* (L.) Cass.
yerba de canz (del cancer), hoja de negra		*Tournefortia hartwegiana* Steud.
yerba de conejo	škʷan kunef	*Tridax coronopifolia* (H.B.K.) Hemsl.
yerba de chapulín	škʷan.gušat	Unidentified
yerba dulce		*Phyla scaberrima* (A. L. Juss.) Moldenke *Lippia dulcis* Trev. (Martínez 1959: 166-7)
yerba de guajolote		*Chenopodium berlandieri* Moq.
yerba maestra		*Artemisia* sp.

APPENDIX II

SPANISH NAMES	ZAPOTEC NAMES	SCIENTIFIC IDENTIFICATIONS
yerba mora	bityuš bä$^{\textrm{ʔ}}$k^w	*Solanum* (*nigrum* group)
yerba de negra		*Rivina humilis* L.
yerba de ojo	šk^{w}am.bižeʔ	*Tournefortia volubilis* L.
yerba santa	bala.šoh	*Piper* sp.
yerba santa del campo	bala.šoh.gihš	*Marsdenia mexicana* Decne.
	yäb	Several genera; see "acahual"
	yäb dahn	*Viguiera dentata* (Cav.) Spreng.
	yäb gid.gai	*Tithonia tubaeformis* (Jacq.) Cass.
	ya.banuh	*Ipomoea pauciflora* Mart. & Gal.
	ya.bišuih	*Quercus glaucoides* Mart. & Gal.
	yahn	*Alternanthera repens* (L.) Kuntze
	yak.čiỷ	*Dodonaea viscosa* Jacq.
	yak.čiv	*Calliandra malacophylla* Benth.
	yak.kučar	*Quercus urbanii* Trel.
	yak.šeh	*Baccharis salicifolia* (R. & P.) Pers.
	yak.tsin	*Quercus obtusata* Humb. & Bonpl.
	yak.tsun	*Montanoa* sp.
zapote blanco	madokh	*Casimiroa edulis* Ll. & Lex.
	zeh.La (zeh.La.gič)	*Salvia amarissima* Ort.
	zi.gon	*Cissus* sp.
	žob	*Zea mays* L.
	žob.leh	*Lantana camara* L.
		L. velutina Mart. & Gal.
	žob.nihd	*Arctostaphylos polifolia* H.B.K.
	žob.štil	*Punica granatum* L.
	žob.yâs	*Condalia mexicana* Schlecht.

RESUMEN EN ESPAÑOL

(por *David J. Wilson*)

Este es un estudio etnobotánico de la comunidad de Mitla, que está ubicada en el este del Valle de Oaxaca. La población de Mitla es mayormente bilingüe, hablando zapoteco y español, aunque cierto porcentaje de la gente también es monolingüe. Durante cuatro temporadas de campo en Mitla, la Dra. Ellen Messer investigó la manera por la cual los zapotecas de la actualidad clasifican a las plantas, cómo las utilizan y cómo comunican el conocimiento de ellas. Se hicieron extensivas colecciones de plantas, y se utilizaron tanto informantes monolingües como bilingües.

Los zapotecas de hoy tienen una sola palabra, *yahg*, que significa "planta," "árbol" y "madera." En un nivel inferior de la jerarquía clasificatoria, *yahg*, o sea "árbol," se contrasta con *kʷan*, "yerba," y *giš*, "pasto." Cada una de estas categorías puede dividirse más. Los árboles, por ejemplo, pueden ser clasificados como espinoso o sin espinas. Las hierbas pueden ser clasificadas en cuanto a la forma de la hoja, el ambiente donde crecen, el color, y si son silvestres o domesticadas. El maíz *(yähl)* tiene su propio vocabulario, y las varias partes de la planta hasta tienen nombres distintos a las partes correspondientes de las hierbas o el pasto.

Como es de suponer, tanto el idioma español como el zapoteco ha prestado mucho el uno del otro. El español ha apropiado palabras del zapoteco (esp. togoles, del zap. *gi togol*, "flor de muerto"); el zapoteco ha apropiado palabras del español (zap. *lečug*, del esp. lechuga). En el caso de algunas plantas europeas introducidas, el zapoteco ha adoptado el mismo término español (v.gr., mostaza). En el caso de otras plantas introducidas, se ha inventado el término zapoteco; por ejemplo, la granada se llama *žob štil* (*žob* = grano de maíz; *štil* = de Castilla) porque sus semillas se parecen a los granos de maíz.

Las varias plantas silvestres todavía son utilizadas extensivamente por la gente de Mitla, o se sabe que son utilizadas por la gente de los pueblos vecinos. Algunas de estas plantas—la bellota, la vaina de mezquite, la semilla de guaje, la tuna, la fruta del cardón—eran comidas por los habitantes precerámicos de la Cueva de Guilá Naquitz, cerca de Mitla. Otras son hierbas que se ocurren como malas hierbas en la milpa, y sus hojas se recogen y se comen como verduras. Este grupo de hierbas comestibles incluye *Chenopodium (bitiaʔ)*, *Amaranthus (guládz)*, *Anoda (lakh)*, *Crotalaria (šiž)*, *Galinsoga (bäldohb)* y *Portulaca (dzědz)*.

Los zapotecas también tienen bastantes términos para las etapas en el crecimiento de las plantas ("poco crecido," "maduro," "seco" y formas transicionales) y para las variedades de terreno agrícola. Hacen una dicotomía entre tierra de humedad *(yuh kohp)* y tierra seca *(yuh bidz)*, y entre tierra gruesa *(yuh nal)* y tierra delgada *(yuh las)*.

El informe de Messer termina con una lista extensiva de plantas utilizadas por los mitleños, con sus nombres vulgares en español y zapoteco y sus designaciones latinas.

REFERENCES TO PART II

Arber, A.
1953a Herbals: Their Origin and Evolution, 1470-1670. Hafner Publishing Co. Darien, Connecticut.
1953b From Medieval Herbalism to the Birth of Modern Botany. *In:* Science, Medicine, and History: Essays on the Evolution of Scientific Thought and Medical Practice Written in Honor of Charles Singer, Vol. 1. E. A. Underwood, ed. Oxford University Press. London.

Bartlett, H. H.
1940 History of the Generic Concept in Botany. Bulletin of the Torrey Botanical Club 67:349-362.

Bateson, G.
1972 Steps to an Ecology of Mind. Ballantine Books. New York.

Bennett, W. C. and R. M. Zingg
1935 The Tarahumara, an Indian Tribe of Northern Mexico. University of Chicago Press. Chicago.

Berlin, B.
1970 A Universalist-Evolutionary Approach in Ethnographic Semantics. *In:* Current Directions in Anthropology, A. Fisher, ed. Bulletin of the American Anthropological Association 3.3(Pt. 2):3-18.
1972 Speculations on the Growth of Ethnobotanical Nomenclature. Journal of Language and Society 1:63-98.

Berlin, B., D. E. Breedlove, and P. H. Raven
1966 Folk Taxonomies and Biological Classification. Science 154:273-275.
1968 Covert Categories and Folk Taxonomies. American Anthropologist 70:290-299.
1973 General Principles of Classification and Nomenclature in Folk Biology. American Anthropologist 75:214-242.
1974 Principles of Tzeltal Plant Classification. Academic Press. New York.

Berlin, B. and P. Kay
1969 Basic Color Terms: Their University and Evolution. University of California Press. Berkeley.

Borah, W. W.
1941 The Collection of Tithes in the Bishopric of Oaxaca During the Sixteenth Century. Hispanic American Historical Review 21:386-409.

Breedlove, D. E. and N. A. Hopkins
1970- A Study of Chuj (Mayan) Plant Names with Notes on Uses. I, II, III. The Wasmann Journal of Biology
1971 28, 29.

Briggs, E.
1961 Mitla Zapotec Grammar. Instituto Lingüístico de Verano and Centro de Investigaciones Antropológicas. México, D.F.

Brown, C. H.
1974 Unique Beginners and Covert Categories in Folk Biological Taxonomies. American Anthropologist 76:325-327.

Buckley, W. F., ed.
1968 Modern Systems Research for the Behavioral Scientist: A Sourcebook. Aldine. Chicago.

Bulmer, R.
1970 Which Came First, the Chicken or the Egg-head? *In:* Échanges et Communications, Mélanges Offerts à Claude Lévi-Strauss à l'Occasion de son 60ème Anniversaire. J. Pouillon and P. Miranda, eds. Mouton. The Hague.

Castetter, E. F. and R. M. Underhill
1935 The Ethnobiology of the Papago Indians. University of New Mexico Bulletin 275:1-84. Biological Series 4(3).

Chevalier, F.
1963 Land and Society in Colonial Mexico: The Great Hacienda. A. Eustis, trans. University of California Press. Berkeley.

Cole, M. and S. Scribner
1974 Culture and Thought. John Wiley and Sons, Inc. New York.

Conklin, H. C.
1954 The Relation of the Hanuóo Culture to the Plant World. Ph.D. Dissertation. Yale University.
1962 Lexicographical Treatment of Folk Taxonomies. *In:* Problems in Lexicography. F. W. Householder and S. Saporta, eds. Indiana University Research Center in Anthropology, Folklore, and Linguistics, Publication 21. Indiana University Press. Bloomington.

Díaz-Cisneros, H.
1974 An Institutional Analysis of a Rural Development Project: The Case of the Puebla Project in Mexico. Ph.D. Dissertation. The University of Wisconsin, Madison.

Drennan, R. D.
1976 Fábrica San José and Middle Formative Society in the Valley of Oaxaca. Prehistory and Human Ecology of the Valley of Oaxaca, Vol. 4. Memoirs of the Museum of Anthropology, University of Michigan, No. 8. Ann Arbor.

Durkheim, E. and M. Mauss
1963 Primitive Classification. R. Needham, trans. The University of Chicago Press. Chicago.
[1903]

Flannery, K. V.
1968 Archeological Systems Theory and Early Mesoamerica. *In:* Anthropological Archeology in the Americas. B. J. Meggers, ed. The Anthropological Society of Washington. Washington, D.C.
1973 The Origins of Agriculture. Annual Review of Anthropology 2:271-310.

Flannery, K. V., A. V. Kirkby, M. Kirkby, and A. W. Williams
1967 Farming Systems and Political Growth in Ancient Oaxaca. Science 158:445-454.

Flannery, K. V. and J. Schoenwetter
1970 Climate and Man in Formative Oaxaca. Archaeology 23:144-152.

Flannery, K. V. et al.
1970 Preliminary Archeological Investigations in the Valley of Oaxaca, Mexico, 1966-1969. Report to the National Science Foundation and the Instituto Nacional de Antropología e Historia, México. Mimeographed.

Fowler, C. S.
1977 Ethnoecology. *In:* Ecological Anthropology. D. Hardesty, ed. John Wiley and Sons. New York.

Fowler, C. S. and J. Leland
1967 Some Northern Paiute Native Categories. Ethnology 6:381-404.

Galván-Rivera, M.
1971 Calendario para 1971. Mexico.

Harmon, L. D.
1973 The Recognition of Faces. Scientific American 229(5):70-83.

Iszaevich, A.
1969 Soledad Etla. Estudio de un Proceso de Modernización. Tesis Profesional (M.A.). Escuela Nacional de Antropología e Historia México, D.F.

Kay, P.
1970 Some Theoretical Implications of Ethnographic Semantics. *In:* Current Directions in Anthropology. A. Fisher, ed. Bulletin of the American Anthropological Association 3.3(Pt. 2):19-31.

Kearney, M.
1972 The Winds of Ixtepeji: World View and Society in a Zapotec Town. Holt, Rinehart, and Winston. New York.

King, L.
1966 Weeds of the World. Interscience Publishers, Inc. New York.

Kirkby, A.V.T.
1973 The Use of Land and Water Resources in the Past and Present Valley of Oaxaca, Mexico. Prehistory and Human Ecology of the Valley of Oaxaca, Vol. 1. Memoirs of the Museum of Anthropology, University of Michigan, No. 5. Ann Arbor.

Leslie, C. M.
1960 Now We Are Civilized. Wayne State University Press. Detroit.

Levey, M.
1966 The Medicinal Formulary of Aqrābādhīn of Al-Kinkī. The Univeristy of Wisconsin Press. Madison.

Lévi-Strauss, C.
1966 The Savage Mind. University of Chicago Press. Chicago.

REFERENCES

Lévy-Bruhl, L.
   1926   How Natives Think. Allen and Unwin. London.

Lloyd, G. E. R.
   1964   The Hot and the Cold, the Dry and the Wet in Greek Philosophy. Journal of Hellenistic Studies 84:92-106.

Loyola Montemayor, E.
   1956   La Industria del Pulque. Departamento de Investigaciones Industriales. Banco de México, S.A.

Mannheim, K.
   1946   Ideology and Utopia: An Introduction to the Sociology of Knowledge. Harcourt, Brace, and Company. New York.

Martínez, M.
   1959   Las Plantas Medicinales de México. Ediciones Botas. Mexico.

Mazess, R. B.
   1968   Hot/Cold Food Beliefs in Peru. Journal of the American Dietetic Association 53:109-113.

McBryde, F. W.
   1945   Cultural and Historical Geography of Southwest Guatemala. Smithsonian Institution Publications in Social Anthropology, No. 4.

Merleau-Ponty, M.
   1964   The Primacy of Perception and Other Essays. J. A. Edie, ed. Northwestern University Press. Evanston, Illinois.

Messer, E.
   1975   Zapotec Plant Knowledge: Classification, Uses, and Communication About Plants in Mitla, Oaxaca, Mexico. University Microfilms. Ann Arbor.
   1976   The Pragmatics of Folk Classification. Michigan Discussions in Anthropology 2:91-106.
   n.d.   Cool Hands: Traditional and Modern Curing in Mitla, "Town of the Souls."

Metzger, D. and G. Williams
   1963   Tenejapa Medicine I: The Curer. Southwestern Journal of Anthropology 19:216-234.

Miller, G.
   1956   The Magical Number Seven, Plus or Minus Two: Some Limits on Our Capacity for Processing Information. The Psychological Review 63:81-97.
   1967   The Psychology of Communication: Seven Essays. Basic Books. New York.

Miracle, M. P.
   1966   Maize in Tropical Africa. University of Wisconsin Press. Madison.
   1967   Agriculture in the Congo Basin: Tradition and Change in African Rural Economies. University of Wisconsin Press. Madison.

Needham, J.
   1956   Science and Civilization in China, Vol. 2. Cambridge University Press. Cambridge.

Odum, E. P.
   1966   Ecology. Prentice-Hall. Englewood Cliffs, New Jersey.

Paddock, J., ed.
   1966   Ancient Oaxaca. Stanford University Press. Stanford.

Parsons, E. C.
   1936   Mitla, Town of the Souls. University of Chicago Press. Chicago.

Paso y Troncoso, F. del
   1905   Relación de Tlacolula y Mitla. F. Horcasitas and R. George, trans. Mesoamerican Notes 4(1955):13-24.

Pennington, C. W.
   1963   The Tarahumar of Mexico. Their Environment and Material Culture. University of Utah Press. Salt Lake City.
   1969   The Tepehuan of Chihuahua, Their Material Culture. The University of Utah Press. Salt Lake City.

Perchonock, N. and O. Werner
   1969   Navajo Systems of Classification: Some Implications for Ethnoscience. Ethnology 8:229-242.

Polanyi, M.
   1967   The Tacit Dimension. Doubleday and Company, Inc. Garden City, New York.

Price-Williams, D. B.
   1962   Abstract and Concrete Modes of Classification in a Primitive Society. British Journal of Educational Psychology 32:50-61.

Raven, P. H., B. Berlin, and D. E. Breedlove.
1971 The Origins of Taxonomy. Science 174:1210-1213.

Reko, B. P.
1919 De Los Nombres Botánicos Aztecos. El México Antiguo 1:113-157.
1945 Mitobotánica Zapoteca. Tacubaya, D. F.

Sanders, W. T.
1957 Tierra y Agua. Ph.D. Dissertation. Harvard University.

Sauer, J. D.
1950 The Grain Amaranths: A Survey of Their History and Classification. Annals of the Missouri Botanical Garden 37:561-632.

Schmieder, O.
1930 The Settlements of the Tzapotec and Mije Indians, State of Oaxaca, Mexico. University of California Publications in Geography, Vol. 4.

Schoenwetter, J.
1974 Pollen Records of Guilá Naquitz Cave. American Antiquity 39:292-303.

Simon, H.
1974 How Big is a Chunk? Science 183:482-488.

Simpson, G. G.
1961 Principles of Animal Taxonomy. Columbia University Press. New York.

Soustelle, J.
1961 The Daily Life of the Aztecs on the Eve of the Spanish Conquest. Stanford University Press. Stanford.

Standley, P. C.
1920- Trees and Shrubs of Mexico. (2 vols.) Smithsonian Institution. United States National Museum.
1926 Contributions from the United States Herbarium, Vol. 23.

Standley, P. C. and J. A. Steyermark
1946- Flora of Guatemala. Fieldiana: Botany 24(1-6).
1958

Stross, B.
1973 Acquisition of Botanical Terminology by Tzeltal Children. Janua Linguarum 158:107-141.

Taylor, W. B.
1972 Landlord and Peasant in Colonial Oaxaca. Stanford University Press. Stanford.

Whalen, M.
in Evolution in a Formative Community in the Valley of Oaxaca, Mexico: Excavations at Santo Domingo
press Tomaltepec. Prehistory and Human Ecology of the Valley of Oaxaca, Vol. 6. Memoirs of the Museum of Anthropology, University of Michigan, No. 11. Ann Arbor.

Wightman, W. P. D.
1962 Science and the Renaissance. Oliver and Boyd for the University of Aberdeen. Edinburgh.

Wilden, A.
1972 System and Structure. Tavistock. London.

Womack, J.
1970 Zapata and the Mexican Revolution. Vintage Books. New York.

Plate 1. *a (above)*. Water standing on poorly drained land. *b (below)*. Milpa with herbs, maguey, and borders of thorny, leguminous trees.

Plate 2. *a*. Gathering *chilillos (ya.bidi)*. The woman uses a stick to avoid being scratched by spines. *b*. Corral del Cerro—gathering of *manzan.giš* among hill vegetation.

Plate 3. *a*. Winnowing maize. *b*. Making tortillas in an outdoor *carrizo* shed.

Plate 4. *a.* Gathering herbs from the fields for animals to eat. *b.* Planting beans in second class land with milpa and maguey. Note squash and herbs, including *chipiles*.

Plate 5. *a*. Early sowing along the lower alluvium. *b*. Regular (June) sowing along the upper alluvium.

Plate 6. *a*. Cleaning milpa. *b*. Hilling milpa.

Plate 7. *a*. First class land along the river's edge. *b*. Cleaning milpa on second class (thin) land.

Plate 8. *a*. The harvest. *b*. Harvesting *guías* and *calabacitas*.

Plate 9. *a*. Transporting the maize by traditional oxcart. *b*. Storing and shelling the maize.